The Power of Language

Francis Ponge

THE POWER OF LANGUAGE

*Texts
and
Translations*

Introduction and Translations by

Serge Gavronsky

UNIVERSITY OF CALIFORNIA PRESS
Berkeley   Los Angeles   London

University of California Press
Berkeley and Los Angeles, California

University of California Press, Ltd.
London, England

ISBN 0-520-03441-4
Library of Congress Catalog Card Number 77-71060
Copyright © 1979 by The Regents of the University of California

Printed in the United States of America

Translator's dedication

To Roy Breunig
who first opened the door

Contents

Introduction   1
Texts   45
  The Object is Poetics   47
  Metatechnical Fragments   55
  Reasons for Living Happily   61
  Some Reasons for Writing   65
  The Augean Stables   69
  Rhetoric   73
  Introduction to the Pebble   75
  The Tree Trunk   85
  French Bread   87
  The Oyster   89
  Blackberries   91
  A Fire   93
  Words on Paper   95
  Reading the Sun on Radio   97
  The Meadow   109
  Joca Seria   121
  Braque or Modern Art as an Event and a Pleasure   143
  Text on Electricity   157
  Ardens Organum, Selections from *Pour un Malherbe*   215
Bibliography   275

Introduction

I

For centuries, rhetoric played such a considerable role in literary criticism that it nearly became synonymous with poetics. By the end of the nineteenth century, however, owing to the multiple and fundamental discoveries in science, mathematics, and economics, as well as the new directions in the arts and literature, the traditional views of the *ancien régime* of the mind were dispelled and as a result, rhetoric seemed to have died a natural death. In a subtle manner, the thematic emphasis, though inescapable and evident, gave way to a new appreciation of the nature of language itself and the poetic forms it would adopt. As language no longer appeared to be the duplicate of the world, the soul of nature, so thinking about rhetoric, the art of expression, equally underwent a transformation in order to demonstrate its pertinence in the new world. Out of what Mallarmé called the "exquisite crisis" came a new literary language that redefined the site of poetry.

Until the end of the century, avant-garde criticism focused on aesthetics and metaphysics. With the coming of the twentieth century and particularly with the advent of DADA which corresponded to the outbreak of World War I, the avant-garde proclaimed the necessity of rejecting apparently inalienable realities of a bankrupt past, that is, all that had been sanctioned by the era of the bourgeoisie. The connection was underlined between poetics, the literary artifact, and reality as reality had been circumscribed ideologically. The so-called meaninglessness of the DADA text was meant to introduce the Trojan Horse of Revolution into the citadel

1

of French letters. In order to overthrow the poetic medium, along with the dissolution of classic rhetoric, new words were introduced. Some of them reflected their African origins; others were pure sounds, absolute signifiers. Genres, too, followed this definitive break with ancient practices.

Surrealism, acting concomitantly, suggested a more complex program. As DADA had explicitly condemned the writing of manifestos, so the first critical act carried out by André Breton was to write one, in accordance with a long history of manifestos going back to the *Pléiade* in the sixteenth century. In this new discourse on method, Breton assailed the relics of positivism and scientific reality as they had distorted the representation of the world. Henceforth, he declared, only automatic writing would salvage poetry and the language of expression from the obscurantism of a censorship imposed on the poet by aesthetics, morality, and politics. Pleading for another experience, one that would reveal to mankind the world of dreams, of the imagination, of the marvelous, where all opposites would eventually be reconciled, Breton insisted that if the automatic text initially made no sense that was not to be taken as its last word. On the contrary, and aligning himself with Freud's research, Breton was convinced that the pristine text would reveal, in time, a significant surreality of the mind not perceivable through ordinary language.

As the Romantics had insisted, one hundred years earlier, on the novelty of their "I," their consciousness of the world, and found it imperative to reiterate their literary distinctiveness, so Breton and his followers, with equal vehemence, asserted that the ego, if not the self, had to discover an untrammeled path to the text of the unconscious, as Lacan was soon to define it. Language, for the Surrealists, was a transparency, a bridge to the unconscious. If it translated symbolic information through rhetorical patterns, then its value accrued but in the meantime, the very postulation of automatic writing sufficed for its earliest practitioners.

This disquietude on the part of those who confronted traditional poetics in a world in flux was not limited to post-Romantic Surrealism. In the twenties, there was a European-wide interest in

theories of language and the application of these theories to poetics. So, too, in a parallel critique, ideologues wrote about the need to transform society. As linguists in Europe were postulating a new reality commensurate with the times, so the theoreticians of the Russian revolution addressed themselves to a similar need.

It is within this ambiance that one must situate Francis Ponge, born in 1899, and introduce him not so much biographically, since he has not led an adventurous life, but through an appreciation of his role in French letters. There, he has occupied a significant and unchallenged place for over fifty years, attracting the attention and admiration of leading intellectuals, writers, and painters, a notable feat in France where reputations are periodically reassessed and undone with the oncoming of a new literary-philosophic school. In isolation, like a carved stone, Francis Ponge has had no disciples. There have been no literary schools formed as a result of his work. But for that reason perhaps, he has maintained his absolute integrity as a poet, varying little over the years in the statement, Mallarmé-like, that he has been constructing in his work.

From the beginning of the twenties, Francis Ponge has been preoccupied with the relationship between consciousness, poetic language, and reality; but so were the Surrealists. The specificity of the Pongian text lies in the answers provided; answers that insisted on the definition of language not as a transparency, unquestionably not as a toy to be played with, but as a materially interconnective element between man and reality. The poet's consciousness of the world is incorporated in the world of language. Because of this, everything that pertains to language, to the things it is meant to apprehend, was of interest to Francis Ponge. Sharing the Surrealists' suspicion of contemporary poetic language, of the French language in its cultural context, as it had been debased ideologically, as it had been corrupted by the marketplace as well as by the academies, Ponge first declared the necessity of resisting words, of cleaning them of their impurities: to take words seriously as Mallarmé and Lautréamont had done before him. Automatic writing was formally excluded as a procedure. For Ponge, who considers himself to have a "positive, Bolshevik mind" (see my interview with the

poet in *Francis Ponge: The Sun Placed in the Abyss and Other Texts* [New York: SUN, 1977], 86).[1] To this new version of idealism and its insistence on the spiritual and the unconscious, he opposed his own materialist approach to semantics as well as to philosophy. Rather than adhering to Surrealism then, Francis Ponge found himself temperamentally and aesthetically closer to a new classicism, one that affirmed the significance of language without in any way resembling André Gide's formal principles of clarity and discipline. For Francis Ponge, classicism was exemplified in Malherbe's poetics, in the play of light and dark, the persistency of the Baroque in the emphatic verbal pronouncements of this early seventeenth-century poet. Such a classicism first required that language be treated in conformity with its importance: as the poet's privileged means of translating what his consciousness of the world had grasped. For this reason, Ponge selected objects, especially those that had been the least worked linguistically. Those objects that crowded his poetry served to sharpen his language outside a Romantic perspective which had so long dominated poetry.

But it cannot be said of Ponge that he is a poet of things, that these things are attractive in themselves. Nor, of course, can he be accused of obscuring the reality of things by tracing them through an anthropomorphic experience. His primal and consistent interest has been in language and not in the things he has used language to describe. Ultimately, what counts for Francis Ponge is the polyvalent complexity of language, its hardness, and its gravity. The poetic definition of things illustrates these characteristics as it ornaments language itself.

Materialism, however, even in its semantical attribution, does not exclude ethics. Marx's influence, which left a visible mark on many Surrealist texts, was also present in Ponge's own formulations. Before Jean-Paul Sartre ever proposed his theory of commitment, it was perfectly clear that an aesthetic statement was unthinkable without an ethical corollary. The innocent text had disappeared in a post-Parnassian world. As the title of Ponge's *Le Parti*

1. Unless otherwise noted, all works in this Introduction are published by Gallimard; all translations are my own.

pris des choses so convincingly establishes, if he assumed the voice of the silent world, such a decision was not solely dictated by aesthetics. There was, in this new poetics, a rejection of the Romantics and the overblown significance they had attributed to the self in poetry. There was another purpose too and it was a cosmological one. Ever since the Renaissance, Ponge believes, reality has been distorted by the disproportionate importance that man has had in the universe. By taking the side of things, Ponge tended to undermine this psycho-poetic disposition. According to him, man should recognize his place in what he calls the universal machinery: his is an important one, though not the only one. As Ponge seeks the propriety of linguistic terms, so he has attached to that task the discovery of the propriety of man's place in the world. The selection of things thus becomes doubly noteworthy: it refines poetic language and it puts man back in his proper place.

Many of these considerations were perceived distinctly by the best readers of the times, if not by the general public. The earliest one to take stock of Ponge's contribution was Jean Paulhan, one of the most astute literary critics, himself a writer fascinated by linguistics and rhetoric, friend of the Surrealists, and the editor of the prestigious *Nouvelle Revue Française*. In the twenties, when Ponge's texts are published in that magazine, he finds himself next to Gide, Claudel, Proust, and Valéry. He is then considered a classicist, a purist in matters of language. This indeed corresponded to his intentions but only in a partial manner since it did not fully account for the comprehensive critique of language and rhetoric. The second phase of his literary reputation occurred when Jean-Paul Sartre and Albert Camus both praised his work as a poetic demonstration of phenomenological principles. The concrete things he had taken as his own, the new cosmology he had constituted, seemed to the Husserlian Existentialists to match their own concern with reality, with the thing-in-itself. Sartre wrote what was soon to be a classic essay on Ponge and quoted him in his *Existentialism is a Humanism*. Once again, the importance of his texts was only partially understood: the thematic orientation of Existentialist readers denied the linguistic insistency in Ponge's writings. "Man is the

future of man" as Sartre had admiringly quoted Ponge but he should have been perspicacious enough to observe that language too was the future of man, as it represented his past, irrevocably.

Mallarmé had already commented on the need to constitute a science of language within an intellectual technology. In the late fifties, Existentialism was first challenged and then displaced from its ruling position by the Structuralists who, among other directions, introduced the works of Saussure, Freud, and Nietzsche into literary criticism, thereby placing a more synchronic, less historical and moral focus on literature and its production. One of the significant voices of this movement was the group of writers who formed the magazine *Tel Quel*. They recognized the emphasis Ponge had placed on the linguistic phenomenon, on the scriptural practice, on criticism, as well. They were also cognizant of Ponge's reformulation of a poetics that coincided with their own particular political and philosophic views. Philippe Sollers, editor-in-chief, wrote an important study on Ponge, and in 1970, his interviews with the poet were published. Jean Thibaudeau, member of the board, contributed a book-length presentation of Ponge while two other colleagues, Marcelin Pleynet and Denis Roche, were equally interested in the works of this materialist poet.

One of the first of Ponge's texts the *Nouvelle Revue Française* had taken was entitled "Logoscope." The true intent of this poem, whose subject was the word, the reading of language, only became apparent thirty years later. For the *Tel Quel* group, Ponge incarnated a "scientific" approach to poetry and the poetic discourse. Far from being a typical confessional poet or a metaphysical one, he thoroughly suited the description of the writer as researcher in the laboratory of language, guided not so much by an anterior production of poetry as by the critical texts of some of these poets, especially Lautréamont and Mallarmé, and those of Marx and Nietzsche. And above them all, the *Littré* dictionary.

As Existentialism had succumbed to the Structuralist school, so in turn that school was destined to diminish in importance with the increasing attention paid to a political-philosophic perspective that still maintained the linguistic and psychoanalytical interpreta-

tions intact. Claude Lévi-Strauss, in this typically French *mise en scène*, was relegated to the background as Foucault, Deleuze, and Guattari, and Jacques Derrida moved to the fore. Lacan, Barthes, and Kristeva were among the fortunate survivors. It is not necessary here to detail the differences between these two groups of interests: what is necessary to note, however, is that once again the works of Francis Ponge were to be appreciated, and this time, by one of the leading younger French philosphers, Jacques Derrida. In his course at Yale University, as a participant at the Francis Ponge Decade at Cerisy-la-Salle in 1975, and in his published essay on Ponge, the poet had found one of the most gifted contemporary readers, a commentator who could do justice to Ponge's signature (Jacques Derrida, "Signéponge," in *Francis Ponge, Colloque Cerisy*, 10/18 [1977], 115-144).

In the United States, Ponge's reputation has not gone unobserved. He first came to this country in 1965 under the auspices of the French government for a tour of American colleges and universities. The following year, he was named visiting Gildersleeve professor at Barnard College where he gave a seminar on French poetics from Malherbe to Lautréamont. In 1970 he was invited to participate in the International Festival of Poetry organized by the Library of Congress, and two years later, he was awarded the Ingram Merrill Foundation Prize. More recently, he received the International Books Abroad/Neustadt prize.

And yet there is relatively little known about this major French poet and thinker in this country. It is to fill this absence of information that I have selected a number of texts that not only show his talents as a poet but also the perspicacity of his views on literature, rhetoric, and poetics, topics that closely define the position of the writer in France and allow the reader the possibility of placing Ponge in an aesthetic and ideological context. One thing is clear when dealing with contemporary French poetry: at no time is a poet ever satisfied with making a purely poetic statement. The conditions of his work are such that he will have to justify his place in literature, and in a wider sense, in culture as well. This usually takes the form of a critical discourse wherein the poet-turned-critic

explains his views and rejects those of others, thereby situating himself within the tradition of French letters. Tristan Tzara condemned manifestos in a manifesto and André Breton wrote two manifestos and a prolegomena to a third one. Francis Ponge has never accepted this solution. More in line with Malherbe and Flaubert, his opinions are directly found in his writings. As a consequence, one of the characteristics of Ponge's work is the stylistic continuity between the two traditionally antithetical discourses: the critical one and the creative one. As a poet, Francis Ponge has always been interested in language and aesthetic problems; as a critic, he has been specifically aware of the terms of the poetic discourse and their relationship to reality. The result has been a harmonious voice that, in an exemplary fashion, as it has revealed Ponge's ways of writing has also described his ways of being.

II

In the following pages, I shall examine Ponge's views on language and on rhetoric; views he has communicated with an exuberance equal to that of the most passionate voice in traditional poetry. And to begin with, this statement: "In order for a text to expect in any way to render an account of reality of the concrete world (or the spiritual one), it must first attain reality in its own world, the textual one" (*Pour un Malherbe* [1965], 48). The immediacy of the warning is an indication of the need to reconsider the nature of the text. The poet can never successfully translate his linguistic impressions of the universe without first recognizing and clarifying its own domain. He must weigh the relationship between language and things, and in so doing, grant primary importance to the linguistic phenomenon. For once, the poet has to be conscious not only of what he says but how he says it, and especially what allows him to express himself—his tools, and the rules that dictate their usages.

As a result, it is not surprising that Ponge initially assumed the responsibility of elaborating the specific linguistic confines within

which his own works exist, an area that stands halfway between the language of the street and the academic one. "We must differentiate our position in relationship, *on the one hand*, to journalism, radio, and to this vulgar, slovenly, dirty, undisciplined language, which is also taking over publishing, and, *on the other hand*, to that academic language, lucid but dead, simplistic, so-called litotic, in reality, worn-out . . ." (ibid., 163). For such a writer, there is no innocence left in the act of writing, in the act of possessing language. There are revolutionary consequences to this aesthetic and linguistic judgment.

Throughout his life, Ponge has most forcefully reacted against a naïve interpretation of both prose and poetry. "But there is perhaps one possible stance which consists in denouncing this tyranny at every turn: I will never retort except in the guise of a *revolutionary* or a *poet*" (*A Chat-perché, Tome premier* [1965], 180). One might slightly modify this declaration and rewrite it thus: revolutionary as a poet, since Francis Ponge has consistently fought a battle with a strategy based on the precise use of language, a language aware of itself, of its connection with the socioeconomic reality as well as its own etymological realities. Only under such circumstances will language once again be able to discover its fitting correspondence with material objects in the world. In so defining language, Ponge refuses to accept the hermetically closed structures that some believe language and the world to be. Rather, he would insist on the dual materiality of both and the connection therein contained. Language does not exist in a void: objects remind the poet of the constant weightiness of language itself, a weight that time has accorded to it, that etymology demonstrates in the *Littré* dictionary. There is, as a consequence, no epistemological gulf between words and things, between our capacity of verbalizing the world and the world itself. This emphatic posture is also characteristic of Ponge's particular brand of vanity, his combination of pride and temerity which is inherent in his statements. For him, it is the language of the poet that has to reach out to grasp the world: nothing else has the proper materiality to translate his views. "The power of language . . . the verbal functioning, without any lauda-

tory or pejorative coefficient. . . ." (*Le Soleil placé en abîme, Le Grand Recueil*, II [1961], 166). Language thus becomes the most demanding, the most serious preoccupation since it puts on paper those basic elements that account not only for the world and our capacity to perceive it (and allow ourselves to become conscious of it as a result) but our very selves as we are differentiated from beasts in the universe.

In the twenties and thirties, Ponge focused his attention on things that he sought to render textually. In order to free himself from a long historical lyrical continuum, to situate himself outside of the major evolution of French poetry as of the Renaissance, Ponge refused to commit his emotions to paper, as so many of his predecessors had done and that in such an expansive fashion. This denial of the lyrico-subjective is not a novel position in French letters. It was practiced by those writers whom Ponge openly claims as his models. And for example, Mallarmé's writings especially in *Divagations* and *Igitur*, Rimbaud's denunciation of subjectivism in his famous letter to Paul Demeny, and Lautréamont's vociferous criticisms of the same topic in *Poésies I* (one might also refer to Artaud's *En finir avec les chefs d'oeuvres*). The Surrealists were themselves, in their theoretical texts, also assertive in rejecting the ego-centered, confessional type of poetry, believing that automatic writing would reveal a universal imaginative substructure that would demonstrate the validity of Lautréamont's own dictum that poetry could be written by anyone.

For Ponge, the decision to exclude formally any allusion to his own subjectivity, to his own emotions, to his relationship with his wife or daughter, to his commitment to politics, rests both on affective and intellectual reasons. If his elimination of nearly all such personal references was applauded as a poetic application of a phenomenological disposition, other reasons exist as well and should be identified in order to appreciate the proper place of this ambition in his work. In *Tentative orale*, he declares that, finding himself on the edge of a precipice, he grasped at a pebble as the only thing left at hand. This non-Pascalian image is a very powerful one, and belies any reading of Ponge that would solely attend to the thing

grasped and not to the despairing situation that preceded it (*Tentative orale, Le Grand Recueil,* II, 247).

For one who found speaking nearly impossible (he had also failed a major oral examination), writing became his only means to "grasp" the object that was to save him. Objects, therefore, are not careless elements in Ponge's poetry; they were not lightly chosen. On the contrary, it is upon them that his fate depends; upon them that, metaphorically speaking, his fate as a poet will be decided. If objects are endowed with such significance and language considered as the only medium capable of describing them, of "holding" them, it thus becomes essential to filter out all the impurities of language, everything that would tend to weaken its effectiveness, given the fact that such definitions of things assure the poet's salvation, in a purely material way, of course.

According to Francis Ponge, these impurities that have left their traces on language go back to Humanism, a period where, for the first time, man's relationship with the world became so obsessively dominant that he came to ignore all previous attention paid to the complex order of nature, to its entirety. In a grandiose oversimplification, perhaps warranted by the very dimensions of the struggle, Ponge excoriates both the obscurantist reign of the Middle Ages, and man's fall from modesty as of the Renaissance. The blame is squarely put on a "system of values which we have inherited from Jerusalem, Athens, Rome . . ." (*Entretiens avec Breton, Le Grand Recueil,* II, 292). In accordance with this "system of values," man finds himself apotheosized, the center of the universe, much as Christian theologians once believed God had centered the world in the cosmos. Beginning in the sixteenth century, both earth and man were put in the center of the universe. The consequences of this counter-Copernician positioning were such as to call into being an equally powerful argument on the part of Francis Ponge. To redress the wrong done to man (that is, to language itself), Ponge sought to reestablish a vibrant (living) accord between man and the only monument that he could truly claim as his own: his word. "Our true blood: words" (*Des raisons d'écrire, Tome premier,* 185).

Unlike DADA and Surrealism's polemical declarations against

rationalism (Descartes as the aweful Father figure in French letters), Ponge's revolutionary undertaking had to be modest (and rational) as he worked in verbal fields that had previously been neglected and doing so in opposition to Breton's insistence on automatic writing as the solitary means of uncovering an uncensored reality. Language was too important, its procedures, its polysemic structures, its manifestations, to be disregarded or assigned to the uncontrolled workings of the mind, expulsing whatever happened to have been lodged inside it. If Breton acknowledged the marvelous role the analogy played in poetry, that was far from being enough. What had to occur was a radical reappreciation of rhetoric itself, especially since its role had increasingly diminished in contemporary expression. If its successes had been founded on the triad Jerusalem, Athens, and Rome, in a Marxist recognition of the interrelationship between language and reality, Ponge claimed that as of the 1870s its powers had waned. The connection, he found, was between Euclid and such rhetorical figures as the ellipse and the parabole, and the rise of a non-Euclidean geometry where such figures were no longer applicable. Those who continued to use them were not only reactionary but inexpressive, and in the long run, oppressive, since they maintained at the heart of the writing experience a dogma that had been rejected for its inappropriateness in a world newly defined by mathematicians and scientists.

Francis Ponge is so sure, in a positivist sense, of his ability to found a new rhetoric, suitable to his total work and to each one of his written texts, that he is willing to propose a rather hyperbolic metaphor to define his own place in French Literature. The image he suggests is the poet as a branch on the tree of literature, carrying it still farther, perpetuating it. The roots of this tree are in the works of Lucretius and Cicero, contain Malherbe and end up with Francis Ponge himself, thereby assuring him not only a place on Mt. Parnassus but perhaps, eventually, in the Pantheon. The reference to Lucretius and Cicero is justified, for Ponge, in that both these writers had so ardently worked in the language at their disposition. As they had put rhetoric through its paces, had, indeed, defined its practice in their own works, so Ponge considers his own medita-

tions on the topic of equal weight, his observations, made as early as the twenties on the need to reform rhetoric, of equal importance —within the French language to rediscover its virile condition; within the antiquated definitions of classical rhetoric to rediscover a scriptural practice.

This conviction of belonging to the tree of French Literature, all the while occupying what effectively is an eccentric position, attests to the radical nature of his interpretation of the evolving substance of language as it has been made visible in the works of some of his favorite writers (La Fontaine, Malherbe, Mallarmé . . .). His own statements on this matter have permitted him not only to elucidate the linguistic transmutations of an object but have become object lessons in poetics itself. All poetic texts, in this light, serve as metapoetical indicators. They comment upon their own existence as poems; they elaborate their own rules, their own rhetoric. In pursuing such a venture, the past has never hesitated to correlate words and things. As Ponge works through his descriptions of a piece of soap, an oyster, a blackberry, or a meadow (without ever adopting the evident solutions of Apollinaire's *Calligrammes* or the more esoteric typographical demonstrations in Mallarmé's *Un Coup de dés*), the unity becomes apparent between language and form (rhetorical figures), language and the extralinguistic cosmos. This double existence is visually defined in the poem, *L'Huître* (*The Oyster*). Here, as he himself explains it, the number of words ending in-*âtre* were found, consciously or not, because of the way the circumflex accent seemed to duplicate, within language itself, the oyster's own cover. It is only by understanding the expressive nature of language, its signifier as well as its signified, that one can approximate the actual physical reach of the hand to the thing and, thereby, through the perception and description of objects, attain a more complex objective. Ponge defines this next objective as the New Man, the one who bears little relationship to the Judeo-Christian-Humanistic perversions that have prohibited man from picking up the signals emitted by "silent" objects, by a world that is not entirely made in man's own image. New Man's lexical operations provide these objects, recuperated from the world of silence, with

such a precise rhetoric, such succinct form and vocabulary that they are once again able to reveal their presence in the world of literature. If for no other reason, this achievement would have assured Ponge of his place as a branch on the tree of French Literature.

The most instructive text at the beginning of Ponge's career as a published writer is unquestionably *Le Parti pris des choses*. Far from being an assortment of poems, loosely connected by a thematic insistence on things, it purports to teach us how to read, how to be guided and instructed by objects themselves as they are transcribed poetically. As a result, this collection is both a seminal work in French poetry and a most significant one in the area of didactic poetics. Here, things will not permit themselves to be neatly arranged by the author. On the contrary, "things have got to disturb you" writes Ponge (*Tentative orale, Le Grand Recueil*, II, 257). Bounded by the physicalness of the objects under consideration, Ponge limits his philosophic engagements to material definitions, a form of nominalism that leads back to Marx himself. However, more pertinent still, the antecedent can be found for this type of reflection in the writings of Epicurus, and especially in their poetic interpretation in Lucretius's *De natura rerum*. And Ponge had declared that his intention in writing poetry was not to assemble disparate texts and put them together in one volume but to duplicate Lucretius's own methodological approach to the universe, to the universe of language, too.

Far from inventing a new world, dependent on subjective events, on "inspiration," on a projection of one's mood on the world, and thus an imperial effort to make it *one's* world, Ponge prefers to consider himself as a laboratory technician, as a worker (in opposition to the apparently uncommitted poet, the one who believes he can exist far from the actual world). "The artist's function is thus quite clear: he must open up a workshop and take in the world for repair, as it comes to him, in pieces" (*Le Murmure, Le Grand Recueil*, II, 193). Language, of course, should be thought of as one of these pieces and as such, once reassembled, once cleaned and ready to work again, made to assume its responsibilities. Words are now in a position (mobile or immobile) to claim

14

(declaim) their proper nature. All they require is a servant, an admirer, one who is ready to discard the usual transformational expressions (unjustified metaphors) that impose man's sentimentality (his optics) on all things.

In this, Ponge faithfully adheres to Lautréamont's own formula: "The fourth Song shall either be begun by a man, a stone or a tree. . . ." But the poet is not the dupe of his own contained enthusiasm. Objects do not speak: only man does, and that, among other men. Consequently, things are only halfway houses leading to men themselves, to an appreciation of man's nature, still so complex as to limit Ponge's approach to purely descriptive maneuvers, as if he were tracking down an unknown prey by plotting out its proportions from the traces left on the ground (on paper). *Le Parti pris des choses* should then be taken as a prolegomena to the Collected Works, to the *Grand Recueil*, the body of the work. "If I call them reasons [for living], it is because they lead the mind back to things. Only the mind can refresh things. However, these reasons are right or valid insofar as the mind returns to things in a way acceptable to things: when they are not slighted, that is, when they are described from their own point of view" (*Raisons de vivre heureux, Tome premier*, 189).

Once again, and in most explicit terms, the emotive self is exiled from the text, in accord with the previously indicated posture. But now a further element is postulated. "The following is a definition of the things I love: they are the ones about which I do not speak, about which I would like to speak, about which I cannot speak" (*Tentative orale, Le Grand Recueil*, II, 246). This recognition of the inability of the poet to "speak" prohibits, in his own declaration, the deepest emotions from being vented, and so they find their way to the visible surface of the text in a sublimated form, taking on the apparent objective reality of the things in question, of the things that his language questions. This destitution of the power of speech energizes the textual expression, that rage that has to explode in order to reveal another world that, otherwise would have remained outside the text, silenced, so to speak.

And yet, if one were to follow Ponge's own reflections

15

throughout his work, it would not be difficult to discover either his tastes or his powerful normative judgments. *Le Parti pris des choses* is a most eloquent portrait of the man himself. Without ever anthropomorphizing the universe he describes, his selection of metaphors, the absolute concurrence between words and things, allow the reader to discover the poet, as poet and as sensitivity. However, the clearest portrayal is to be found in his frequent sorties into art criticism. There, immodestly, though obliquely, through individuals he praises, one comes to appreciate, nearly intact, the Francis Ponge that had willfully escaped attention in the absence of specific texts dealing with his person. Speaking about the Breton painter Kermadec, Ponge writes: "The most important thing to note . . . is the intransigence of his libertarian mind, egotistical *and* the elegance of a life style, his way of living. . . . A man who is neither modest nor vain" (*Quelques notes sur E. de Kermadec, Nouveau Recueil* [1967], 116).

It would not be difficult to find other telling characteristics in the portraits he draws of others and for instance, his comments on Giacometti. But the most illuminating, and at once the most fascinating, joyous and at times unbearably pretentious exercise is unquestionably his alliance (his confusion) with François Malherbe, founder of modern French poetics. It was this seventeenth-century poet who, single-handedly, reformed the extravagances of the *Pléiade*, and as a result paved the way for the classical writers of the latter part of the century. Often with tongue in cheek but frequently in absolute earnestness, Ponge aspires to a similar position of responsibility. He too would like to be the next determinant within French poetry and for the French language itself. These appreciations are thus to be construed as ideal projective portraits. In all of them, the reader can catch a glimpse of what Ponge has incompletely defined as the New Man, that creature standing diametrically opposed to the Renaissance man. "Let us put man back in his place in nature: it is a rather honorable one. Let us give back to man his proper rank in nature: it is a rather high one" (*Notes premières de l'homme, Tome premier,* 240).

This enterprise constitutes a major redefinition of poetics.

Ponge not only debunks the Romantics and the Surrealists, the Mussets and the Bretons, those who lyricize from the heart or the unconscious, but he has also come prepared with a tonic solution. Poetry can only extricate itself from its predicament by taking seriously its place in language. Then language will transgress old poetic codes and, outfitting the simplest objects in a proper linguistic parallel, will, once again, be correctly apparelled. Nothing could be more disruptive than this insertion of a new body of things (of a new and invigorated language) into the text of poetry. Nothing so materially violates the sacrosanct lyrical world as the appearance, and that en masse (in its double meaning), of the simplest objects, animate and inanimate. Ponge, in so doing, separates himself from nearly all his predecessors with the exception of poets like Rimbaud, Lautréamont, and Mallarmé.

When he turns his attention to contemporary French poetry, he is equally critical of his fellow poets, whether metaphysicians like Yves Bonnefoy, Catholics like Pierre Emmanuel, post-Surrealists like Alain Jouffroy, or lyricists like Jacques Prévert. Neither is he convinced of the manner in which either René Char or André du Bouchet have redesigned the natural landscape or the manner in which Follain maintained a nostalgic overhang on the objects that he described, or the temptation to moralize about them as Guillevic has done. This aggressive criticism is meant to assure the distinctiveness of his own position. "I would like to write a sort of *De natura rerum*" (*Introduction au galet, Tome premier*, 200), an enterprise that would let Ponge integrate things into a new cosmogony founded on a new phenomenological dictionary and perhaps even a new cosmetic (which, according to the *Littré*, shares the same root with cosmos: world, order, ornament). This declaration makes it clear that the realm of ideas must share equal status with words themselves. Such words must be cleared of all taints in order to be faithful to their vowels and consonants in a positive, symphonic, and material way.

If Ponge turns to the sun, it is not to offer himself as victim, in a Rimbaldian sacrifice but to capture the sun in a linguistic webbing, thereby marking man's particularity, his specific difference:

17

the manipulation of language. That is man's deed and the one that he passes on and which defines him. As a consequence, Ponge exercises great prudence when he uses analogies or metaphors since such rhetorical figures tend to define by restriction rather than similitude. This is not to say that such figures are absent from his work. They consistently appear whether he is describing a rowboat as a bucking horse or an apricot as a baby's bottom. But they are sanctioned by the thing described. The imagination in these pursuits is not excluded; it is bounded by a respect for language. Whereas the scientist uses language to clarify his intentions, the poet submits language to its own arbitration in order to honor it as both word and thing. At the beginning then, a specific ambition: "I intend to formulate descriptions—definitions—literary *objets d'art*" (*My Creative Method, Le Grand Recueil*, II, 17). The rule for this circumscription of the verbal universe is given in a pithy and all-important formula: "SPEAKING FOR THINGS *equals* A RECOGNITION OF WORDS" (ibid., 19). At no time in his poetic practice has Francis Ponge ever slighted one or the other and any explanation of his work which tends to accentuate the one in favor of the other is bound to be erroneous, that is, off balance.

To redo the world linguistically: "In every sense of the word, *remake*, due to the character simultaneously concrete and abstract, interior and exterior of the VERB! due to its semantical thickness" (*Nous ferons une oeuvre classique, Tome premier*, 228). This gravity, this weightiness of words acts upon the poem itself. Ponge disallows the text the pleasure of self-involvement as the Surrealists had done. The unraveling of the poem is neither generated by homophonic associations nor is it produced by the automatic movement of the pen. Rather, more in line with the scribe working his style on matter, the language of poetry is as dense and as formal as any hieroglyph. And thus Ponge literally prohibits his text from "taking off," in unforeseen directions. When, by chance, as it occurred in the case of the fig, a chance association does occur, he is unduly preoccupied with its elimination, its reduction to a meaning contextually acceptable. (*Comment une figue de paroles et pourquoi* [Flammarion, 1977], 1). In *Le Savon*, for example, he was

first tempted to use red ink and box in a duplicate of the plane's instructional panel but the idea was discarded because he found it too easy, too DADA, as he says. In that same text, where effervescent words do accumulate, where they do indeed collude and resuscitate each other, the reasons are self-evident and self-contained: it is in the nature of soap to act out this frothy comedy. As it lathers, so must the text be enriched with synonyms, with verbal forms that approximate its physical presence. The source of these words, however, is not found in the unconscious, and liberated through free association; it is located in the dictionary and requires patience, and especially taste, the most intuitive and also the most rational demonstration of man's being in the world.

This critical posture is also directed against the tenets of classical formalism. In the seventeenth century, Le Brun and the Academy had declared that a portrait stood higher on the normative scale than a still-life. Ponge has reversed this qualitative system by attributing a superior rank to a still-life, to Chardin's as well as to his own. After all, treating still-lives represents the material first step of a cognitive process: the perfect practice of naming things, of being trained by things as one learns to respect them. Can any such ambitious project succeed? Ponge is the first to recognize the limits that are placed on it but in fact, derives a certain satisfaction from this very difficulty. All that remains, as he wrote in 1941 about Camus's *Le Mythe de Sisyphe*, is the artist's effort to render an account of his own "abortive descriptions" (*Réflexions en lisant "L'essai sur l'absurde," Tome premier,* 206). This pessimistic disposition is rare in Ponge's writings. More often than not, his exuberance cancels out such dark thoughts as he proclaims, and with disarming forthrightness, the manner in which he plans to go about the description of a segment of the material world.

If he has taken things in hand and has stood by them as the basic elements of his poetic reconstruction of the world (with a posture as intransigent as Breton's), Ponge, nevertheless, prefers the company of La Fontaine and Chardin, Bach, Mozart, and Rameau to a blade of grass. And this out of human vanity. Ponge much prefers an object made by man—a poem, a musical score, a painting—

to an object with no purpose (one might say, without an author). Fundamentally, things underscore both the betrayal of language and the nonsignificance of the world (*Vous me demandez, Tome premier*, 221). Despite this attitude, reminiscent of a Nietzschean reading of Schopenhauer (two authors Ponge greatly appreciated as a young man), only things (language, now) could save man from his distress, from the predicament that Camus had described in his own work. The sun, the sea, and the Greek equilibrium of the Mediterranean world would not suffice. The manipulation of language became Ponge's way of living happily, of making life bearable.

Finally, if language is a way of transcending difficulties in one's own life, it does so not only by allowing the poet to create an aesthetic experience but an ethical one. The two are inextricably connected. The text defines ways of living, ways of thinking, congruent to the event at hand, not molded by the hand but cautioned by the object itself, proceeding affirmatively and directly, with those metaphorical inventions suggested by the object itself. "It is especially (perhaps) against a mealy-mouthed ideological tendency that I came up with my own particular bias" (*C'est surtout [peut-être], Tome premier*, 211). Therefore, to be at the disposal of things meant to act in conformity with a position rejecting hidden correspondences and a search for "deep" or metaphysical meanings.

If an alliance with words justifies language (the term justification taken here both at its primary and typographical levels), such an arrangement does not warrant an uncritical inclusion of Ponge's work within a phenomenological argument as Jean-Paul Sartre had written in his article on *Le Parti pris des choses* in *Situations I*. Instead, as Ponge would have it, nuances have to be added to such an outright philosophical reading in order to recognize Saussure's influence (here as the paradigm of linguistics) alongside Husserl's. But such a reading had to be held in abeyance until the existential discourse had given way to another, one less heavily indebted to Kantian idealism and to a humanistic morality. According to this new intellectual grid, the structural one, defined in part by Claude Lévi-Strauss and Roman Jakobson, language and its structures, the

semiotic approach, could provide not just an approximation of the intent of thought but its very order and nature.

At one with Foucault's argument in *Les Mots et les choses*, Ponge would be the first to agree that the question is now one of recognizing that language is our only means of ordering the world, of converting the insignificant into the significant; the unmentionable into the spoken, nature into culture, or as one might venture to say, suppression into expression. But this evolution has led civilization farther and farther away from its initial roots (its etymologies, archaeologically speaking).

Claude Lévi-Strauss has projected a Rousseauistic pessimism over his own works, condemning, at a distance, the world in which he lives. He sees it as a deliberate destruction of our natural habitat. The apocalyptical message is clear: if we do not stop considering apparent linear progress as automatically beneficial, if we do not reverse a trend that goes back to the Middle Ages, and which Jean-Jacques Rousseau had already warned us about in the eighteenth century, then we shall ruin ourselves and the world about us. Language responds to our needs to order nature but it also provides us with a means of destroying it. If Ponge refuses to speak as magniloquently as Lévi-Strauss, he does share with him both his suspicions about the Occidental solution and his insistence on the primacy of linguistics.

At a time when Literature as a body of consequent writing is being questioned by critics like Todorov who would prefer to overlook it in order to perfect their own signifying analyses, at a time when critics such as Roland Barthes are formulating, in a post-Saussurian world, an *arcana verba* in metalinguistics, removed from the materiality of the world, at a time when both Maoism and, indirectly, a return to Sartrean preoccupations are evident in the recent directions taken by *Tel Quel*, Francis Ponge, and with insistence, reverts back, or more exactly, deepens his initial explanation which he had devised early on in his life as a writer. "Things are *already as close to words* as they are to things, and reciprocally, words are *already as close to things* as they are to words" (*La Fabrique du pré*

21

[Skira, 1971], 23). This undeniable material consolidation removes the poetic text from a reading which considers it as decorative or illustrative of a linguistic theory, an appendage of criticism. The reading that is imposed by the Pongian text insists on its phonemic qualities and its form as well as its content. Lacan in his 1953 essay on "Fonction et champ de la parole et du langage en psychanalyse," defined the unconscious in terms of a quadratic field where the function of language is to preserve history, that otherwise censured truth. Lacan initially defined the unconscious as monuments, or the body itself, the hysterical nucleus of our neurosis "where the hysteric symptom reveals the structure of a language and deciphers itself like an inscription..." (*Ecrits I* [Seuil, 1961], 136). Second, the unconscious as the archival document—it contains the impenetrable and unknown origins of childhood memories; third, the unconscious as a semantical evolution containing our particular lexical stock, as specific as our life style and our personality. Last, Lacan proposes to treat traditions as another form of our unconscious, "In truth, legends that, under a heroical form, express my life" (ibid., 137). Though Francis Ponge might shun such a ready transcription of his work through a Lacanian interpretation, I believe he would recognize the pertinency of the fourfold presentation: he has himself underlined them in interviews and in his own writings. The difference, and a notable one, is that Ponge personally assumes the responsibility of both discovering the elements to be analyzed and the analysis as well. Ponge, of all contemporary poets, prides himself on his eminent lucidity. It is reason above all, and reason tempered by the dialectical appreciation of the place of man in the world.

III

No poetic text can exist without rhetoric; there is no "outside" position. What the poet does confront is the absolute need to refashion a rhetoric, or perhaps, more accurately, to allow the rhetoric of the text to be fashioned by its own discourse. For Ponge, rhetoric is

inescapable: it is codeterminant with the text itself. As a metalanguage, it formalizes the textual surface, taking itself as its own reference, a discourse on discourse itself.

Ponge, of course, is far from being alone in his appreciations of the rhetorical act. Rather, he assumes a perfect consciousness of it and of that tradition which goes back to Aristotle. To valorize rhetoric is to recognize the structural determinants of Western culture and its ideological basis. It implies an assessment of its literary and literal values. Initially, as a technique, it was the art of persuasion, a set of rules that, once learned, provided the manipulator with sufficient power to convince his listeners, his readers. Oral in the beginning, it was called eloquence. Then, as it assumed a written identity, it found its place in stylistics, and eventually came to be identified with literature itself, with its profound mechanisms. But rhetoric was also a science, applying itself to a delimited field with homogeneous elements: the "effects" of language, the classification of these elements (the "figures" of rhetoric), and a metalanguage, that is, a compilation of rhetorical treatises where language itself was described. These attributes would have assured it a central position within the culture but its rule extended further to include a moral-aesthetic code, as it defined the permissible, and consequently acknowledged certain transgressive divergences. The distinction between so-called ordinary speech and literary writing constituted one such polarization while a similar duality was constituted in an ethical model where behavior was equally well defined. Finally, rhetoric, as Roland Barthes has pointed out, sanctions a particular social practice (*Communications*, 16 [1970], 173). As a learned technique, it is not a neutral phenomenon. Indeed, it is still closely associated with the middle class in France for which language is one of the principal (and expensive) means of attaining social status.

Rhetoric, however, does not exist in a void. Through a series of complex historical and cultural phenomena, its position in French schools was first weakened in the 1870s and then destroyed. The *classe de rhétorique*, though it still continued to exist in name, was phased out in the 1880s. Such a decision on the part of the

Introduction

Ministry of Education might mislead a reader into thinking that what had up to then been dominant was now on its way out. Such, of course, was not the case. The truth of the matter is more organic; less dramatic, in fact. If French schoolchildren stopped learning rhetoric as a subject in the last year of their lycée careers (as did Francis Ponge, for example, and his father before him) that did not indicate the disappearance of the subject. The curriculum had merely changed labels and introduced rhetoric in literature courses, the backbone of a French education. The emphasis on the *explication de texte*, the close textual analysis, and on the *morceau choisi* method, too clearly reminded one of the digests of expressions (rhetorical figures) that clerics in the Middle Ages had to memorize in order to perform with sufficient grace (eloquence) in their future sermons. Thus as rhetoric slowly retreated as an official subject, it was reintroduced in the study of literature, where it became the sine qua non of its explanation.

And yet alongside these rather regressive tendencies, the study of rhetoric has once more, in our time, preoccupied leading critics of literature and language. In Russia, Switzerland, France, Belgium, and the United States, interest in rhetoric has been emblematic of the most adventurous sectors of the university and the world of critics. If classical figures and tropes no longer exclusively provide the grid for interpreting literature (its intentions, its forms, and its language), they do provide metalinguistic terms that allow for a systematic treatment of language as a privileged area of expression, not to speak of the useful transference of this vocabulary to nonlinguistic, semiotic fields. Stylisticians, semioticians, linguists, philosophers, and psychoanalysts have all, either explicitly or implicitly, turned back to Aristotle's formulations in the hope of perfecting their decoding potential. Far from being a peripheral interest, applicable to the analysis of literary "ornaments," rhetoric has become one of the key analytical mechanisms leading to an understanding of the foundations of the text, of meaning in communication itself.

These observations lead to one conclusion: as a poet, it is impossible to use the French language (or any other language, for that matter) and avoid finding oneself operating within the rules,

practices, and historical definitions of rhetoric. As a result, one way of affirming one's independence is to assume a deliberate stance in the face of rhetoric, to deny its hold and simultaneously to constitute a parallel rhetoric. Francis Ponge has done precisely that in a conscious effort to situate himself within the confines of French literature. "I also feel that I have another mission *as well*, which is to discover verbal forms, original expressive formulations. A way of marking the language with my style, making the spirit of the French language walk forward step by step, working in the verbal laboratory, providing examples, models . . ." (*Pour un Malherbe*, 70). The poet does not invent language. Rather, his task is one of validating it through a complex process involving etymological meanings and homophonic elements. That decision marks a departure of consequence given the avant-garde tradition of twentieth-century French poetry. If the poet cannot lay claim to the making of his own language, if he will not let himself be "carried away" by free associations, he can, nevertheless, act against the old and persistent forms of rhetoric. "At that moment, teaching the art of *resisting words* becomes useful, the art of saying only what one wants to say, the art of doing them (the words) violence, of forcing them to submit. In short, of founding a rhetoric . . ." (*Rhétorique, Tome premier*, 177). By what other means can the poet rid himself of ready-made expressions, of the Babelian noises of contemporary civilization?

Such reactions against the world had already become part of the intellectual heritage of the century, having been preceded by Romantic criticism of bourgeois materialism, Nietzschean denunciation of Christian models of culture, and Mallarmé's frontal attack against the language of poetry, the very means whereby civilization expresses itself. So that, by the mid-twenties, to assail the word (world) was no longer a novelty. The poet had to find a more hyperbolic formula. In 1928-29, with what appears as an excessive show of bravura, Ponge allied himself with Stravinsky and Picasso, two other men of his own conviction who had systematically refused what to others had seemed the absolute rules of the game (*Raisons de vivre heureux, Tome premier*, 190). Alongside these

two self-appointed peers, stands Lautréamont who succeeded in demolishing the system of poetics that Malherbe had legislated in the seventeenth century.

Still, the selection of models is not to be equated with a doctrine that would permit the reformulation of ways of being as a writer. But Ponge, like Flaubert and Malherbe before him, is not a theoretician. What he shares with those two Normans is the capacity of rendering explicit some of his fundamental assumptions and for example: to write "against all existing rules" (*La Rage de l'expression, Tome premier*, 379). The decision is not part of a program but rather textually demonstrable and always in a unique situation. For Francis Ponge, this deliberate act entails the perfection of a lucid technique, a condition defining the approach to the object. "The poet must never put forth a thought but an object, that is to say, that even upon thought itself, he must impose the stance of an object" (*Natare piscem doces, Tome premier*, 148). This modification of things by words themselves, this collaboration between words and things, as we have seen, is such that they intermesh harmoniously. Besides, as Ponge declared in "Le Pain," at times, such objects are less a matter of respect, and in the case of bread, of religious respect, than they are of consumption. Poems must be "eaten" as the Japanese poet Takoboku said. Finished is the sacrosanct nature of the poetic text, the awe in which the poet and his precious object must be regarded. It is this decision to jump off the merry-go-round of centuries of words that Ponge sees as the beginning of a new rhetoric of things, as a new poetic posture in front of things. Words themselves have their semantical thickness; therein lies the overture to the text itself.

Words must not be thought of as abstractions, as transparencies, as means to an end. For Ponge, words are not to be solicited in order to gain access to some transcendent realm that would permit the poet to correspond with a spiritual world wherein words would be metaphorical translations of a Platonic ideal. Words, furthermore, by being in possession of themselves (not being dependent on others), reject anthropomorphic ambitions, the projection of the

writer's feelings onto the world about him. Consequently, words, for once, attain their own paradise. They are perfect in themselves, revealing the triple characteristics (as Ponge notes in *Pour un Malherbe*, and as he had previously done in *My Creative method* and in *Proclamation et petit four*) that the Greeks had already defined as phanopia and melopia (the signifier), and logopoeia (the signified). Words have shapes, sounds, and meaning(s). Together, these elements constitute the articulation of the sign on the textual surface.

Now that classical rhetoric has been overturned, Ponge cries out: "Long Live Rhetoric!" But this time, rhetoric informs the work in a less visible manner. It is a skeleton, a fetus (*My Creative method, Le Grand Recueil*, II, 36). And thus, "if we find it impossible to believe that an object deliberately begins to speak (prosopopeia) which, in any case, would be too easy a rhetorical form and would eventually become monotonous, nevertheless, every object must impose on the poem a particular rhetorical form" (ibid.). That form, as the skeletal analogy implies, is far removed from either the Apollinairian effects or the Mallarmean experiments. Ponge defines it in the following way: "This clockwork mechanism is in fact the rhetoric of the object...." (*Tentative orale, Le Grand Recueil*, II, 260). The clockwork metaphor is not a fortuitous one; it is meant to remind the reader of a Newtonian eighteenth century and also a century of French materialism which was one of the primary influences on Marx's philosophy.

The object (become subject) imposes its form on the poem. The *Seine* assumes a certain verbal fluidity but it is also the scene, and as of that moment, the polysemic elements begin to manifest themselves, because in French the word scene is a homonym for Seine and thus the poem is at once text, stage, and river (it may also be a pun on the Last Supper, *La Cène*, in French). Nothing consequently is transparent. All the polyvalencies catch the eye and the mind and guide them through an elaborate system of textual indicators. Ponge presents us with a text within a text; he makes of that double scene the very matter of his description of the Seine (the

river, the poem). He forces the reader to acknowledge his limpid prose as a means of capturing and being captured by the physical requirements of the object rhetorically defined.

Rhetoric becomes the generating event, the source of the text (ibid., 532), without, however, ever misleading the reader (leading him astray, drowning him), or misrepresenting either the literal Seine or the figurative levels of the scene. Such multiplication of signifiers make us aware of the representational aspects of prose, its material production taken as a constant source of interest by the self-reflecting writer who makes it perfectly clear that he is dealing with *his* Seine which we are equally asked to trace as it evolves out of the line of print, scripted by Ponge who now becomes a resograph, effacing the image of the traditional, imaginative, intuitive poet. Adopting the role of scriptor, he has at his command all the possible resources of the writer, together with a far greater degree of objectivity. The rhetorical figures become both pre-text and the object of the text itself. The verbal discourse corresponds to the thing it designates, and which cannot exist without it. It is edified by it and invented by it. In this way, the text is a continuous series of interferences—crossings made with the subject of the text—and, as a result, language becomes cognizant of itself, responsible for its being on the page. The text is open, accessible to a reading that is regulated by signals emitted by it and that authorize the evolution of the writing itself, the body of the work.

Addressing a German radio audience through a speaker, Ponge begins *Le Savon* by underlining its own emergence *as a text*. "I am in the process of writing these initial lines. I am no further than you are. I am *no further ahead* than you are. We are going to *move* forward, we are already *moving* forward, *together*, you listening, I speaking (*Le Savon* [1967], 9). The incorporation of the reader in the evolution of the allegory is reminiscent of Lautréamont's prefatory warning in the first stanza of *Les Chants de Maldoror* and, in a more distant past, that other model reader, Memmius, for whom Lucretius had composed his epic poem.

Such an intention on the part of Ponge indicates an effort not only to build his work in full view (on the page) but also to associ-

ate the reader in all its developments, the periphrastic periods that antecede the actual and stabilized text that is now in the process of being, read, being born, in a manner of speaking. The reader in this enterprise becomes a supplementary justifier of the reality of the text. As a rhetorical figure (in both sense of the word *figure*), the "dear reader" is a synchronic branch of reality grafted onto the tree of poetics. The historical factor has been neutralized in Ponge's work; the traditional role of social or polemical reflections associated with the reader's perceptions have been eliminated. He is now stateless and timeless; he observes, and in that function satisfies the essential quality that is required of him. He has no other trait to contribute to the text, to its reading. The scriptor conjures him up as a needed dialectical fiction (reality?), and from that moment on, he is on a par with the text itself, bringing no other references to it, defined internally by it, and defining it as well for the reader, the observer. The reader (the eye) in this order of things, operates wholly within an extratemporal dimension, marked solely by material (linguistic) modifications. In *Le Savon*, for example, the soap disintegrates as the poem wears itself out. The reader too comes to the end of the piece he is reading, he is holding. The dialectical relationship does not pretend to connect the reader to a historical reality as much as it associates him to a textual phenomenon, and in this instance, allows the reader not only to cast his eyes on the text but to hold the object (the book, the theme of the book) in his hand. Few texts lend themselves as well to this conceit as does the bar of soap in its formal representation.

The association writer/reader has become increasingly apparent in recent years as Ponge has decided to publish, alongside the finished manuscript, the evidence of the selective process that culminates in the book. This diary or journal method structures *Le Savon, Pour un Malherbe,* and the texts published in *Tel Quel* ("L'avant-printemps," no. 3 [1968]) and in *Ephémère* ("L'Opinion changée quant aux fleurs," no. 5 [1968]). Such a procedure shows how rhetoric can be modified and Ponge's decision to substitute his own in the place of the conventional one. A new rhetoric conscious of itself. "RHETORIC, why should I recall your name? You are

now only a word with columns, the name of a palace I detest, from which my blood has forever excluded itself. Poetry? a ruined newspaper-stand in its gardens; and you, literature of our time, at best a nocturnal party that the enemy offers itself" (*Prologue aux questions rhétoriques, Le Grand Recueil*, II, 182-183). The object is a literature without illusion, as he declared in *Pour un Malherbe*; a literature that can partially free itself from the priorities accorded to the signified as it admits in the text the function of disguise, and what had rendered it inert, idealist, and monological in the past. In order to understand it, the reader does not need to duplicate empathetically the affective disposition of the poet nor must he try to guess what extratextual conditions may have contributed to the author's intentions. It is a curious and unforeseen justification of Pope's line: "WHATEVER IS IS RIGHT," and a closer approximation to Mallarmé's observation, in *Un Coup de dés*, that "Nothing will have occurred but the occurrence itself."

IV

So far, I have tried to indicate a certain number of elements pertaining to the mechanics of Ponge's writing. These have included approaches to the work itself, the double sense in which the word text must be taken: first, as the object in question (the *things* in *Le Parti pris des choses*), and second, the text as a linguistic phenomenon. But as it was evident in the case of the *Seine*, the secondary reading is coequal in importance with the first; in fact, fuses with the first, so that the reader is absolutely clear as to the integrity of the text.

I would now like to analyze the generative qualities of the text itself, the manner in which it is shaped, and how it determines what Ponge calls the obgame and Mallarmé had called the literary game. Perhaps one should begin with a few notations about Ponge's character, or more exactly, about his taste, especially since this aspect is so prominent in his early works. There, he appears as a turn-of-the-century dandy, reviling contemporary materialism. He is sensitive

Introduction

and haughty as he happily considers literature as the only significant pursuit. This disdain for the vulgar introduces a stylistic perspective reminiscent of the Parnassian Mallarmé, intent upon purifying the language of his tribe. For Ponge, then, literature (perhaps
it should be capitalized) represented a form of deliverance from the
overbearing crassness of a bourgeoisie that had soiled (spoiled) the
linguistic object. Literature, as it should now be understood, becomes an isolated and grandiose declaration of a way of living
against the world, outside the world; in fact, the pursuit of the literary grail comes to represent a quasi-religious purpose or, put in
another way, a political act far removed from the abstract ruminations of utopists or madmen. Literature then becomes a parallel
existence in this world, and yet totally unconcerned with the social
mores of the times, infected with bad taste and "illiterate commercialism" (*R. C. Seine, No . . . , Tome premier,* 75). In this particular
world, even those who were excluded from the marketplace were
not immune from criticism. "Down with intellectual merit! That's
an acceptable cry of revolt. I would not like to leave it at that—and
I would rather suggest stupefying oneself in an excess of technical
exercises, any one; and of course, my preferences would go to
those of language itself, to RHETORIC" (*Pas et le saut, Tome premier,* 135). Writing, and a comprehensive understanding of what
that implies, thus became a way of living, defining one's existence
in the world. In opposition to much of the subjective poetry then in
vogue, however, Francis Ponge's appeared to be more scientific
than "literary." To avoid Terpander's fate, Ponge practiced on his
lyre, keeping only the tautest strings. In this manner, the music of
the *proêmes* begins. But these few strings are guaranteed by the
Littré itself where words are defined historically and their meanings
illustrated through literary selections that reveal the richness of
each entry; the dimensions of a term as concrete as matter itself.
After that, all that is required is a degree of linguistic sensitivity,
intuition, and a passion for the literary act. Ponge has never failed
to accept, alongside this scientific determination, the profound and
necessary presence of intuition, and the need to be constant to one's
initial intuition, even in the face of apparent contradictions coming

31

from the dictionary itself. The origin of numerous puns, and for example, the sequence *pré, près, prêt,* in *Le Pré,* comes from this intuition founded on the signifier.

In his *Tentative orale,* Ponge describes writing as a very active form of contemplation, where the nominative function occurs almost immediately. It is similar to an alchemical action or, as he states parenthetically, to a political one. Rather than finding himself in a state of ecstasy "that insipid round" (*Tentative orale, Le Grand Recueil,* II, 254), the poet operates with the care and disinterestedness of the scientific researcher ("Déclaration: Condition et destin de l'Artiste," *Tel Quel* [Printemps 1968]). The fabrication of the text implies the composition of a vocabulary; this procedure, however, is totally unlike Michel Leiris's efforts in *Biffures,* or prior to that, any number of Surrealist texts, including perhaps the most illustrative one, Raymond Roussel's *Impressions d'Afrique.* The creation of a vocabulary cannot be left to chance invention. Thus, if through an intuitive act, Ponge is able to associate certain linguistic signs that, on the signified level, do not immediately belong to the same etymological category, these terms in the text become necessary in the linguistic structure that defines the text. Such rapprochements are one of the signals of the literary act. It is a signifying act made up of word-objects that leads to the definition of man himself (*certainement, en un sens, Tome premier,* 215). Through this austere and laboratorylike approach to language, and to what it contains, the poet succeeds in expressing "something, that is to say, himself, his will to live . . ." (ibid., 217). The emergence of the text becomes equivalent to a self-creation, and for Ponge, this is further guaranteed by the scriptural introduction of the reader into the game: "Since you are reading me, dear reader, therefore I am; since you are reading us (my book and I), dear reader, therefore we are (You, it and I)" (*Pour un Malherbe,* 203). This is a binding contract:

FABLE

By the word *by* the text thus begins
Whose first line states the truth,

But this tain under one and the other,
Can it be tolerated? There, dear reader,
You can already judge
Our difficulties...
[*Tome premier*, 144.]

This two-letter proposition initiates the text. It invites us to feast on words, provokes us to speech, and makes us observe the difference between ourselves and the rest of dumb nature. "And we are then invited to recognize it, and to say it, that is, to invite our words there, and in turn these words invite us to say it" (*Pour un Malherbe*, 250). The power of language is not only omnipresent but nothing else can rival it. It is the one that authorizes Nature (according to the *Littré*, that word shares a common origin with to be born, birth) to emerge, and in a very material manner since, as Ponge declares, *Le Pré* can only be rendered accurately by language: painting cannot achieve the same objective. Such an endeavor is not wasted effort. It means what it says, and what is said corresponds to reality—to Nature itself.

Take a tube of green and spread it on the page,
That's not the way to make a meadow.
They are born differently.
They spring up from the page.
And then only from a brown page.
[*Le Pré, Nouveau Recueil*, 203.]

The complete *La Fabrique du Pré* (unpaginated) becomes, as a result, not only an eulogy to the natural processes of the meadow and its growth but also to the expressivity of language itself and its capacity to surface on the page. The correlation between words and things is then assured: both rising from the same inspiration. The published text begins with a replica of the handwritten manuscript as if the author wanted to equate his own preparatory work with the meadow itself and its preliminary activity, below the surface, before it becomes what we can see or sit upon. The text is then fol-

lowed by photographs and reproductions of paintings, landscapes, musical scores, *Littré* definitions, botanical sketches, buildings, and maps—all situating the meadow in question; the meadow upon which we lie and which the poet lays on the page. In this way, the meadow is before our eyes. It actually springs from the brown paper. This section of the text is followed by the printed manuscript on green paper, thereby closing the circle (the natural cycle) which includes, most prominently, language itself, its ancient history brought up-to-date, participating in the cycle that is the one shared by man in nature.

Le Savon, long in the making, reveals the same procedural advances. The poet, like the painter, keeps his sketches facing the wall until he is ready to finish them. He then turns them around, works them up, and when they are completed, has them carried to the printer who affixes them on the page. So it was with *Le Savon*, containing the sum of Ponge's aesthetics and materialist ethics, containing also his belief in the supremacy of language as it becomes the object of the text: the text-object. This work, perhaps one of the longest running metaphors in literature, slowly unwinds, bubbles in verbal inventions, and finally evaporates, leaving the water slightly troubled, slightly darker, but the hands clean, really clean. Unlike Holy Water, the bar of soap is not metaphysical or theological; it is, first of all, a phenomenological acquisition. In fact, it is a part of the nominalist game, a linguistic exercise rarely found in poetry. The bar of soap is then a redemptor. Out of murky literary habits, Ponge has devised a way of cleaning his text, and through it, man himself, his vocabulary, and as a consequence, his way of being in the world. Because, quite clearly, for the poet, the soap in question is not a poetic image but a functional item, and it must be used, even abused, without any pejorative connotations appended to that expression. "And thus we slide from words to meaning, with drunken lucidity, or rather effervescence, an irridescence though a cold and lucid ebullition, out of which we emerge with our hands purer than at the beginning of this exercise" (*Le Savon*, 19).

At the outset, the leitmotif is indicated, as it were, by a musical

key. The work itself is a series of anaphoric constructions (*Pour un Malherbe* and *Le Pré* are other examples of this figure) that, fugue-like, establish, with increasing emphasis, a perpetual reviewing of the matter in hand. It is a growing body of work (a paradox, since the piece of soap is meant to dissolve) that clarifies the areas of pertinence through numerous devices such as diary entries, a dramatic scene, interstitial observations in italics and, finally, a full-fledged declaration, in caps, that THE BOOK IS FINISHED. Before this statement, however, Ponge interjects (facetiously?) his own refutation of Sartre's famous "Hell is others" in *No Exit*. Given the reworking of Descartes's *cogito ergo sum* in *Pour un Malherbe* (previously quoted), it is perfectly reasonable to end *Le Savon* with the following declaration: "In conclusion, shouldn't our paradise be *the other?*" (*Le Savon*, 128). Had the reader any lingering doubts, the next paragraph cleared them up: "As for the paradise in this book, what is it, after all? What could it be, if not, reader, *your reading* (as it bites its tail at the end of these concluding lines)" (ibid.).

V

If the fabrication of the text implicitly contains a sexual imagery, there is even less doubt about that imagery in the procreation of the New Man, a series of affirmations that Ponge has made over the years, and especially in his *Proêmes* and which constitute the initial step in the exploration of a difficult, and for him, new topic meant one day to form a work on Man, such as Buffon might have considered. These affirmations taken as a whole constitute a succession of probes, tentative efforts, sketches of a demonstration of the technique to be employed, of an attitude to be adopted. In so doing, as it will become evident in these concluding pages, Ponge has frequently used himself both as man and as poet for the subject of these meditations. The result is a tantalizing approach to the poet and to his imagination, as well as to a distantiation forced upon us by the sobriety of the matter in question, and Ponge's refusal to

35

deliver himself through his text, other than in the fashion he had previously assumed as the master builder. The form he is about to draw is man become a species to be observed. Man as a lesson in measurement, something to be accounted for, as an eighteenth-century paleontologist would have done for vertebrates, or a draftsman might execute by lining up his materials on the side of his worktable.

The first striking aspect of his adumbration of the New Man is the absence of any personification: he is nameless, atemporal, and ahistorical. Unlike Nietzsche's project in *Thus Spake Zarathustra*, where, in a prophetic time, the New Man shall become himself, Ponge, although an early admirer of the German philologist-philosopher, preferred in his instance Flaubert's technique, which the novelist related in his correspondence with Turgenev. There, he informed him about the writing of *Un Coeur simple*. As Flaubert wrote, he placed before himself a stuffed bird in order to portray it with the greatest accuracy. The New Man, though infinitely more complex, resembles such a project, and therefore, requires similar verbal precision in order to be blocked out. He is, furthermore, though barely formed in these first pages, often compared with Ponge himself: stripped of all personal and social configurations.

But as a Marxist, in the years prior to World War II, it would have been inconceivable to situate such a material being outside the world. Ponge does not fail to account for the exigencies of class and economic factors, as these influence and even determine man's condition. Though Ponge has steadfastly drawn a distinction between poetics and political commitment (unlike his close friend, Eluard), he has not failed to acknowledge the need to modify man's economic life in this world. At one point, the "magical party"—the Communist party, was entrusted with the mission of alleviating man's impossible existence. Before turning away from the party after the war, Ponge, like many other French intellectuals, supposed there were no other alternatives. But even during the war itself, unlike Aragon and Guillevic, for instance, Ponge refused to accommodate the party by altering his views on poetry and its relationship to politics. Man, as Ponge first considered him, exists out-

side of time, at least in the early pieces devoted to the subject. In these texts, there are no allusions to the war or to the German Occupation; there are no lyrical or patriotic poems meant to bolster French morale; there are no emotional displays over the fate of France or the tragedy of mankind (*Le Savon* does contain an *ex post facto* comment on the scarcity of soap during the Occupation, and *Le Platane* had an undercurrent of nationalistic pride, according to some appreciative readers). But for Ponge himself, the distinction had to be preserved between poetry and polemic, between what was essentially a laudatory voice and the voice of criticism and hate. Consequently, as he composed the features of the New Man, he refused to become a committed *littérateur*.

With this refusal, he drew the line between himself and the two major French literary-philosophic movements of the first six decades of the century. André Breton had recognized the need for a Marxist social philosophy to accompany his own Rimbaldian orientation (*Position politique du surréalisme*, J. J. Pauvert [1962]), and though Jean-Paul Sartre had little understanding of Surrealism, he, too, in a nonpoetic fashion, before his official break with the Communist party (*Critique de la raison dialectique* [1960]), insisted on the need for that party to represent the workers' demands. If both Surrealism and Existentialism incorporated Marxism in the fabric of their humanistic and literary theories, Ponge, a member of the party right before and during the war, with less enthusiasm, settled for a new world but did not allow his political convictions to determine his poetic preoccupations. If he envisaged in 1943 the party as a nonbrutal and yet radical solution to the question of the individual (*C'est bien là que nous étions restés, Tome premier*, 213-214), his more personal convictions appear with less ambiguity in this formulation: "Brotherhood and happiness (or rather virile joy): that is the only heaven toward which I aspire. The Hereabove" (ibid., 214). When such apolitical statements do surface, they tend to disappoint (both for their echoes of Mallarmé, in this instance, and for their self-centeredness). However, they do indicate the direction that Ponge has been following with greater and greater insistency—not so much the definition of man as a social

37

animal, affected by class structures and those materialist considerations underlined by Marx himself, but a New Man defined as a physical and spiritual being. Thus, the New Man will emerge out of the verbal orbit designed by the presence of things, by words, also, as they exist between their etymological past and their synchronic presence.

The point of departure for the creation of the New Man is a Roman vision that Rousseau had defined in his *First Discourse:* pride, honor, fortitude, and virility; a man who is not at the center of the universe, though justly aware of himself and his capacities. Of all his capacities, the linguistic one would loom largest. This faculty unquestionably conforms to Ponge's own disposition, to his philosophic belief, stressing the linguistic superiority of man, if "superiority" can be used legitimately in this context, since Ponge refuses to valorize man above all other creations on earth. Each element in the world has its specificity, its distinguishing mark, its difference, and it is exactly that distinction which must be developed. For man, speech expresses himself and his relationship to things in the world, thus marking the intercession of the poet's word with the materiality of the world. Language becomes tantamount to life itself. It is only because of his power of speech that man has been able to constitute the past, describe the present, decipher it, and propose, via the future tense, events that are to come.

Silence, on the other hand, absolutely intolerable for Ponge, is the sign of death. The poet, as one might have expected it, cannot desert language. If some writers have accepted the invalidity of language, questioned its ability to come to terms with reality, or claimed that the horror of the world is such that one has a moral obligation to keep silent, Ponge cannot and will not figure among them. "One must talk, one must hold the pen...." (*Méthodes, Le Grand Recueil*, II, 67). One is here reminded of Beckett's line in the opening page of the *Unnamable:* "I am obliged to speak. I shall never be silent. Never." This is the exulting fate of man and not some deplorable Pascalian condition that proposes a metaphysical man thrown into a Providential scheme of things. "I must reread Pascal (in order to demolish him)" (*Notes premières de l'homme, Tome premier*, 245).

Ponge is as opposed to the Christian view of mankind as he is to the Existentialist emphasis on the absurd. Although the absurd undeniably exists, there is no reason to attribute to it a tragical quality. At a time, near the end of the war, and then for a number of years thereafter, when the fashion proclaimed the dire consequences of the Absurd, when every Existentialist author prided himself on seeing the world as bleakly as possible, and his own station within it as hopelessly involved in the nonsignification of things, Ponge rebelled and countered in an eighteenth-century manner. "The New Man will not *care* (in the Heideggerian sense of *anxiety*) about ontological or metaphysical problems, which are still, for Camus, of primary importance, whatever he says. He will consider the absurdity of the world as definitely accepted (or rather the relationship man-world). As for Hamlet, yes, of course, I know all about that. He will be Camus's absurd man always standing on the cutting edge of the problem, but his (intellectual) life will not be spent trying to balance himself on the edge like high-wire artists of the XXth century. He will balance himself with *ease*, and will be able to do other things, without falling" (*Réflexions en lisant "l'essai sur l'absurde,"* Tome premier, 218).

Evidently old debates do not interest Ponge nor the accrued philosophical arguments of the past which have enmeshed man in a web of his own making, thereby prohibiting him from finding workable solutions. Therefore, let there be a new attitude, one that will help remove the obstacles that have distorted his vision. There *is* something the New Man can do, and will do with a degree of elation, and that is, turn his attention to significant things, things that he can actually deal with, and that are commensurate with his stature in the world (precisely what these things are to be, after the elementary, though essential reobjectification of poetry, remains unsaid in Ponge's initial observations). Part of the project, however, depends on a type of Spartan independence, as well as an Epicurean understanding of the world and man's place in it. Once again, Lucretius has surfaced on the text, and via that author, Rousseau himself. Let man avoid, like the plague, all forms of debilitating pessimism, anything "that flatters human masochism" (*C'est surtout [peut-être]*, Tome premier, 212). This Nietzschean inclination

integrally rejects the part of the victim: the image of the individual overwhelmed by circumstances, beaten, frightened, searching desperately for himself, exhibiting his tear-soaked handkerchief to a psychiatrist. Ponge will have none of that. Literature has more important tasks to perform. "What should man do? Live, continue to live, and live happily" (*Elle décrit, Tome premier*, 224).

In order for man to "live happily" Ponge suggests a twofold enterprise. First let man turn his attention to concrete objectives. The starting point is in *Le Parti pris des choses* and the comments found in his observations on the New Man. There, with great and deliberate caution, he writes down a brief description of man's face, his eyes, his body, his vibrations (*Notes premières de l'homme, Tome premier*, 245). Ponge then goes on to define his contact with nature and his character. He is gay, enthusiastic, courageous, thirsting for the absolute, and capable of living in an absurd world (a telling parallel to Nietzsche's own joyous vision). As the psychological difficulties increase, the poet moves away as if to gain a better perspective on his subject. However reluctant he is, certain metaphysical facts are still in order. Those that Francis Ponge makes are rather basic ones, made with reluctance given both his distaste for religion and the fear of falling prey to a rebaptized humanism. Nevertheless, man's desire to transcend his organic nature in the world has to be comprehended, and the poet must codify these aspirations as part of the definition of the text on man. In order to do so, "man must, and the poet first of all, find his law, his key, his god within himself" (*certainement, en un sens, Tome premier*, 216). This curious mixture of heretical (the heresy of the Free Spirit?) and Protestant elements is not totally unexpected. After all, Ponge lived in a Cathare region of France and if we are to listen to him, in some of his more self-consciously conceited moments, he will attribute to members of his family the belief that the Ponges are distantly related to the Henri IV branch of Protestantism. But the poet speaks in this matter, too. "Man is a god who is unaware of himself" (*Notes premières de l'homme, Tome premier*, 238). The internalization of the divine corresponds to the metaphysical aspect of the definition of man. But it is a god in lower case, stripped of the omnipo-

tence that is his to begin with. Having evicted god from his body, man committed the first error of his being. The poet suggests man recognize the divinity within and yet remain modest enough in the world. In this rediscovered simplicity, man can then proceed to an aesthetic theory that would be its natural counterpart: a New Classicism.

In the context of French literature, this proposal raises innumerable questions and associations. Classicism is a word around which the nineteenth century did battle; a word that is still, like a shibboleth, uttered by critics of the right, followers of Charles Maurras, for example, who associate classicism with the monarchy, and critics of the left who concede that association, and revere the Romantic movement because of its association with the revolutionary struggle of the post-Napoleonic world. Classicism seems to encompass the French tradition, at least that one which the university and the lycées have consecrated as the French genius. If the heroes in French history are kings and saints and at best a saintly king, so is it that Racine becomes the paradigm of the French mind. Classicism, in other words, is at the center of a cultural and political experience. When Francis Ponge revitalizes this term, he is counting on all the implicit and explicit associations that the term suggests. For him, the adjective marks the absolute distinction between the traditional vision of that aesthetics and his own proposal. For him, New Classicism is the tautest string on the lyre, the most direct achievement of poetry. It is also the question of rhetoric restated and as a consequence New Classicism has nothing to do with either a political perspective or aesthetic rules as these had been formulated by academicians in the seventeenth century. Furthermore, it has nothing to do with a characterological definition which posits that a classic is one who conceals his vanity, who understates his emotions, whose work is the very result of the presence of formal obstacles placed in his way. As man himself had been corrupted by the philosophical-theological vision coming out of Jerusalem, Athens and Rome, so classicism, too, had become a mock production of a papier-mâché antiquity. It had to be reclaimed from the history-of-literature past. As the old rhetoric is

now sclerotic, so the new one must envisage the perpetuation of a classic man: pure, instinctual, with dimensions as proper as those the Greek sculptors had given him.

This dialectical relationship with the medium of language, with rhetoric, with the universe that is contained in it, is perfectly set forth in the long poem *Le Soleil placé en abîme*. There, Ponge describes the manner in which the God of all the gods is mastered by the poet's mastery of language, by the rules of rhetoric as the poet charts out a new genre proportionate with the subject (that is, fitted out with its own rhetorical figure). This rhetorical infrastructure, seemingly the effortless result of the topic itself, acknowledges the fundamental dialectic that defines man/sun in the text and in the world, or more precisely, man-language as this combination succeeds in capturing the sun in a complex show of linguistic strength. In a metaphorical sense, the poet becomes as brilliant as his subject, has the subject assume, by the fact of it being subjected to the poet's attention, a condition that allows itself to be defined and contemplated. Language, and the power of language, in the text, subjugate the sun. The poet, and the reader after him, are now in a different position vis-à-vis the sun. Without ever fooling himself into thinking that the poet has indeed become the greater of the two, the reader can at least admit that it is, once more, the victory of language over the silence of the world.

In this way, Ponge puts an end to the argument that had gone on since Plato pitted Hermogenes against Cratylus, the former holding to the theory that words were founded on an artificial agreement among men and the latter that words had some intrinsic relationship with the things they designated; that words were the surnames of things, that they mimicked them, in fact. Ponge refuses to accept as definitive either of the terms of the debate. Language contains both the onomatopoeic element and the arbitrary designation; it has its own historic rights that impose themselves upon the eye as well as the ear, the mind as well as the senses. One thing is clear: the poet does not have to invent the origins of his own language, nor does he have to preoccupy himself with the ontological problems that surround them. He lives in a linguistic community

where language, as Saussure described it, is recognized as the treasure wherein the poet finds his verbal stability. "Call it *nominalist* or *cultist*, or by any other name, it doesn't matter to us: we have baptized it the Obgame" (*Le Soleil placé en abîme, Le Grand Recueil*, III, 156).

The poet does the sun over in prose (and verse) and he succeeds in this task by admiring it, praising it, and especially, naming it at the top of the page. The poet's sun is tamed by verbal precision; it is rendered accountable to the text itself. There is, as of the initiation of the text, a logic that the text must follow: a linguistic fatality entrapping the sun in words. The verbal exercise (the obgame) acknowledges the reality of the text (its metatextuality). In so doing, Ponge recognizes the power of language which is at the disposal of the New Man—a language that will translate as accurately as possible the function and the evolution of the sun, that will, in fact, recreate it, but now on the horizon of the printed page. As a consequence, the poet conjures up, through the language that he has newly minted, the New Man who will use it and whose task, like the poet's, begins with his daily confrontation with the sun. If man is to assume his own happiness, this confrontation will end in the adjudication of that rivalry, admitting the superiority of the sun on the page, over the text but submitting it to the same linguistic and rhetorical legislation.

Should one insist on the sexual motif apropos the man/sun relationship? The sun as phallus, as the Father supreme? Philippe Sollers made such a proposition ("Ponge caché," TXT, 1971, 3/4). Should one draw attention to the connection between the brilliant sperm-maker and the Earth? Ponge specifically defines it as a bursting sun, one that illuminates the world in the same way as the title of a page fecundates the text below with its particular rays. "In the great cask of the sky, it is the radiant bung, often enveloped in a cloth of dull clouds but always humid, the interior pressure of the liquid being so powerful, its nature so impregnating" (*Le Soleil placé en abîme, Le Grand Recueil*, III, 159). If it is proper for man to receive the sun, it is also within his power to welcome it, to exclaim in its favor in a language filled with onomatopoeias and

syllables; a language that also contains the totality of man's history, his existence under the sun, as well as his final decision: "Therefore, we must 'remake' it metalogically. . . . Change evil into good. Forced labor into Paradise" (ibid., 166). What other Paradise can there be for Ponge but the scriptural one with its weighty materiality?

We are finally led to the reconciliation of two apparently disparate concerns. One has been Ponge's insistence on language, and the other, his eloquent plea for a New Man whose traits would no longer be cast in the disproportionate mold of ancient humanism. The resolution of the differences that separated language and the New Man is to be found in Ponge's autotelic text that also contains its own gloss, that is, its own running interpretation (translation), its own series of annotations. Thus, while disregarding the traditionally grander aspects of man, those aspects that have contributed to his weakness and hollowness, Ponge throws a truer mantle of etymological accuracy over him: the propriety of terms, con-fusing man's linguistic propensities with those of a theory of rejuvenated classicism, found through the pages of *Pour un Malherbe*. Ponge has thus created a fool-proof object. It neither fools the reader nor can it be faulted by him. The words that Ponge quotes from the *Littré* act as verification for the correctness of his initial intuition and also as a source of inspiration. Out of it, the New Man arises. Out of it comes the *summa* of his poetics, derived from the *Littré, mon bible* as he wrote, despite the ungrammatical turn (*Le Savon*, 118). That dictionary is then the final arbiter in all deliberations about the strength of language. It is also the final authority (a reconciliation between father and son?), and it assumes the significance of a New Testament in the form of a poetic statement, self-reflecting, and providing the reader with at least one joyous definition of his place under the sun.

Texts

L'OBJET, C'EST LA POÉTIQUE[1]

Le rapport de l'homme à l'objet n'est du tout seulement de possession ou d'usage. Non, ce serait trop simple. C'est bien pire.

Les objets sont en dehors de l'âme, bien sûr; pourtant, ils sont aussi notre plomb dans la tête.

Il s'agit d'un rapport à l'accusatif.

*

L'homme est un drôle de corps, qui n'a pas son centre de gravité en lui-même.

Notre âme est transitive. Il lui faut un objet, qui l'affecte, comme son complément direct, aussitôt.

Il s'agit du rapport le plus grave (non du tout de *l'avoir*, mais de *l'être*).

L'artiste, plus que tout autre homme, en reçoit la charge, accuse le coup.

*

Par bonheur, pourtant, qu'est-ce *l'être*?—Il n'est que des façons d'être, successives. Il en est autant que d'objets. Autant que de battements de paupières.

D'autant que, devenant notre régime, un objet nous concerne, notre regard aussi l'a cerné, le discerne. Il s'agit, dieux

---

1. L'expression est de Braque.

THE OBJECT IS POETICS [1]

The relationship between man and object is not at all limited to possession or use. No, that would be too simple. It's much worse.

Objects are outside the soul, of course; and yet, they are also ballast in our heads.

The relationship is thus in the accusative.

*

Man is a curious body whose center of gravity is not in himself.

Our soul is transitive. It needs an object that affects it, immediately, like a direct complement.

It is a matter of the most serious relationship (not at all with *having* but with *being*).

The artist, more than any other man, bears the burden, reacts.

*

But what, luckily, is *being*, after all? Only a succession of ways of being. There are as many objects. As many blinkings of an eyelid.

Furthermore, becoming our object,[2] an object concerns us; we have also visually embraced it, discovered it. Thank

1. Braque's expression (F. P.).
2. In the grammatical sense (S. G.).

47

merci, d'une « discrétion » réciproque ; et l'artiste aussitôt touche au but.

Oui, seul l'artiste, alors, sait s'y prendre.

Il cesse de regarder, tire au but.

L'objet, certes, accuse le coup.

La Vérité se renvole, indemne.

La métamorphose a eu lieu.

*

Ne serions-nous qu'un corps, sans doute serions-nous en équilibre avec la nature.

Mais notre âme est du même côté que nous dans la balance.

Lourde ou légère, je ne sais.

Mémoire, imagination, affects immédiats, l'alourdissent ; toutefois, nous avons la parole (ou quelque autre moyen d'expression) ; chaque mot que nous prononçons nous allège. Dans *l'écriture*, il passe même de l'autre côté.

Lourds ou légers donc je ne sais, nous avons besoin d'un contrepoids.

*

L'homme n'est qu'un lourd vaisseau, un lourd oiseau, sur l'abîme.

Nous l'éprouvons.

Chaque « battibaleno » nous le confirme. Nous battons du regard comme l'oiseau de l'aile, pour nous maintenir.

Tantôt au sommet de la vague, et tantôt croyant nous abîmer.

God, it's a matter of reciprocal "judgment"; and just as soon, the artist's goal is in sight.

Yes, only the artist, then, knows how to handle it.

He stops looking, reaches his goal.

The object also reacts.

Truth takes off again, undamaged.

The metamorphosis has occurred.

*

Were we only a body, we would undoubtedly be in a state of equilibrium with nature.

But our soul is on the same side of the scale as we are.

Heavy or light, I cannot tell.

Memory, imagination, sudden reactions, a growing heaviness; still, we have speech (or some other means of expression); each word that we pronounce relieves us. In *writing*, it even reaches the other side.

Whether heavy or light, I cannot say, but we need a counterweight.

*

Man is just a heavy ship, a heavy bird, on the edge of an abyss.

We feel it.

Each "battibaleno" confirms it. Our eyelids beat like the wings of a bird, to keep us steady.

Sometimes at the crest of a wave, sometimes ready to sink.

Eternal vagabonds, at least as long as we're alive.

Éternels vagabonds, du moins tant que nous sommes en vie.

Mais le monde est peuplé d'objets. Sur ses rivages, leur foule infinie, leur collection nous apparaît, certes, plutôt indistincte et floue.

Pourtant cela suffit à nous rassurer. Car, nous l'éprouvons aussi, chacun d'eux, à notre gré, tour à tour, peut devenir notre point d'amarrage, la borne où nous appuyer.

Il suffit qu'il fasse le poids.

Plutôt que de notre regard, c'est alors l'affaire de notre main, —qu'elle sache filer la manoeuvre.

*

Il suffit, dis-je, qu'il fasse le poids.

La plupart ne font pas le poids.

L'homme, le plus souvent, n'étreint que ses émanations, ses fantômes. Tels sont les objets subjectifs.

Il ne fait que valser avec eux, chantant tous la même chanson; puis s'envole avec eux ou s'abîme.

*

Il nous faut donc choisir des objets véritables, objectant indéfiniment à nos désirs. Des objets que nous rechoisissions chaque jour, et non comme notre décor, notre cadre; plutôt comme nos spectateurs, nos juges; pour n'en être, bien sûr, ni les danseurs ni les pitres.

Enfin, notre secret conseil.

Et ainsi composer notre temple domestique :

Chacun de nous, tant que nous sommes, connaît bien, je suppose, sa Beauté.

But the world is peopled with objects. On its shores, we see their infinite crowd, their gathering, even though they are indistinct and vague.

Nevertheless, that is enough to reassure us. Because we also feel that all of them, according to our fancy, one after the other, may become our point of docking, the bollard upon which we rest.

It only needs to be the proper weight.

Then, rather than our looking at it, it is up to our hands —let them spin out the line.

*

As I said, it only needs to be the proper weight.

Most of them do not make the weight.

In most cases, man only grasps his emanations, his ghosts. Such are subjective objects.

He only waltzes with them, and they all sing the same song; then he flies away with them or sinks.

*

Therefore, we must choose true objects, constantly objecting to our own desires. Objects that we would select again and again, and not as our decor or milieu; rather like our spectators, our judges; without our being, of course, either dancers or clowns.

At last, to have our secret council.

And thus furnish our domestic temple:

I suppose that each one of us, as long as we exist, recognizes his own Beauty.

It keeps to the center, always untouched.

Elle se tient au centre, jamais atteinte.
Tout en ordre autour d'elle.
Elle, intacte.
Fontaine de notre patio.

(Février 1962.)

Everything in order around it.
It remains intact.
Fountain in our patio.

February 1962
in *Nouveau Recueil*, pp. 143-148.

FRAGMENTS MÉTATECHNIQUES

On peut se moquer de Littré, mais on doit user de son dictionnaire.

Outre la syntaxe en usage, il règle au mieux l'étymologie. Quelle science est plus nécessaire au poète? Tel « matériau » (selon Bourdelle) aide mieux l'esprit, pour faire la beauté. Et Michel-Ange reconnaissait longuement l'élite des marbres dans les montagnes de Carrare.

Il est ainsi certains mots qui tiennent plus d'esprit et de beauté que nos plus riches idées. Respectueux et prudents, nous pouvons entrer dans leur gloire, si nous ménageons à proprement parler toutes leurs susceptibilités.

Et d'abord retrouvons-les. Soignons notre palette. C'est une condition de la beauté littéraire : il faut choisir des mots qui ajoutent à la pensée.

*

Au contraire de la vertu, le style ne demande pas d'exemples. L'excellence y est singulière; le sublime caractéristique.

L'état de grâce est donc celui de table rase. Pour s'y tenir, il faut quitter non seulement les ouvrages des auteurs, mais jusqu'à la plus vague habitude de leur manière. A cette fin, le mieux est de bourrer la mémoire avec des tournures et des rythmes impossibles, qui ne tentent pas le style. Ainsi usait Stendhal du Code civil.

Le plus grand danger peut, ici, venir de la syntaxe, piège

METATECHNICAL FRAGMENTS

You can make fun of Littré, but you must use his dictionary.

Besides ruling on proper syntax, he is also the best there is for etymology. What knowledge is more necessary for the poet? Such "materials" (according to Bourdelle) help the mind create beauty. And Michelangelo patiently recognized the high value of the marble from Carrara.

thus, there are certain words that contain more beauty and intelligence than our richest ideas. Respectful and prudent, we can share in their glory if we observe, so to speak, their susceptibilities.

And first of all let us find them again. Let us take care of our palette. The following is a condition for literary beauty: words must be chosen that will add to one's thought.

*

Contrary to virtue, style does not require examples. There, excellence is singular; the sublime characteristic.

The state of grace is therefore a *tabula rasa*. In order to abide by it, one must not only put aside authors and their works but also the slightest trace in ourselves of any of their ways of writing. Toward that end, the best solution is to stuff one's memory with impossible turns of the phrase and rhythms that style would not find attractive. Stendhal used the Civil Code in this fashion.

Here, the greatest danger might come from syntax, the

du bon sens, triomphe de l'école. Pour lier les mots, c'est une sauce, dont l'excès abîme le goût.

*

On veut que l'art vive pour lui-même. Je n'y entends rien. Il n'y a là que de l'homme; et il faut plaire : c'est tout.

Certes, l'oeuvre d'art mène immortellement sa vie propre, émue par la multiplication intérieure des rapports, et par cette mystérieuse induction de l'âme dans les proportions choisies. Mais partout où il y a de l'âme, on est encore chez l'homme. Pour vivre, il faut l'habiter et subir ses catégories. D'où les genres :

L'artiste peut aborder le public par un cap, ou par un golfe, ou par une rivière qu'il remonte jusqu'au coeur; il peut le survoler, et que son ombre seulement en amuse la surface; il peut le conquérir à pied, longuement, par tous les sentiers.

On voit ce que l'art doit céder à la nature. Ici, le génie fait moins que le talent. Ici, tout l'appareil de la société se retrouve : l'État et les moeurs. Il faut bien qu'on les considère, mais surtout les constantes du plaisir esthétique, jusqu'à l'éternité du goût.

*

C'est moins l'objet qu'il faut peindre qu'une idée de cet objet. Mais j'entends qu'on crie : « Romantique; il nous faut la nature au lieu de ton idée; la nature et ses traits éternels.

—Où les voyez-vous qu'en vous-mêmes, où les verrais-je qu'en moi?

—La nature existe. —En nous.

—La beauté existe. —En nous.

—Les chefs-d'oeuvre la montrent. Fais un chef-d'oeuvre.

triumph of the academics, which traps common sense. It holds words together like a sauce, but in excess, it spoils the taste.

*

You want art to live for itself. That doesn't mean anything to me. There's only man here; and one must please: that's it.

No doubt, the work of art leads its own immortal life, moved by the multiplication of internal relationships, and by that mysterious induction of the soul into the proportions decided upon. But wherever the soul is found, man shall be found. In order to live, one must live with him, and submit to his categories—hence the genres:

The artist can reach the public by way of a cape, or a gulf, or a river which he can travel back to its heart; he can fly over it, and only allow his shadow to amuse the surface; he can conquer it by foot, and in time take all the paths.

That is what art must yield to nature. Here, genius does less than talent. Here, all the social paraphernalia reappears: the State and customs. One must consider them, but especially the constants of aesthetic pleasure, and that, as long as taste exists.

*

It is less the object that one must paint than an idea of that object. But I hear them clamoring: "Romantic! What we need is nature and not your idea of it; nature and its eternal features.

—Where do you see them if not in yourselves? Where would I see them if not in myself?

57

—Ah! laissez-moi le faire. Je peins, forcé. Un corps idéal m'oblige au labeur. Pitié! J'accouche. Laissez! Je vous l'habillerai d'un genre, la caresse de mon style fera l'expression de son visage, mais sa chair est mon idée : je fais ce que je peux.

—Il faut nous plaire.

—O double torture, élaboration enfin réussie! Voici : ceci est mon sang, qui jamais n'a coulé. Et c'est aussi le tien, critique intérieur, voix des hommes.

—Miracle : ô neuve image de moi-même : c'est beau! »

(1922.)

—Nature exists. —In us.

—Beauty exists. —In us.

—Masterpieces reveal it. Make us a masterpiece.

—Ah! Let me make one. I paint, under duress. An ideal body holds me to the task. Have pity! I give birth. Enough! I will dress it up for you in a genre; the caress of my style will lend expression to its face, but its flesh is my idea: I do the best I can.

—You must please us.

—O double torture, elaboration finally come to fruition!

Here it is: this is my blood which has never flowed. And it is also yours, interior critic, the voice of men.

—Miracle! o new image of myself: how beautiful!"

1922
in *Nouveau Recueil*, pp. 15-17.

RAISONS DE VIVRE HEUREUX

L'on devrait pouvoir à tous poèmes donner ce titre : Raisons de vivre heureux. Pour moi du moins, ceux que j'écris sont chacun comme la note que j'essaie de prendre, lorsque d'une méditation ou d'une contemplation jaillit en mon corps la fusée de quelques mots qui le rafraîchit et le décide à vivre quelques jours encore. Si je pousse plus loin l'analyse, je trouve qu'il n'y a point d'autre raison de vivre que parce qu'il y a d'abord les dons du souvenir, et la faculté de s'arrêter pour jouir du présent, ce qui revient à considérer ce présent comme l'on considère la première fois les souvenirs : c'est-à-dire, garder la jouissance présomptive d'une *raison* à l'état vif ou cru, quand elle vient d'être découverte au milieu des circonstances uniques qui l'entourent à la même seconde. Voilà le mobile qui me fait saisir mon crayon (Étant entendu que l'on ne désire sans doute conserver une *raison* que parce qu'elle est *pratique,* comme un nouvel outil sur notre établi). Et maintenant il me faut dire encore que ce que j'appelle une raison pourra sembler à d'autres une simple description ou relation, ou peinture désintéressée et inutile. Voici comment je me justifierai : Puisque la joie m'est venue par la contemplation, le retour de la joie peut bien m'être donné par la peinture. Ces retours de la joie, ces rafraîchissements à la mémoire des objets de sensations, voilà exactement ce que j'appelle raisons de vivre.

Si je les nomme raisons c'est que ce sont des retours de l'esprit aux choses. Il n'y a que l'esprit pour rafraîchir les choses. Notons d'ailleurs que ces raisons sont justes ou valables seulement si l'esprit retourne aux choses d'une

REASONS FOR LIVING HAPPILY

One should be able to give to all poems the title: Reasons For Living Happily. In my case, at least, those that I write are all like the note that I try to reach on the heels of a meditation or a contemplation when a flare of words springs from my body, refreshes it, and convinces it to live on a few more days. If I pursue this analysis, I find first that the only reasons for living are the gift of memory and then the ability to pause in order to enjoy the present, which amounts to saying that the present is like the first time we remember: that is, keeping that presumptive joy of a *reason* in its raw or vibrant state when it has just been discovered in the midst of unique circumstances that surround it at that very second. That is what makes me pick up my pencil (with the understanding that we only keep a *reason* because it is *practical*, like a new tool on our workbench). But now, I've got to say that what I consider a reason might appear to others to be a simple description or narration, or a painting with no preconceived object or use. This is the way I would justify myself: since I felt joy come from contemplation, that same feeling of joy might well return upon looking at a painting. What I call reasons for living are exactly those moments when joy returns, when the memory of sensate objects is refreshed.

If I call them reasons, it is because they lead the mind back to things. Only the mind can refresh things. However, these reasons are right or valid only insofar as the mind returns to things in a way acceptable to things: when they are not slighted, that is, when they are described from their own point of view.

61

manière acceptable par les choses : quand elles ne sont pas lésées, et pour ainsi dire qu'elles sont décrites de leur propre point de vue.

Mais ceci est un terme, ou une perfection, impossible. Si cela pouvait s'atteindre, chaque poème plairait à tous et à chacun, à tous et à chaque moment comme plaisent et frappent les objets de sensations eux-mêmes. Mais cela ne se peut pas : Il y a toujours du rapport à l'homme... Ce ne sont pas les choses qui parlent entre elles mais les hommes entre eux qui parlent des choses et l'on ne peut aucunement sortir de l'homme.

Du moins, par un pétrissage, un primordial irrespect des mots, etc., devra-t-on donner l'impression d'un nouvel idiome qui produira l'effet de surprise et de nouveauté des objets de sensations eux-mêmes.

C'est ainsi que l'oeuvre complète d'un auteur plus tard pourra à son tour être considérée comme une chose. Mais si l'on pensait rigoureusement selon l'idée précédente, il faudrait non point même une rhétorique par auteur mais une rhétorique par poème. Et à notre époque nous voyons des efforts en ce sens (dont les auteurs sont Picasso, Stravinsky, moi-même : et dans chaque auteur une manière par an ou par oeuvre).

Le sujet, le poème de chacune de ces périodes correspondant évidemment à l'essentiel de l'homme à chacun de ses âges; comme les successives écorces d'un arbre, se détachant par l'effort naturel de l'arbre à chaque époque.

1928-1929.

But this is an impossible goal or enterprise. If this could be achieved, each poem would please everybody and everyone, at all and every moment, in the way that sensate objects please and strike us. But this cannot be: man must always be reckoned with.... Things do not speak among themselves, but men among themselves speak about things, and thus it is impossible to get away from man.

At least we will try by molding and through a primordial disrespect of words, etc., to give the impression of a new idiom that will produce effects of surprise and novelty similar to those produced by sensate objects themselves.

In this manner, at a later time, the complete works of an author in their turn may be considered as a thing. But if one were to think rigorously along the preceding lines, it would require not just a rhetoric for each author but a rhetoric for each poem. In our time, a number of individuals have worked in that direction (Picasso, Stravinsky and myself: and for each author a style per year or per work).

The subject, the poem of each one of these periods obviously corresponding to the essential of the individual in each one of his stages; similar to the successive barks of the tree, peeled off by the natural efforts of the tree in each one of its periods.

1928-1929
From *Proêmes* in *Tome premier*, pp. 188-190.

DES RAISONS D'ÉCRIRE

I

Qu'on s'en persuade : il nous a bien fallu quelques raisons impérieuses pour devenir ou pour rester poètes. Notre premier mobile fut sans doute le dégoût de ce qu'on nous oblige à penser et à dire, de ce à quoi notre nature d'hommes nous force à prendre part.

Honteux de l'arrangement tel qu'il est des choses, honteux de tous ces grossiers camions qui passent *en nous*, de ces usines, manufactures, magasins, théâtres, monuments publics qui constituent *bien plus* que le décor de notre vie, honteux de cette agitation sordide des hommes non seulement *autour* de nous, nous avons observé que la Nature autrement puissante que les hommes fait dix fois moins de bruit, et que la nature *dans l'homme*, je veux dire la raison, n'en fait pas du tout.

Eh bien! Ne serait-ce qu'à nous-mêmes nous voulons faire entendre la voix d'un homme. Dans le silence certes nous l'entendons, mais dans les paroles nous la cherchons : *ce* n'est plus rien. C'est des paroles. Même pas : paroles sont paroles.

O hommes! Informes mollusques, foule qui sont dans les rues, millions de fourmis que les pieds du Temps écrasent! Vous n'avez pour demeure que la vapeur commune de votre véritable sang : les paroles. Votre rumination vous écoeure, votre respiration vous étouffe. Votre personnalité et vos

SOME REASONS FOR WRITING

I

You may be quite sure that we needed a few imperious reasons to become and to stay a poet. Our first motive was undoubtedly the disgust we felt about what we were obliged to think and say; what, as human beings, we were forced to deal with.

Ashamed of the way things were arranged, ashamed of all those heavy trucks that pass *through us*, those industries, factories, stores, theaters, public monuments that constitute *much more* than the backdrop of our lives, ashamed of the sordid movement of men and not just *around us*, we saw that Nature, so much more powerful than men, makes ten times less noise, and that nature *within man*, I mean reason, doesn't make any at all.

Well! were it only for ourselves, we would want to let one man's voice be heard. We hear it in silence, but we seek it out in words. *It* is no longer negligible. *It*'s a word. Not even: words are words.

O mankind! Formless molluscs, crowds that emerge into the streets, millions of ants crushed by the feet of Time! Your only residence—the common vapor of your true blood: words. You're sickened by the food you eat, your breath makes you choke. Your personality and your expressions consume each other. Such words, such ways, o society! All is words.

expressions se mangent entre elles. Telles paroles, telles moeurs, ô société! Tout n'est que paroles.

II

N'en déplaise aux *paroles* elles-mêmes, *étant données les habitudes que dans tant de bouches infectes elles ont contractées*, il faut un certain courage pour se décider non seulement à écrire mais même à parler. *Un tas de vieux chiffons pas à prendre avec des pincettes, voilà ce qu'on nous offre à remuer, à secouer, à changer de place.* Dans l'espoir secret que nous nous tairons. Eh bien! relevons le défi.

Pourquoi, tout bien considéré, un homme de telle sorte doit-il parler? Pourquoi les meilleurs, quoi qu'on en dise, ne sont pas ceux qui ont décidé de se taire? Voilà ce que je veux dire.

Je ne parle qu'à ceux qui se taisent (un travail de suscitation), quitte à les juger ensuite sur leurs paroles. Mais si cela même n'avait pas été dit on aurait pu me croire solidaire d'un pareil ordre de choses?

Cela ne m'importerait guère si je ne savais par expérience que je risquerais ainsi de le devenir.

Qu'il faut à chaque instant *se secouer de la suie des paroles* et que *le silence est aussi dangereux dans cet ordre de valeurs que possible.*

Une seule issue : parler contre les paroles. Les entraîner avec soi dans la honte où elles nous conduisent de telle sorte qu'elles s'y défigurent. Il n'y a point d'autre raison d'écrire. Mais *aussitôt conçue* celle-ci est absolument déterminante et comminatoire. On ne peut plus y échapper que par une lâcheté rabaissante qu'il n'est pas de mon goût de tolérer.

1929-1930.

II

With all due respect for *words, given the habits they have contracted in so many foul mouths*, it actually takes courage not only to write but even to speak. *A pile of old rags not to be touched with tweezers—that's what we're given to move, to shake, to turn about.* And all that in the secret hope that we'll keep quiet. Well! Let us accept the challenge.

All things considered, why should such a man speak? Aren't the best, whatever is said about them, those who have decided against keeping quiet? That's what I want to say.

I speak only to those who keep quiet (a matter of arousing them), be it only to judge them afterward on their words. But even if I hadn't said that, would you really have believed that I might have agreed with such an order of things?

This would not have bothered me had I not been aware, from experience, that I ran the risk of accepting it.

That at every moment, it is necessary *to shake yourself free of the soot of words* and that *silence is as dangerous as possible in this system of values.*

There is only one way out: to speak against words. Drag them along in shame to where they lead us, and there, they will be disfigured. There is *no other reason for writing.* But *once this is understood*, it becomes absolutely determining and comminatory. One can only escape it by a degrading cowardice which my taste finds intolerable.

1929-1930
From *Proêmes* in *Tome premier*, pp. 184-186.

LES ÉCURIES D'AUGIAS

L'ordre de choses honteux à Paris crève les yeux, défonce les oreilles.

Chaque nuit, sans doute, dans les quartiers sombres où la circulation cesse quelques heures, l'on peut l'oublier. Mais dès le petit jour il s'impose physiquement par une précipitation, un tumulte, un ton si excessif, qu'il ne peut demeurer aucun doute sur sa *monstruosité*.

Ces ruées de camions et d'autos, ces quartiers qui ne logent plus personne mais seulement des marchandises ou les dossiers des compagnies qui les transportent, ces rues où le miel de la production coule à flots, où il ne s'agit plus jamais d'autre chose, pour nos amis de lycée qui sautèrent à pieds joints de la philosophie et une fois pour toutes dans les huiles ou le camembert, cette autre sorte d'hommes qui ne sont connus que par leurs collections, ceux qui se tuent pour avoir été « ruinés », ces gouvernements d'affairistes et de marchands, *passe encore*, si l'on ne nous obligeait pas à y prendre part, si l'on ne nous y maintenait pas de force la tête, si tout cela ne parlait pas si fort, si cela n'était pas seul à parler.

Hélas, pour comble d'horreur, *à l'intérieur de nous-mêmes*, le même ordre sordide parle, parce que nous n'avons pas à notre disposition d'autres mots ni d'autres grands mots (ou phrases, c'est-à-dire d'autres idées) que ceux qu'un usage journalier dans ce monde grossier depuis l'éternité prostitue. Tout se passe pour nous comme pour des peintres qui n'auraient à leur disposition pour y tremper leurs pinceaux qu'un même immense pot où depuis la nuit des temps tous auraient eu à délayer leurs couleurs.

THE AUGEAN STABLES

The shameful order of things in Paris strikes you in the eye and deafens your ear.

Of course, at night, when the traffic has stopped for a few hours in darkened neighborhoods, one can forget about it. But in the early morning hours, it imposes itself physically with a rush, a tumult, such an excessive pitch that its *monstrosity* is beyond question.

This onrush of trucks and cars, these neighborhoods that no longer house anyone but the goods or the files of companies that ship them, these streets where the honey of production flows freely, where nothing else ever counts anymore—for our High-School friends who jumped headlong, after their final year of Philosophy, and for a lifetime, into oils and camemberts, those other men, who are only known for their collections, those who kill themselves after going into "bankruptcy," those administrations filled with opportunists and merchants—*all that could still be tolerated*, were we not forced to participate, to keep our heads in it, if all of it did not speak so loudly, if that were not the only voice.

Unfortunately, to cap this horror, *within ourselves*, the same sordid order speaks, because we have no other words at our disposal, no high sounding words (or sentences, that is to say, ideas) except for those that have been, and from the beginning of time, prostituted on a daily basis in this crass world. We are like painters who, from as far back as can be remembered, would all have to dip their brushes in the same immense can in order to thin out their paints.

. . . But having become aware of it we are nearly saved;

69

... Mais déjà d'en avoir pris conscience l'on est à peu près sauvé, et il ne reste plus qu'à se crever d'imitations, de fards, de rubriques, de procédés, à arranger des fautes selon les principes du mauvais goût, enfin à tenter de faire apparaître l'idée en filigrane par des ruses d'éclairage au milieu de ce jeu épuisant d'*abus mutuels.* Il ne s'agit pas de nettoyer les écuries d'Augias, mais de les peindre à fresques au moyen de leur propre purin : travail émouvant et qui demande un coeur mieux accroché et plus de finesse et de persévérance qu'il n'en fut exigé d'Hercule pour son travail de simple et grossière *moralité.*

1929-1930.

there is nothing left to do but to fill ourselves up on imitations, artifices, headlines, deals; to arrange errors according to principles of bad taste, and in the end, attempt to bring out the filigree of an idea through artful lighting in the midst of this exhausting game of *mutual abuses*. We are not interested in sweeping out the Augean stables but in painting them in frescoes with their own manure: exciting work which requires a stouter heart and more finesse and perseverance than Hercules needed for his task involving a simple and crass *morality*.

1929-1930
From *Proêmes* in *Tome premier*, pp. 175-176.

RHÉTORIQUE

Je suppose qu'il s'agit de sauver quelques jeunes hommes du suicide et quelques autres de l'entrée aux flics ou aux pompiers. Je pense à ceux qui se suicident par dégoût, parce qu'ils trouvent que « *les autres* » ont trop de part en eux-mêmes.

On peut leur dire : donnez tout au moins *la parole* à la minorité de vous-mêmes. Soyez poètes. Ils répondront : mais c'est là surtout, c'est là encore que je sens les autres en moi-même, lorsque je cherche à m'exprimer je n'y parviens pas. Les paroles sont toutes faites et s'expriment : elles ne m'expriment point. Là encore j'étouffe.

C'est alors qu'enseigner l'art de *résister aux paroles* devient utile, l'art de ne dire que ce que l'on veut dire, l'art de les violenter et de les soumettre. Somme toute fonder une rhétorique, ou plutôt apprendre à chacun l'art de fonder sa propre rhétorique, est une oeuvre de salut public.

Cela sauve les seules, les rares personnes qu'il importe de sauver : celles qui ont la conscience et le souci et le dégoût des autres en eux-mêmes.

Celles qui peuvent faire avancer l'esprit, et à proprement parler changer la face des choses.

1929-1930.

RHETORIC

I assume that we are talking about saving a few young men from suicide and a few others from becoming cops or firemen. I have in mind those who commit suicide out of disgust, because they find that *others* own too large a share of them.

To them one should say: at least let the minority within you have the right to *speak*. Be poets. They will answer: but it is especially there, it is always there that I feel others within me; when I try to express myself, I am unable to do so. Words are ready-made and express themselves: they do not express me. Once again I find myself suffocating.

At that moment, teaching the art of *resisting words* becomes useful, the art of saying only what one wants to say, the art of doing them violence, of forcing them to submit. In short, it is a matter of public safety to found a rhetoric, or rather, to teach everyone the art of founding his own rhetoric.

This saves those few, those rare individuals who must be saved: those who are aware, and who are troubled and disgusted by the others within them.

Those individuals who make the mind progress, and who are, strictly speaking, capable of changing the reality of things.

1929-1930
From *Proêmes* in *Tome premier*, pp. 177-178.

INTRODUCTION AU GALET

Comme après tout si je consens à l'existence c'est à condition de l'accepter pleinement, en tant qu'elle remet tout en question; quels d'ailleurs et si faibles que soient mes moyens comme ils sont évidemment plutôt d'ordre littéraire et rhétorique; je ne vois pas pourquoi je ne commencerais pas, arbitrairement, par montrer qu'à propos des choses les plus simples il est possible de faire des discours infinis entièrement composés de déclarations inédites, enfin qu'à propos de n'importe quoi non seulement tout n'est pas dit, mais à peu près tout reste à dire.

Il est tout de même à plusieurs points de vue insupportable de penser dans quel infime manège depuis des siècles tournent les paroles, l'esprit, enfin la réalité de l'homme. Il suffit pour s'en rendre compte de fixer son attention sur le premier objet venu : on s'apercevra aussitôt que personne ne l'a jamais observé, et qu'à son propos les choses les plus élémentaires restent à dire. Et j'entends bien que sans doute pour l'homme il ne s'agit pas *essentiellement* d'observer et de décrire des objets, mais enfin cela est un signe, et des plus nets. A quoi donc s'occupe-t-on? Certes à tout, sauf à changer d'atmosphère intellectuelle, à sortir des poussiéreux salons où s'ennuie à mourir tout ce qu'il y a de vivant dans l'esprit, à progresser—enfin! —non seulement par les pensées, mais par les facultés, les sentiments, les sensations, et somme toute à accroître *la quantité de ses qualités*. Car des millions de sentiments, par exemple, aussi différents du petit catalogue de ceux qu'éprouvent actuellement les hommes les plus sensibles, sont à connaître, sont à éprouver. Mais non!

74

INTRODUCTION TO THE PEBBLE

If, after all, I consent to existence, it is on the condition that I accept it fully, because it puts everything in doubt again. Even though my means may be weak, since they obviously fall more into the literary and the rhetorical order, I don't see why I shouldn't begin, arbitrarily, by showing that, about the simplest things, it is possible to make countless speeches entirely constituted of original statements, and therefore not only has little been said about anything but practically everything remains to be said.

From a number of points of view it is really unbearable to think in what a lowly rink, and for centuries, words have gone around, the mind and even the reality of men. In order to understand this, one only has to focus one's attention on the first object in sight: it is immediately apparent that no one has ever really looked at it, and that the most basic things remain to be said about it. Of course, I don't mean to say that it is *essential* for man to observe and describe objects; however, it is a sign, and one of the clearest. What takes up our time? Everything, except changing the intellectual climate, getting out of those musty drawing rooms where everything alive in one's mind is bored to death: to move ahead—finally! —not just by thinking but by mental powers, feelings, sensations, and, all in all, to increase the *quantity of those qualities.* Clearly millions of feelings, for example, as different from the little catalog of those that the most sensitive men feel, remain to be known, to be felt. But no! For a long time to come, man will be satisfied to be "proud" or "humble," "sincere" or "hypocritical," "gay" or "sad," "sick"

L'homme se contentera longtemps encore d'être « fier » ou
« humble », « sincère » ou « hypocrite », « gai » ou « triste »,
« malade » ou « bien portant », « bon » ou « méchant »,
« propre » ou « sale », « durable » ou « éphémère », etc., avec
toutes les combinaisons possibles de ces pitoyables qualités.

Eh bien! Je tiens à dire quant à moi que je suis bien autre
chose, et par exemple qu'en dehors de toutes les qualités que
je possède en commun avec le rat, le lion, et le filet, je prétends à celles du diamant, et je me solidarise d'ailleurs entièrement aussi bien avec la mer qu'avec la falaise qu'elle attaque
et avec le galet qui s'en trouve par la suite créé, et dont l'on
trouvera à titre d'exemple ci-dessous la description essayée,
sans préjuger de toutes les qualités dont je compte bien que la
contemplation et la nomination d'objets extrêmement différents me feront prendre conscience et jouissance effective par
la suite.

*

A tout désir d'évasion, opposer la contemplation et ses
ressources. Inutile de partir : se transférer aux choses, qui
vous comblent d'impressions nouvelles, vous proposent un
million de qualités inédites.

Personnellement ce sont les distractions qui me gênent,
c'est en prison ou en cellule, seul à la campagne que je
m'ennuierais le moins. Partout ailleurs, et quoi que je fasse,
j'ai l'impression de perdre mon temps. Même, la richesse de
propositions contenues dans le moindre objet est si grande,
que je ne conçois pas encore la possibilité de rendre compte
d'aucune autre chose que des plus simples : une pierre, une
herbe, le feu, un morceau de bois, un morceau de viande.

Les spectacles qui paraîtraient à d'autres les moins com-
pliqués, comme par exemple simplement le visage d'un

or "in good health," "nice" or "mean," "clean" or "dirty," "lasting" or "ephemeral," etc., with all the imaginable combinations of those pitiful qualities.

Well! I insist upon saying that, as for me, I am of another breed, and, for instance, besides all the qualities that I have in common with the rat, the lion, and the net, I hold to those that belong to the diamond, and besides, I am entirely at one with the sea and the cliff that it attacks, and with the pebble that finds itself created as a result, and that you will find, further on, in the form of a sample, an initial description, without prejudicing all the qualities that will make me aware and joyous as I contemplate and name extremely different objects.

*

Every time we want to escape, let contemplation and its resources stand in the way. No sense in going: transfer yourself into things that gratify you with new impressions, that offer you a million new qualities.

As for me, distractions bother me: I would be the least bored in a prison or a cell, alone in the country. Anywhere else, and whatever I do, I have the feeling of wasting my time. The very wealth of propositions contained in the least object is so great that I cannot yet conceive of the possibility of accounting for any but the simplest things: a stone, an herb, fire, a piece of wood, a piece of meat.

What would appear to others as devoid of any complexity, such as, for example, the face of a man about to speak, or a man asleep, or any display of an activity by a living being, still seem to me to be much too difficult and charged with new meanings (to be discovered, then linked dialectically) for me to dream of harnessing myself to such a

homme sur le point de parler, ou d'un homme qui dort, ou n'importe quelle manifestation d'activité chez un être vivant, me semblent encore de beaucoup trop difficiles et chargés de significations inédites (à découvrir, puis à relier dialectiquement) pour que je puisse songer à m'y atteler de longtemps. Dès lors, comment pourrais-je décrire une scène, faire la critique d'un spectacle ou d'une oeuvre d'art? Je n'ai là-dessus aucune opinion, n'en pouvant même conquérir la moindre impression un peu juste, ou complète.

*

Tout le secret du bonheur du contemplateur est dans son refus de considérer *comme un mal* l'envahissement de sa personnalité par les choses. Pour éviter que cela tourne au mysticisme, il faut : 1° se rendre compte précisément, c'est-à-dire expressément de chacune des choses dont on a fait l'objet de sa contemplation; 2° changer assez souvent d'objet de contemplation, et en somme garder une certaine mesure. Mais le plus important pour la santé du contemplateur est la *nomination*, au fur et à mesure, de toutes les qualités qu'il découvre; il ne faut pas que ces qualités, qui le TRANSPORTENT le transportent plus loin que leur expression mesurée et exacte.

*

Je propose à chacun l'ouverture de trappes intérieures, un voyage dans l'épaisseur des choses, une invasion de qualités, une révolution ou une subversion comparable à celle qu'opère la charrue ou la pelle, lorsque, tout à coup et pour la première fois, sont mises au jour des millions de parcelles, de paillettes, de racines, de vers et de petites bêtes jusqu'alors

task for a long time to come. As a result, how could I describe a scene, review a play or a work of art? I have no opinion on such matters, since I have not even gained the slightest impressions about them.

*

For an individual who has a contemplative disposition, the whole secret of happiness is not to consider *as an evil* the invasion of his personality by objects. In order for that experience to avoid becoming a mystical one, it is necessary (1) to arrive at a precise inventory of each thing that one has made the object of one's contemplation; (2) to change objects of contemplation rather frequently to assure a degree of equilibrium. But for a contemplative individual, what is most important is the progressive *nomination* of all the qualities that he discovers; those *qualities* that TRANSPORT him should not transport him further than their measured and exact meanings.

*

I suggest that each individual opens up a series of interior trapdoors; travels through the thickness of things; an invasion of qualities, a revolution or a subversion comparable to the one effected by the plow or the shovel when, all of a sudden, and for the first time, millions of parcels, grains, roots, worms, and tiny beasts, up to then buried in the ground, appear in the light of day.

O infinite resources of the thickness of things, *brought out* by the infinite resources of the semantical thickness of words!

enfouies. O ressources infinies de l'épaisseur des choses, *rendues* par les ressources infinies de l'épaisseur sémantique des mots!

*

La contemplation d'objets précis est aussi un repos, mais c'est un repos privilégié, comme ce repos perpétuel des plantes adultes, qui porte des fruits. Fruits spéciaux, empruntés autant à l'air ou au milieu ambiant, au moins pour la forme à laquelle ils sont limités et les couleurs que par opposition ils en prennent, qu'à la personne qui en fournit la substance; et c'est ainsi qu'ils se différencient des fruits d'un autre repos, le sommeil, qui sont nommés les rêves, uniquement formés par la personne, et, par conséquence, indéfinis, informes, et sans utilité : c'est pourquoi ils ne sont pas véritablement des fruits.

*

Ainsi donc, si ridiculement prétentieux qu'il puisse paraître, voici quel est à peu près mon dessein : je voudrais écrire une sorte de *De natura rerum*. On voit bien la différence avec les poètes contemporains : ce ne sont pas des poèmes que je veux composer, mais une seule cosmogonie.

Mais comment rendre ce dessein possible? Je considère l'état actuel des sciences : des bibliothèques entières sur chaque partie de chacune d'elles... Faudrait-il donc que je commence par les lire, et les apprendre? Plusieurs vies n'y suffiraient pas. Au milieu de l'énorme étendue et quantité des connaissances acquises par chaque science, du nombre accru des sciences, nous sommes perdus. Le meilleur parti à prendre

*

The contemplation of specific objects is also a rest, but a privileged rest, like the perpetual rest of adult plants that bear fruits. Special fruits, nurtured as much by the air or the surrounding area, at least for the form to which they are limited and the colors that they assume in opposition to it, as they are by the person who provides them with substance; such fruits can be differentiated from others, called dreams, in that other rest—sleep—where they are solely shaped by the person, and consequently, indefinite, shapeless and useless: that is why they are not truly fruits.

*

Here, and however ridiculously pretentious this may appear, is a rough draft of my project: I would like to write a sort of *De natura rerum*. This is obviously different from the work of contemporary poets: I do not want to compose poems, but a single cosmogony.

But how can this project come about? I take stock of the present state of the sciences: whole libraries are devoted to each of their subdivisions. . . . Should I then begin by reading them? Learning them? One life would not be enough. We are lost in the midst of the enormous extent and quantity of knowledge acquired by each science, and the increased number of sciences. Therefore, the best solution is to consider all things as unknown, and to walk or rest in the woods or on the grass and to start everything over from the very beginning.

*

est donc de considérer toutes choses comme inconnues, et de se promener ou de s'étendre sous bois ou sur l'herbe, et de reprendre tout du début.

*

Exemple du peu d'épaisseur des choses dans l'esprit des hommes jusqu'à moi : du *galet*, ou de la pierre, voici ce que j'ai trouvé qu'on pense, ou qu'on a pensé de plus original :

Un coeur de pierre (Diderot);

Uniforme et plat galet (Diderot);

Je méprise cette poussière qui me compose et qui vous parle (Saint-Just);

Si j'ai du goût ce n'est guère

Que pour la terre et les pierres (Rimbaud).

Eh bien! Pierre, galet, poussière, occasion de sentiments si communs quoique si contradictoires, je ne te juge pas si rapidement, car je désire te juger à ta valeur : et tu me serviras, et tu serviras dès lors aux hommes à bien d'autres expressions, tu leur fourniras pour leurs discussions entre eux ou avec eux-mêmes bien d'autres arguments; même, si j'ai assez de talent, tu les armeras de quelques nouveaux proverbes ou lieux communs : voilà toute mon ambition.

1933.

Examples of the limited thickness of things in the minds of men who came before me: about the *pebble* or the stone, here are a few thoughts that I have found and that have been considered as most original:

A heart of stone (Diderot)

A pebble flat and uniform (Diderot)

I despise this dust that composes me and speaks to you (Saint-Just)

Of the things that I care for

Earth and stones and nothing more (Rimbaud).

Well! stones, pebbles, dust, such trite feelings albeit so contradictory have been expressed about you; I will not judge you so hastily because I want to judge you on your own merits: and you will serve me, and henceforth, you will serve mankind for many other expressions; you will provide them with arguments when they speak among themselves or to themselves and, if I have enough talent, you will even arm them with a few proverbs or platitudes: that's the extent of my ambition.

1933
From *Proêmes* in *Tome premier*, pp. 196-202.

LE TRONC D'ARBRE

Puisque bientôt l'hiver va nous mettre en valeur
Montrons-nous préparés aux offices du bois

Grelots par moins que rien émus à la folie
Effusions à nos dépens cessez ô feuilles
Dont un change d'humeur nous couvre ou nous dépouille

Avec peine par nous sans cesse imaginées
Vous n'êtes déjà plus qu'avec peine croyables

Détache-toi de moi ma trop sincère écorce
Va rejoindre à mes pieds celles des autres siècles

De visages passés masques passés public
Contre moi de ton sort demeurés pour témoins
Tous ont eu comme toi la paume un instant vive
Que par terre et par eau nous voyons déconfits
Bien que de mes vertus je te croie la plus proche

Décède aux lieux communs tu es faite pour eux
Meurs exprès De ton fait déboute le malheur
Démasque volontiers ton volontaire auteur...

Ainsi s'efforce un arbre encore sous l'écorce
A montrer vif ce tronc que parfera la mort.

THE TREE TRUNK

Soon winter will put us to the task so
Let us be prepared for the rites of the wood

Bells moved to folly by hardly a thing
Outpourings at our expense stop o leaves
Whose change of mood covers us or strips us bare

With difficulty we try to imagine you
You who are already so hard to believe

Split yourself from me my bark too sincere
Go join at my feet those of other centuries

Bygone masks of bygone faces public
Against me they have stayed to witness your fate
Like you, all have had for an instant, their palms alive
That, on the ground and in the water, we see discomfited
Although I find you to be the closest to my virtues

Die in the commonplaces you are made for
Die on purpose By your act misfortune dismissed
Unmask willingly your willing author . . .

Thus still under the bark a tree attempts
To show living this trunk that death will finish.

From *Le Tronc d'arbre, Tome premier*, pp. 251-252.

LE PAIN

La surface du pain est merveilleuse d'abord à cause de cette impression quasi panoramique qu'elle donne : comme si l'on avait à sa disposition sous la main les Alpes, le Taurus ou la Cordillère des Andes.

Ainsi donc une masse amorphe en train d'éructer fut glissée pour nous dans le four stellaire, où durcissant elle s'est façonnée en vallées, crêtes, ondulations, crevasses... Et tous ces plans dès lors si nettement articulés, ces dalles minces où la lumière avec application couche ses feux, — sans un regard pour la mollesse ignoble sous-jacente.

Ce lâche et froid sous-sol que l'on nomme la mie a son tissu pareil à celui des éponges : feuilles ou fleurs y sont comme des soeurs siamoises soudées par tous les coudes à la fois. Lorsque le pain rassit ces fleurs fanent et se rétrécissent : elles se détachent alors les unes des autres, et la masse en devient friable...

Mais brisons-la : car le pain doit être dans notre bouche moins objet de respect que de consommation.

FRENCH BREAD

The surface of a French bread is marvelous, first of all because of that quasi-panoramic impression it gives: as if one had at one's fingertips the Alps, the Taurus, or the Andean Cordillera.

Thus an amorphous mass in the process of belching was slipped into the stellar oven for us, where, hardening, it fashioned itself into valleys, peaks, ondulations, crevasses... And, as of that moment, all those planes, so distinctly articulated, those thin tiles where the light carefully lays down its fires—heedless of the ignoble underlying softness.

This loose and cold subsoil we call the white part has a texture similar to a sponge's: there, leaves or flowers, like Siamese twins, are fused together by all their elbows. In stale bread, these flowers wilt and shrink; they separate one from the other and the mass becomes easily crumbled...

But let's break it off here: after all, bread in our mouth must be eaten rather than respected.

From *Le Parti pris des choses, Tome premier*, p. 51.

L'HUÎTRE

L'huître, de la grosseur d'un galet moyen, est d'une apparence plus rugueuse, d'une couleur moins unie, brillamment blanchâtre. C'est un monde opiniâtrement clos. Pourtant on peut l'ouvrir : il faut alors la tenir au creux d'un torchon, se servir d'un couteau ébréché et peu franc, s'y reprendre à plusieurs fois. Les doigts curieux s'y coupent, s'y cassent les ongles : c'est un travail grossier. Les coups qu'on lui porte marquent son enveloppe de ronds blancs, d'une sorte de halos.

A l'intérieur l'on trouve tout un monde, à boire et à manger : sous un *firmament* (à proprement parler) de nacre, les cieux d'en-dessus s'affaissent sur les cieux d'en-dessous, pour ne plus former qu'une mare, un sachet visqueux et verdâtre, qui flue et reflue à l'odeur et à la vue, frangé d'une dentelle noirâtre sur les bords.

Parfois très rare une formule perle à leur gosier de nacre, d'où l'on trouve aussitôt à s'orner.

THE OYSTER

The oyster, the size of an average pebble, looks rougher, its colors less uniform, brilliantly whitish. It is a world stubbornly closed. And yet, it can be opened: then you've got to hold it in the hollow of a dish towel, use a jagged and rather tricky knife, repeat this several times. Curious fingers cut themselves on it, nails break: it's tough work. Hitting it that way leaves white circles, like halos, on its envelope.

Inside, one finds a whole world to drink and eat: under a nacreous *firmament* (strictly speaking), the heavens above recline on the heavens below, and form a single pool, a viscous and greenish sachet that flows in and out when you smell it or look at it, fringed with blackish lace along the edges.

Sometimes, a very rare formula pearls in its nacreous throat and right away you've found an ornament.

From *Le Parti pris des choses, Tome premier*, p. 48.

89

LES MÛRES

Aux buissons typographiques constitués par le poème sur une route qui ne mène hors des choses ni à l'esprit, certains fruits sont formés d'une agglomération de sphères qu'une goutte d'encre remplit.

*

Noirs, roses et kakis ensemble sur la grappe, ils offrent plutôt le spectacle d'une famille rogue à ses âges divers, qu'une tentation très vive à la cueillette.

Vue la disproportion des pépins à la pulpe les oiseaux les apprécient peu, si peu de chose au fond leur reste quand du bec à l'anus ils en sont traversés.

*

Mais le poète au cours de sa promenade professionnelle, en prend de la graine à raison : « Ainsi donc, se dit-il, réussissent en grand nombre les efforts patients d'une fleur très fragile quoique par un rébarbatif enchevêtrement de ronces défendue. Sans beaucoup d'autres qualités, — *mûres*, parfaitement elles sont mûres — comme aussi ce poème est fait. »

BLACKBERRIES

On typographical bushes constituted by the poem along a road that leads neither beyond things nor to the spirit, certain fruits are formed by an agglomeration of spheres filled by a drop of ink.

Black, pink, and khaki, all on a cluster, they look more like members of an arrogant family of varying ages than a very lively temptation to pick them off.

Given the disproportion of the pits to the pulp, birds find little to appreciate, so little in the end remains by the time it has traveled from the beak to the anus.

But the poet on his professional walk mulls this over in his mind: "Clearly," he says to himself, "the patient efforts of a very delicate flower are mostly successful although protected by a forbidding tangle of brambles. Lacking many other qualities—blackberries are perfectly ripe, the way this poem is ready."

From *Le Parti pris des choses, Tome premier*, pp. 41-42.

LE FEU

Le feu fait un classement : d'abord toutes les flammes se dirigent en quelque sens...

(L'on ne peut comparer la marche du feu qu'à celle des animaux : il faut qu'il quitte un endroit pour en occuper un autre; il marche à la fois comme une amibe et comme une girafe, bondit du col, rampe du pied)...

Puis, tandis que les masses contaminées avec méthode s'écroulent, les gaz qui s'échappent sont transformés à mesure en une seule rampe de papillons.

A FIRE

A fire classifies: to begin with, all the flames go in a particular direction...

(One can only compare the way a fire walks to that of animals: it's got to leave a place in order to occupy another; it walks like an amoeba as well as a giraffe, leaping from the neck and crawling on its feet)...

Then, while the contaminated masses methodically disintegrate, the escaping gases are successively transformed into a single file of butterflies.

From Le Parti pris des choses, Tome premier, p. 52.

PAROLES SUR LE PAPIER

Paroles, fondez du haut des airs sur ce papier!
Vous voliez jadis... et ne nichiez, par occasion, que dans le marbre.
Jetez-vous aujourd'hui sur cet indigne support :
Noircissez, décriez, déchirez ce papier!

Aujourd'hui les écrits volent, comme oiseaux de basse-cour, et ne nichent qu'aux cabinets.

Effrayez cette monstrueuse prolifération d'oiseaux infirmes,

Puis revolez aux frontons!

O regrettés ramiers,
Rares et farouches,
Alertes et bruyants,
De faîte en faîte vous voliez...

Vous renicherez dans le marbre
Pour avoir piétiné ce papier.

(1950.)

WORDS ON PAPER

Words! Swoop down from above on this paper!
Long ago, you flew . . . and rarely came to nest except in
marble.
Throw yourselves today on this worthless support:
Blacken, disparage, destroy this paper!

Today, texts fly like barnyard birds and only nest in
toilets.

Frighten this monstrous proliferation of invalid
birds,

They fly back to your pediments!

O regretted ring-doves,
Rare and fierce,
Alert and noisy,
You flew from peak to peak . . .

You will nest again in marble
For having stamped on this paper.

1950
Nouveau Recueil, p. 49.

LE SOLEIL LU À LA RADIO

1

Puisque tel est le pouvoir du langage,
Battrons-nous donc soleil comme princes monnaie,
    Pour en timbrer le haut de cette page?
    L'y ferons-nous monter comme il monte au zénith?

OUI

Pour qu'ainsi réponde, au milieu de la page,
L'acclamation du monde à son exclamation!

2

« Brillant soleil adoré du Sauvage... »
Ainsi débute un choeur de l'illustre Rameau.
Ainsi, battons soleil comme l'on bat tambour!
Battons soleil aux champs! Battons la générale!

OUI

Battons d'un seul coeur pavillon du soleil!

3

Pourtant, tel est le pouvoir du langage,
Que l'Ombre aussi est en notre pouvoir.
    Déjà, prenons-y garde,

READING THE SUN ON RADIO

1

Since such is the power of language,
Shall we then mint the sun as princes do money?
    To stamp the top of this page?
    Shall we make it climb as it climbs to the zenith?

YES

So that the answer may be, in the middle of the page,
The acclamation of the world to its exclamation!

2

"Brilliant sun adored by the Savage . . ."
So begins a chorus by the illustrious Rameau.
So, let us beat the sun as we beat a drum!
Let us beat the praises of the sun! Beat the alarum!

YES

Let us beat with a single heart the colors of the sun!

3

But such is the power of language,
That the Shadow is also in our power.
    Already, let us beware,

Le soleil la comporte et ce *oui* la contient :
OUI, je viens dans son temple adorer l'Éternel.
OUI, c'est Agamemnon, c'est ton roi qui t'éveille!
Par la même exclamation monosyllabique
      Débute la Tragédie.
OUI, l'Ombre ici déjà est en pouvoir.

4

Nous ne continuerons donc pas sur ce ton.
La révolte, comme l'acclamation, est facile.
Mais voici peut-être le point.

Qu'est-ce que le soleil comme objet? — C'est le plus brillant des objets du monde.

OUI, brillant à tel point! Nous venons de le voir.

Il y faut tout l'orchestre : les tambours, les clairons, les fifres, les tubas. Et les tambourins, et la batterie.

Tout cela pour dire quoi? — Un seul monosyllabe. Une seule onomatopée monosyllabique.

Le soleil ne peut-être remplacé par aucune formule logique, CAR le soleil n'est pas un objet.

LE PLUS BRILLANT des objets du monde n'est — de ce fait — NON — *n'est pas* un objet; c'est un trou, c'est l'abîme métaphysique : la condition formelle et indispensable de tout au monde. La condition de tous les autres objets. La condition même du regard.

5

Et voici ce qui en lui est atroce. Vraiment, du dernier mauvais goût! Vraiment, qui nous laisse loin de compte, et nous empêche de l'adorer :

The sun allows it and this *yes* contains it:

YES, I come to this temple to adore the Eternal.

YES, it is Agamemnon, it is your king who awakens you!

By the same monosyllabic exclamation
    The Tragedy begins.

YES, the Shadow here is already in power.

4

We shall not, therefore, carry on this way.

Revolt, like acclamation, is easy.

But perhaps that's the point.

What kind of object is the sun?—it is the brightest object in the world.

YES, brilliant to such a degree! We have just seen it.

It takes a whole orchestra: drums, bugles, fifes, tubas. And the tambourines and the timpani.

All that to voice a single monosyllable. A single mono-syllabic onomatopoeia.

The sun cannot be replaced by any logical formula, FOR the sun is not an object.

THE BRIGHTEST of all objects in the world is—conse-quently—NOT—*is not* an object; it is a hole, the metaphysi-cal abyss: the formal and indispensable condition of every-thing in the world. The condition of all other objects. The condition of sight itself.

5

And now that part of it which is atrocious. Really in poor taste! That leaves us really unsatisfied, and prevents us from adoring it:

Cette condition *sine qua non* de tout ce qui est au monde s'y montre, s'y impose, y apparaît.

Elle a le front de s'y montrer !

Qui plus est, elle s'y montre de telle façon qu'elle interdit qu'on la regarde, qu'elle repousse le regard, vous le renfonce à l'intérieur du corps !

Vraiment, quel tyran !

Non seulement, il nous oblige *à être*, je vais dire dans quelles conditions — mais il nous force à le contempler — et cependant nous en empêche, nous interdit de le fixer.

OUI et NON !

C'est un tyran et un artiste, un artificier, un acteur ! Néron ! Ahenobarbus !

6

Voici en quelques mots ce qui s'est passé.

Le Soleil, qui n'est pas la Vie, qui est peut-être la Mort (comme Goethe l'a décrite : « plus de lumière »), qui est sans doute deçà de la Vie et de la Mort, — a expulsé de Lui certaines de ses parties, les a exilées, envoyées à une certaine distance pour s'en faire contempler.

Envoyées, dis-je, à une certaine distance. Distance fort bien calculée. Suffisante pour qu'elles refroidissent, suffisante pour que ces exilées aient assez de recul pour le contempler. Insuffisante pour qu'elles échappent à son attraction et ne doivent continuer autour de lui leur ronde, leur service de spectateurs.

Ainsi elles refroidissent, car il les a vouées à la mort, mais d'abord — et c'est bien pire — à cette maladie, à cette tiédeur que l'on nomme la vie. Et, par exemple, quant à l'homme, à ses trente-sept degrés centigrades. Ah ! Songez

This *sine qua non* condition of everything in the world reveals itself, imposes itself, appears in it.

It has the effrontery to show itself!

What's more, it reveals itself in such a way that it forbids you to look at it, that it forces your eyes back into your head!

Really, what a tyrant!

Not only does it compel us *to be*, I will later say under what conditions—but it forces us to contemplate it—and nevertheless prevents us from doing so, forbids us from staring at it.

YES and NO!

It is a tyrant and an artist, a fireworks specialist, an actor! Nero! Ahenobarbus!

6

Here, in a few words, is what happened.

The Sun, which is not Life, which may be Death (as Goethe described it: "more light"), which is without a doubt beyond Life and Death,—expelled from Itself certain fragments, exiled them, sent them a certain distance in order to be seen by them.

Sent out, I say a certain distance. A well-calculated distance. Enough to let them cool off, enough so that these exiles could still contemplate it. Not far enough for them to escape its attraction, and to stop circling around it, as dutiful spectators.

Thus they cool off, for it has destined them to die, but first—which makes it much worse—to this sickness, to this tepidness called life. And in the case of man, to these ninety-eight degrees. Ah! Think of how much closer to death is life,

combien plus proche de la mort est la vie, cette tiédeur, que du soleil et de ses milliards de degrés centigrades!

J'en dirais autant des formes et des couleurs, qui expriment la damnation particulière de chaque être, de chaque spectateur exilé du soleil. Sa damnation, c'est-à-dire sa façon particulière d'adorer et de mourir.

7

Ainsi les corps et la vie même ne sont qu'une dégradation de l'énergie solaire, vouée à la contemplation et au regret de celle-ci, et — presque aussitôt — à la mort.

Ainsi le soleil est un fléau. Voyez : comme les fléaux, il fait éclater les épis, les cosses. Mais c'est un fléau sadique, un fléau médecin. Un fléau qui fait se reproduire et qui entretient ses victimes; qui les *recrée* et s'en fait désirer.

Car — cet objet éblouissant — un nuage, un écran, le moindre volet, la moindre paupière qu'il forme suffit à le cacher, et donc à le faire désirer. Et il ne manque pas d'en former. Et ainsi la moitié de la vie se passe-t-elle dans l'ombre, à souhaiter la chaleur et la lumière, c'est-à-dire les travaux forcés dans la prison de l'azur.

8

Pourtant, voici que cette fable comporte une moralité.

Car, plongés dans l'ombre et dans la nuit par les caprices du soleil et sa coquetterie sadique, les objets éloignés de lui au service de le contempler, tout à coup voient le ciel étoilé.

Il a dû les éloigner de lui pour qu'ils le contemplent (et se cacher à eux pour qu'ils le désirent), mais voici qu'ils aperçoivent alors ces myriades d'étoiles, les myriades d'*autres* soleils.

this tepidness, than it is to the Sun and to its millions of degrees of fahrenheit!

I would say as much about the forms and colors that express the particular damnation of each being, of each spectator exiled from the sun. His damnation, that is to say, his particular way of adoring and dying.

7

Thus, bodies and life itself are but a degradation of solar energy, doomed to contemplate it and to mourn it, and— almost as soon—to die.

Thus, the sun is a flail. Behold! like a flail, it breaks open the spears of grain, the husks. But it is a sadistic scourge, a curative scourge. A scourge that encourages reproduction and watches over its victims; that *recreates* them and makes itself desired.

For—this blinding object—a cloud, a screen, the lightest shutter, the thinnest eyelid that it forms is enough to hide it and, therefore, to make it desirable. And it does not fail to form them. And thus, half of life is spent in the shade, wishing for heat and light, that is to say, forced labor in the prison of the sky.

8

However, there is a moral to this story.

For, plunged in the shade and the night by the sun's caprice and its sadistic whims, objects in its service that have been placed at a certain distance in order to contemplate it, suddenly see the starry sky.

It had to place them at a distance to be contemplated by

Et il n'a pas fallu longtemps pour qu'ils les comptent. Et ne comptent leur propre soleil *parmi* l'infinité des astres, non comme le plus important. Le plus proche et le plus tyrannique, certes.

Mais enfin, l'un seulement des soleils.

Et je ne dis pas qu'une telle considération les rassure, mais elle les venge...

9

Ainsi, plongé dans le désordre absurde et de mauvais goût du monde, dans le chaos inouï des nuits, l'homme du moins compte les soleils.

Mais enfin, son dédain s'affirme et il cesse même de les compter.

(*Écrit le XXII juin de ma cinquante et unième année : jour du solstice d'été.*)

10

... Cependant le soleil se fait longuement regretter; nuit et nuées; s'éloigne de la terre, conçue vers le solstice d'hiver.

Puis il remonte.

C'est alors qu'il faut continuer par l'expression de la remontée du soleil, malgré nous. Et, bien sûr, cela ne peut finir que par un nouveau désespoir, accru (« Encore un jour qui luit! »).

Il ne reste donc qu'*une* solution.

Recommencer volontairement l'hymne. Prendre décidément le soleil en bonne part. C'est aussi là le pouvoir du langage. Nous en féliciter, réjouir. L'en féliciter. L'honorer, le

them (and to hide itself from them to be desired), but now they see these myriad stars, these myriad *other* suns.

And it did not take them long to count them. And to count their own sun *among* an infinity of stars, and not as the most important. Although the closest and the most tyrannical.

But finally only as one of the suns.

And I do not say that such a consideration reassures them, but it avenges them . . .

9

Thus, plunged in the absurd disorder and poor taste of the world, in the incredible chaos of nights, man at least counts the suns.

But, finally, his disdain asserts itself and he even stops counting them.

(*Written June XXII of my fifty-first year; the day of the summer solstice.*)

10

. . . However, the sun is regretted for a long time; night and clouds; it moves away from the earth, conceived during the winter solstice.

Then it rises again.

Then, we must follow up by expressing the ascent of the sun, despite ourselves. And, naturally, this can only lead to a new and sharpened despair ("Another bright day!")

There is then only *one* solution left.

Start up the hymn voluntarily. And decidedly take the

chanter, tâchant seulement de *renouveler* les thèmes (et variations) de ce los. Le nuancer, en plein ravissement.

Certes nous savons à quoi nous en tenir, mais *à tout prix* la santé, la réjouissance et la joie.

Il faut donc métalogiquement le « refaire », le posséder. En plein ravissement.

« Remonte donc, puisque enfin tu remontes. Tu me recrées. Ah! j'ai médit de toi! Etc..., etc. »

Changer le mal en bien. Les travaux forcés en Paradis.

Puis finir dans l'ambiguïté hautement dédaigneuse, ironique et tonique à la fois; le fonctionnement verbal, sans aucun coefficient laudatif ni péjoratif : l'objeu.

sun in good faith. That is also in the power of language. Congratulate ourselves, rejoice in it. Congratulate it. Honor it, praise it, trying only to *renovate* the themes (and variations) of the gramercy. Be subtle in the midst of this rapture.

Obviously, we know what to expect, but *at all costs*, let's have health, pleasure, and joy.

Therefore, we must "remake" it metalogically, possess it. In the midst of this rapture.

"Rise, then, since you are rising. You recreate me. Ah! I have slandered you! Etc...etc..."

Change evil into good. Forced labor into Paradise.

Then finish up in an ambiguity highly disdainful, ironic and tonic at the same time; the verbal function, without any laudatory or pejorative coefficient: the obgame.

From *Le Soleil placé en abîme, Le Grand Recueil*, pp. 160-166.

LE PRÉ

Que parfois la Nature, à notre réveil, nous propose
Ce à quoi justement nous étions disposés,
La louange aussitôt s'enfle dans notre gorge.
Nous croyons être au paradis.

Voilà comme il en fut du pré que je veux dire,
Qui fera mon propos d'aujourd'hui.

Parce qu'il s'y agit plus d'une façon d'être
Que d'un plat à nos yeux servi,
La parole y convient plutôt que la peinture
Qui n'y suffirait nullement.

Prendre un tube de vert, l'étaler sur la page,
Ce n'est pas faire un pré.
Ils naissent autrement.
Ils sourdent de la page.
Et encore faut-il que ce soit page brune.

Préparons donc la page où puisse aujourd'hui naître
Une vérité qui soit verte.

Parfois donc — ou mettons aussi bien par endroits —
Parfois, notre nature —
J'entends dire, d'un mot, la Nature sur notre planète
Et ce que, chaque jour, à notre réveil, nous sommes —
Parfois, notre nature nous a préparé(s) (à) un pré.

THE MEADOW

When at times Nature when we awaken proposes
Just what we were disposed to do,
Then praise immediately swells in our throat.
We believe we are in paradise.

That is the way it was with the meadow I want to evoke,
Which will comprise my topic today.

Because it deals more with a way of being
Than a dish we have been asked to admire,
Words suit it better than paint,
Which wouldn't do at all.

Take a tube of green, spread it on the page,
That's not the way to make a meadow.
They are born differently.
They spring up from the page.
And then only from a brown page.

Let us then prepare the page upon which
A green truth may be born today.

At times, then—let us say, as well, in certain places—
At times, our nature—
I mean by that, in a word, Nature on our planet
And what we are, when we awake every morning—
At times, our nature has prepared us (for) a meadow.

Le Pré

Mais qu'est-ce, qui obstrue ainsi notre chemin?
Dans ce petit sous-bois mi-ombre mi-soleil,
Qui nous met ces bâtons dans les roues?
Pourquoi, dès notre issue en surplomb sur la page,
Dans ce seul paragraphe, tous ces scrupules?

Pourquoi donc, vu d'ici, ce fragment limité d'espace,
Tiré à quatre rochers ou à quatre haies d'aubépines,
Guère plus grand qu'un mouchoir,
Moraine des forêts, ondée de signe adverse,
Ce pré, surface amène, auréole des sources
Et de l'orage initial suite douce
En appel ou réponse unanime anonyme à la pluie,
Nous semble-t-il plus précieux soudain
Que le plus mince des tapis persans?

Fragile, mais non frangible,
La terre végétale y reprend parfois le dessus,
Où les petits sabots du poulain qui y galopa le marquèrent,
Ou le piétinement vers l'abreuvoir des bestiaux qui lentement
S'y précipitèrent...

Tandis qu'une longue théorie de promeneurs endimanchés, sans y
Salir du tout leurs souliers blancs, y procèdent
Au long du petit torrent, grossi, de noyade ou de perdition,
Pourquoi donc, dès l'abord, nous tient-il interdits?

Serions-nous donc déjà parvenus au naos,
Enfin au lieu sacré d'un petit déjeuné de raisons?
Nous voici, en tout cas, au coeur des pléonasmes
Et au seul niveau logique qui nous convient.

But what is this that obstructs our way?
In this underbrush, half-light, half-shade,
Who throws sticks in our wheels?
Why, when we come forth, bent over the page,
In this single paragraph, all these scruples?

Why then, seen from here, should this limited fragment of space,
Stretched out between four rocks or four hawthorn hedges,
Hardly larger than a handkerchief,
Forest moraine, downpour of an adverse sign,
This meadow, pleasant surface, aureole of the springs
And the initial thunderstorm's gentle sequel
Calling or answering the rain unanimous anonymous,
Suddenly appear to us more precious
Than the thinnest Persian rug?

Delicate but not brittle,
The vegetal earth sometimes regains the upper hand,
Where the young hoofs of the galloping colt marked it,
Or the steady trampling of the animals going to the trough
In a great rush . . .

While a long procession of Sunday strollers without
In any way soiling their white shoes, proceed
Along the little torrent, swollen by drownings or perdition,
Why then, from the outset, should it hold us back?

Might we have already arrived at the naos,
At last at the sacred site of a light lunch of accommodations?
Here we are, in any case, at the heart of pleonasms
And at the only logical level that suits us.

Ici tourne déjà le moulin à prières,
Sans la moindre idée de prosternation, d'ailleurs,
Car elle serait contraire aux verticalités de l'endroit.

Crase de paratus, selon les étymologistes latins,
Près de la roche et du ru,
Prêt à faucher ou à paître,
Préparé pour nous par la nature,
Pré, paré, pré, près, prêt,

Le pré gisant ici comme le participe passé par excellence
S'y révère aussi bien comme notre préfixe des préfixes,
Préfixe déjà dans préfixe, présent déjà dans présent.
Pas moyen de sortir de nos onomatopées originelles.
Il faut donc y rentrer.

Nul besoin, d'ailleurs, d'en sortir,
Leurs variations suffisant bien à rendre compte
De la merveilleusement fastidieuse
Monotonie et variété du monde,
Enfin, de sa perpétuité.

Encore faut-il les prononcer.
Parler. Et, peut-être, paraboler.
Toutes, les dire.

. . . .

(Ici doit intervenir un long passage, où, dans la manière
un peu de l'interminable séquence de clavecin solo du cin-
quième concerto brandebourgeois, c'est-à-dire de façon fastidieuse et mécanique mais mécanisante à la fois, non tellement

The Meadow

Here the prayer box has already begun to chatter,
Without in any way intending to kneel,
Because that would be contrary to the verticalities of the place.

Crasis of *paratus*, according to Latin etymologists,[1]
Near rock and water,
Ready to be cut or eaten,
Prepared for us by nature,
Meadow, adorned, meadow, near, ready,[2]

The meadow lying here like the past participle par excellence
Reveres itself also as our prefix of prefixes,
Prefix already in prefix, present already in present.
No way of avoiding our initial onomatopoeias.
Therefore, let us accept them.

No need, moreover, to reject them,
Their variations are perfectly able to account
For the marvelously fastidious
Monotony and variety of the world,
In fact, its perpetuity.

But we must pronounce them.
Speak. And perhaps parabolate.
Say them, all.

. . . .

(At this point, a long passage must be inserted in which,

1. *Crasis*, Greek for *Krasis*, contraction of vowels; *Paratus*, Latin, prepared for (S. G.).
2. These are all near homonyms in French (S. G.).

de la musique que de la logique, raisonneuse, du bout des lèvres, non de la poitrine ou du coeur, je tâcherai d'expliquer, je dis bien expliquer, deux ou trois choses, et d'abord que si le pré, dans notre langue, représente une des plus importantes et primordiales notions logiques qui soient, il en est de même sur le plan physique (géophysique), car il s'agit en vérité d'une métamorphose de l'eau, laquelle, au lieu de s'évaporer directement, à l'appel du feu, en nuages, choisit ici, se liant à la terre et en passant par elle, c'est-à-dire par les restes pétris du passé des trois règnes et en particulier par les granulations les plus fines du minéral, réimprégnant en somme le cendrier universel, de donner renaissance à la vie sous sa forme la plus élémentaire, l'herbe : élémentarité—alimentarité. Ce chapitre, qui sera *aussi* celui de la musique des prés, sonnera de façon grêle et minutieuse, avec une quantité d'appoggiatures, pour s'achever (s'il s'achève) en accelerando et rinforzando à la fois, jusqu'à une sorte de roulement de tonnerre où nous nous réfugierons dans les bois. Mais la perfection de ce passage pourrait me demander quelques années encore. Quoi qu'il en soit...)

. . . .

L'orage originel a longuement parlé.

. . . .

L'orage originel n'aura-t-il donc en nous si longuement grondé
Seulement pour qu'enfin
                    — car il s'éloigne, n'occupant plus que
                    partiellement l'horizon bas où il fulgure
                    encore —

rather like the endless harpsichord solo of the Fifth Branden-
burg Concerto, that is, in a fastidious and mechanical manner, mechanizing as well, not so much music as logic, reasoning, from the tip of the lips, not from the chest or the heart, I
will try to explain, I repeat, explain two or three things, and
first of all, that if the meadow, in our language, represents
one of the most important and primordial logical notions
imaginable, the same can also be truthfully said about it on
the physical level (geophysical), because, in truth, it represents a metamorphosis of water which, instead of immediately evaporating, beckoned by fire, into clouds, chooses this
place, becoming one with the earth and passing through it,
that is, by the petrified remains of the past three reigns and in
particular, by the finest granulations of minerals, reimpreg-
nating, in fact, the universal ashpit, to give birth to life in its
most elementary form: grass elementarity—alimentation.
This chapter, which will *also* be devoted to the music of the
meadows, will sound high-pitched and detailed with many
appoggiaturas, and then will conclude (if it can conclude) in a
simultaneous *accelerando* and *rinforzando*, culminating in a
roll of thunder, and at that moment, we will run for cover in
the woods. But I might need a few more years to perfect this
passage. Be that as it may . . .)

. . . .

The original thunderstorm spoke for a long time.

. . . .

The original thunderstorm will it have only boomed in us for
such a long time

Parant au plus urgent, allant au plus pressé,
Nous sortions de ces bois,
Passions entre ces arbres et nos derniers scrupules,
Et, quittant tout portique et toutes colonnades,
Transportés tout à coup par une sorte d'enthousiasme paisible
En faveur d'une vérité, aujourd'hui, qui soit verte,
Nous nous trouvions bientôt alités de tout notre long sur ce pré,
Dès longtemps préparé pour nous par la nature,
                    — où n'avoir plus égard qu'au ciel bleu.

L'oiseau qui le survole en sens inverse de l'écriture
Nous rappelle au concret, et sa contradiction,
Accentuant du pré la note différentielle
Quant à tels près ou prêt, et au prai de prairie,
Sonne brève et aiguë comme une déchirure
Dans le ciel trop serein des significations.
C'est qu'aussi bien, le lieu de la longue palabre
Peut devenir celui de la décision.

Des deux pareils arrivés debout, l'un au moins,
Après un assaut croisé d'armes obliques,
Demeurera couché
D'abord dessus, puis dessous.

Voici donc, sur ce pré, l'occasion, comme il faut,
Prématurément, d'en finir.

Messieurs les typographes,
Placez donc ici, je vous prie, le trait final.
Puis, dessous, sans le moindre interligne, couchez mon nom,

The Meadow

Just so that at last
               —because it moves away, now only
               partially occupying the lower horizon
               where it still flashes—
Parrying the most urgent, facing the most pressing,
We left the woods,
Passing through these trees and our last scruples,
And, leaving behind all porticos and all colonnades,
Carried away suddenly by a kind of peaceful enthusiasm
For a truth, today, which will be green,
We soon found ourselves stretched out on this meadow
Long ago prepared for us by nature,
               —now only attentive to the blue sky.

The bird that flies over it in a direction opposite to the way we write
Brings us back to the fact, and its contradiction,
Accentuating the differential note of the meadow
When near or ready, and in the *prai* of prairie,
Rings quickly and sharply like a rent
In the sky too serene with meanings.
For it may just be that the site of these lengthy palavers,
Can become a dueling field.

Of the two who arrived, looking alike and upright, one at least,
After an oblique crossing of the swords,
Will remain on his back,
First above then below.

Here then, on this meadow, the moment has finally come
To put an end to it, prematurely.

Pris dans le bas-de-casse, naturellement,
Sauf les initiales, bien sûr,
Puisque ce sont aussi celles
Du Fenouil et de la Prêle
Quidemaincroîtrontdessus.

Francis Ponge.

The Meadow

Typographers, sirs,
Would you kindly place the final line here.
Then, below, without any spacing, lay down my name,
In lower case, naturally,

> Except for the initials, of course,
> Since they also correspond
> To the Fennel and Parsley
> Thattomorrowwillgrowabove.

Francis Ponge.

Nouveau Recueil, pp. 203-209.

JOCA SERIA

Paris, 30 juillet 1951[1]

I (i), J (je), I (un) : un, simple, single, singularité.

1° Chaos de la matière de l'I (un), parce que, bien qu'il soit un, il est fait pourtant de détails, de parties; 2° Timidité, hésitation, tremblement du J (e) qui l'exprime, le conçoit, le dessine; 3° Jaillissement, évidence, saisissement, apparition.

L'X : où les visions de chacun des deux yeux se croisent. Vue du relief : volume au minimum.

Minceur pour exprimer la multiplicité des I, et que le monde (l'espace en largeur) n'en est que surimpressionné, qu'ils ne l'offusquent pas. Parce qu'ils bougent (par rapport à moi) et que je bouge aussi.

Pas d'ombre. (Comme en rêve.)

Cet I est mon semblable (avalé, accepté tout de suite) : point de contemplation (sinon celle suffisante pour constater qu'il est I, immédiat, évident, *malgré* les parties — que je puis, elles, contempler à loisir).

---

1. Suite de notes ayant servi à la composition du texte intitulé *Réflexions sur les statuettes, figures et peintures d'Alberto Giacometti* qui parut d'abord dans les *Cahiers d'Art*, au début de 1952 et qui a été repris dans *Le Grand Recueil* (Gallimard, 1961, t. I : Lyres, p. 70). *Joca Seria*, expression proverbiale que l'on recontre chez Cicéron : les choses sérieuses et celles qui ne le sont pas, c'est-à-dire toute chose, tout.

JOCA SERIA

Paris, July 30, 1951[1]

I (i), I (aye), I (one): one, simple, single, singularity.

1. Chaos of matter in the I (one), because, although one, it is, nevertheless, made up of details, of parts; 2. Timidity, hesitation, trembling of the I which expresses it, conceives it, draws it; 3. Jack-in-the-box, evidence, surprise, apparition.

The X: where the vision of each of the two eyes crosses. Looking at the relief: volume at a minimum.

Thinness to express the multiple I's, and let the world (space in width) only be overly impressed by them, let them not offend it. Because they move (in relationship to me) and that I, too, am moving.

No shadows. (As in a dream.)

This one is my look-alike (swallowed whole, totally accepted): no contemplation (if not the kind needed to observe that it is the one, immediate, evident *despite* the parts—which I can, in good time, contemplate).

1. Series of notes having served for the composition of a text entitled *Reflections on the Statuettes, Figurines and Paintings of Alberto Giacometti* which first appeared in *Cahiers d'Art*, at the beginning of 1952, and was later reprinted in *Le Grand Recueil* (Gallimard, 1961, Vol. I: *Lyres*, p. 70). *Joca Seria* is a proverbial expression that one finds in Cicero. It means serious things and those that are not, that is, all things, everything (F. P.).

Corps humain non contemplable, c'est-à-dire non à traiter comme une chose (qui se laisse contempler), ni comme un
paysage.

Le contraire du « la regarder dormir ».

Instantanéité.

S'agacerait d'une contemplation (Intolérable de lui
infliger cela).

Voilà qui est proche de moi. Car je ne décris pas dans
l'extension. C'est l'idée simple (la particularité essentielle, la
qualité différentielle) que je veux seulement exprimer, faire
jaillir.

Possession idéale instantanée, parant à l'échec prévu de
la (longue) tentative de possession véritable (l'amour, la
« communication »). S'agit-il d'un complexe?

30 juillet 1951

Les statuettes et figurines de Giacometti, de proportions
très modestes et parfois infimes, qu'en pourrait-on inférer,
quant à la civilisation ou l'homme qui les produisit?

Et d'abord qu'en dirait-on? Dans quelle catégorie d'objets
les classerait-on?

Étant donné qu'elles sont nettement représentatives, l'on
songerait d'abord à mettre leur extraordinaire élongation au
compte d'une nécessité fonctionnelle : chenets, manches
d'outils, épées. Ce seraient alors des piquets métalliques
ciselés.

A human body that cannot be contemplated, that is to say, that can neither be treated as a thing (which allows itself to be contemplated), nor as a landscape.

The opposite of "looking at her sleeping."

Instantaneousness.

Would be annoyed by someone looking at it (Intolerable to inflict that upon it).

That touches me. Because I do not describe in extension. It is only the simple idea (the essential particularity, the differential quality) that I want to express, have spring forth.

Instantaneous ideal possession, warding off the expected failure of the (lengthy) attempt of a true possession (love, "communication"). Is this a complex?

July 30, 1951

Giacometti's statuettes and figurines, of a very modest proportion and sometimes infinitesimal, what could we infer about them, about the civilization or the man that produced them?

But first of all what could be said about them? Under what category could these objects be classified?

Given that they are clearly representational, one might first be tempted to explain their extraordinary elongation by some functional necessity: andirons, sticks, swords. They would then be chiseled metallic pickets.

31 juillet 1951

L'homme — et l'homme seul — réduit à un fil — dans le délabrement — la misère du monde — qui se cherche à partir de rien — sortant du néant, de l'ombre — pour qui le monde extérieur n'a plus ni haut ni bas — à qui apparaît son semblable — délabré, mince, nu, exténué, étriqué, allant sans raison dans la foule. L'individu réduit à un fil.

Il cherche une conception de l'homme.
L'homme en souci de l'homme, en terreur de l'homme.

Suprême élégance. Réduit à un fil, il naît de l'ombre, va et vient dans le monde délabré de l'absurde.

L'individu exténué.

Chaque objet pour lui prend aussi cette apparence à la fois serrée et étique; dur comme une vieille pomme sans raison sur une table branlante dans un atelier délabré.
S'affirme une dernière fois en attitude hiératique d'une suprême élégance. L'homme se regratte, se regrette.

L'homme dans son atelier délabré, seul avec son idée de l'homme, cherchant un homme par (à travers) le plâtre, dans sa misère.
Cherchant aussi une pomme, ou ses paysages (clairières, forêts).

Le pathétique de l'exténuation à l'extrême de l'individu réduit à un fil.

July 31, 1951

Man—and man alone—reduced to a thread—in the decay—the misery of the world—who looks for himself starting from nothing—emerging from nothingness, from the shadows—for whom the exterior world has no above or below—for whom his fellow man appears—sick, thin, naked, exhausted, cramped, going out into the crowd for no good reason. The individual reduced to a thread.

He wants to find the meaning of man.
Man worrying about man, terrorized by man.

Supreme elegance. Reduced to a thread, he appears out of the shadow, comes and goes in the decayed world of the absurd.

The exhausted individual.

Each object also appears to him both compact and emaciated; tough as an old apple put without any reason on a rickety table in a dilapidated studio.
Affirms himself for the last time in a hieratic attitude of supreme elegance. Man once again feels an itch, feels for himself.

Man in his dilapidated studio, alone with his idea of man, looking for man through (by means of) plaster, in his misery.
Also looking for an apple, or his landscapes (fields, forests).

Voilà qui est fait pour me réjouir.
C'est une confirmation pour moi.

L'univers de la disparition de l'homme. Il va mourir.
Suprêmement élégant.
Sursum corda. Le monde va renaître.

Un dernier coup de canif et puis plus rien (rêve anarchiste).

Fragilité, minceur extrême de l'individu, pourtant de plus en plus serré sur lui-même et qui s'affirme avec l'élégance la plus aiguë.

L'homme ne tient plus qu'à un fil.

Presque plus de raison d'être.

(C'est une constatation.)

(il en est de même de ses animaux domestiques.)

Précarité de l'individu réduit à lui-même dans le monde néant.

Laminé par les soucis, l'absurdité de tout.

Plus personne à l'horizon.

Proximité de Seurat.

The pathos of the extreme exhaustion of an individual reduced to a thread.

There's enough to make me rejoice.
That confirms it for me.

The universe of the disappearance of man. He is going to die. Supremely elegant.
Sursum corda. The world will be reborn.

A last thrust of the penknife, and then, nothing more (anarchist dream).

Fragility, extreme thinness of the individual, nevertheless, increasingly drawn upon himself and who affirms himself with the sharpest sense of elegance.

Man now only holds on by a thread.

Hardly any more *raison d'être.*

(That is an observation.)

(The same is true for his domesticated animals.)

Precarious state of the individual reduced to himself in this meaningless world.

Laminated by his worries, the absurdity of everything.

Nobody left on the horizon.

Paris, 2 août 1951

Dans ce monde de l'absurde et de la révolte, de la destruction et refonte des valeurs, où l'individu se sent à la fois amenuisé au maximum et serré sur lui-même,
il y a ceux qui envisagent d'abord l'individu (l'homme), le ressentent, le décrivent tel qu'ils le ressentent (les philolosphes : Sartre, Camus, Nietzsche — et certains artistes : poètes divers, Michaux, Char (?), Giacometti);
ceux qui s'écrient en choeur : allons aux choses (Husserl) ou à la terre (Nietzsche);

— Et puis il y a ceux qui plongent *vraiment* dans le monde, dans la nature, dans la terre : moi d'abord.

Paris, 2 août 1951

La Société, l'Individu, la Nature sont chaos (remous et chaos).

1° La *Société* est *chaos-ruche* : camp de concentration, four crématoire, chambre à gaz, *prison et charnier.*
2° L'Individu (l'homme) est *chaos-minceur extrême* (Giacometti).
3° La *Nature* (le monde extérieur) est *chaos-matière épaisse.* Chaos de passé et avenir : de cimetière et germes, de cadavres en décomposition et vers (gainés d'énergie).

La *Nature* est : *Chaos-nourricier.*
Oui, il faut y plonger (c'est à quoi, sans qu'il le veuille, chaque individu, chaque personne est fatalement conduit

Joca Seria

Close to Seurat.

Paris, August 2, 1951

In this world of the absurd and of revolt, of the destruction and the recasting of values, where the individual feels himself at the same time reduced to the extreme and drawn closer upon himself,

There are those who start off by looking at the individual (man), who are aware of his plight, who describe their feelings about him (the philosophers: Sartre, Camus, Nietzsche—and some artists: various poets, Michaux, Char[?], Giacometti);

Those who cry out in a chorus: let's go to things (Husserl) or to the earth (Nietzsche);

—And then there are those who *really* plunge into the world, into nature, into the earth: myself, first of all.

Paris, August 2, 1951

Society, the Individual, Nature are chaos (swirls and chaos).

1. *Society* is a *chaos-hive:* concentration camp, crematorium, gas chamber, *prison and charnel-house.*
2. The Individual (man) is *chaos-extreme thinness* (Giacometti).
3. *Nature* (the external world) is *chaos-thick matter.* Chaos of past and future; of cemetery and germs, of cadavers decomposing and worms (sheathed in energy).

(par la vie et la mort). Mourir et renaître. (Que le monde renaisse, la moindre chose.)

Paris, 2 août 1951

Il s'agit d'un égarement (peut-être) passager : d'une phase (épique) de mon oeuvre.

Me placer au niveau de la mort de Dieu, et de l'amincissement, extrême amaigrissement de l'individu (homme); de la destruction (et refonte) des valeurs.

Dire le pourquoi de *la Rage de l'Expression* et des *Sapates et Momons* (poèmes rhétoriques) dans le processus logique de mon oeuvre.

Que cela fait partie de ma méthodologie et de mon expérimentation (reprendre aussi à partir du *Prologue aux Questions Rhétoriques*).

Voilà le noeud de la question, l'épisode central de la Tragédie (cette momerie nocturne).

Paris, le 3 août 1951

L'homme de G. Richier, sorte de King-Kong (jamais plus sauvage) réveillé dans la forêt actuelle (primitive) par l'orage actuel (primitif), prêt à étreindre le monde, à l'étrangler..., a maigri... (nouvelles désillusions depuis 1944), s'est exténué dans sa destruction des valeurs (Nietzsche), sans rien à se mettre sous la dent. Laminé de plus en plus par son désespoir, sa solitude, son sentiment exaspéré de la *personne* humaine, de la liberté, de etc., sa volonté de puissance (Socrate, Descartes, Pascal, Nietzsche, Sartre, Camus).

Et ce n'est pas l'article de Sartre (*la Recherche de l'Absolu*) qui aidera Giacometti et son homme, à mourir et à renaître...

Nature is: *Nutritive-chaos.*

Yes, let us plunge in it (whether he knows it or not, each individual, each person is fatally led to it (by life, and by death). Death and rebirth. (Let the world be reborn, the slightest thing.)

Paris, August 2, 1951

This is (maybe) a momentary deviation: an (epic) phase of my work.

To place myself at the level of the death of God, and the thinning down, the extreme slendering of the individual (man); of the destruction (and recasting) of values.

Explain the reason for *The Rage of Expression* and the *Sapates* and *Momons* (rhetoric poems) in the logical sequence of my work.

That this is part of my methodology and my experimentation (take this back to *Prologue to Rhetorical Questions*).

There's the crux of the matter, the capital scene of the Tragedy (this nocturnal mommery).

Paris, August 3, 1951

G. Richier's man, a kind of King Kong (never fiercer) awakened in the actual (primitive) forest by the actual (primitive) tempest, ready to embrace the world, to strangle it . . . lost weight . . . (new disillusions after 1944), exhausted himself as he went about destroying values (Nietzsche), without giving himself anything to bite on. More and more laminated by despair, his solitude, his exasperated feelings about the human *person*, liberty, etc., his will to power (Socrates, Descartes, Pascal, Nietzsche, Sartre, Camus).

And it won't be Sartre's article (*In Search of the Abso-*

131

Ils ont beau jeu, les chrétiens... (« Non, Dieu n'est pas mort »)... et les pathétistes (« l'Homme est divin »)...

L'homme ne se nourrira (« Renaissance ») que par l'oubli de soi-même, sa nouvelle prétention et modestie à se considérer comme un simple élément (animal comme un autre) dans le monde, dans le fonctionnement du monde. Qu'il envisage donc le monde, la moindre chose.

(Giacometti, faites des *bustes*, des *portraits*, faites des *natures mortes*!)

La passion, la nécessité, la sincérité, l'authenticité, le goût avec lesquels Giacometti peint son homme, lui procurent une maîtrise, une technique de la peinture et sculpture (serrées comme Seurat) grâce à quoi il va réinventer le monde (natures mortes, bustes) dès qu'il changera de point de vue. (Jusqu'à présent, c'est le contraire du « *la regarder dormir* ».) Conflit avec le réalisme analytique, photographique.

Ce n'est pas l'ironie qui convient envers de tels artistes (poètes ou peintres métaphysiciens). Seuls les sophistes insensibles, incapables de création, appliqueront actuellement leur ironie, faute de mieux.

Notre attitude est plus difficile, plus profonde, nous devons assumer à la fois l'inspiration et les censures (ne pas choisir entre Horace et Artaud), être à la fois Pascal et Malherbe.

Roméo à la fête des Capulet.

Hamlet sur la plage à Elseneur, avant le drame (encore étudiant), tenant un galet en main, avant que le fossoyeur ne tienne le crâne.

lute) that will help Giacometti or his man to die, and be reborn . . .

Christians have it fine . . . ("No, God is not dead") . . . and the pathetists ("Man is divine") . . .

Man will only nourish himself ("Renaissance") if he can forget himself, his new pretension and modesty in considering himself as a simple element (an animal like any other) in the world, in the functioning of the world. Let him, therefore, consider the world, the slightest thing.

(Giacometti! Execute *busts, portraits,* execute *still-lives!*)

The passion, the necessity, the sincerity, the authenticity, and the taste with which Giacometti paints his man, provide him with a mastery, a technique of painting and sculpting (as compact as Seurat's) thanks to which he is going to reinvent the world (still-lives, busts) as soon as he changes his point of view. (To date, it is the opposite of *"looking at her sleeping."*) In conflict with analytic, photographic realism.

Irony is inappropriate with such artists (poets or metaphysical painters). Only insensitive sophists, incapable of creation, will now apply their irony, *faute de mieux*.

Our position is more demanding, more exhaustive; we must accept both inspiration and criticism (do not choose between Horace and Artaud), be at the same time Pascal and Malherbe.

Romeo at the Capulet's feast.

Hamlet on the beach at Elsinor, before the drama (still a

Les Fleurys, 21 août 1951

Que *Je* soit un autre, voilà l'une des trouvailles récentes de l'homme à propos de lui-même, pour se rendre la vie difficile, pour s'inquiéter.

Vous croyez être ceci? laissez-nous rire; laissez-nous vous expliquer à vous-même. Vous êtes la proie de l'histoire (marxisme). Vous êtes un noeud de complexes (freudisme). Vous êtes un criminel, une vipère lubrique, un petit bourgeois (bolchevisme). Vous n'y pouvez rien. Vous êtes coupable (toutes les religions). Vous devez souhaiter votre propre destruction (dont nous nous chargerons si vous ne vous en chargez). L'Autocritique. La Confession.

Voilà la forme nouvelle du *problème* de la « grâce », de celui du « destin ». Voilà la *Terreur* (et aussi bien la « *Terreur dans les Lettres* »).

Voilà comment on inquiète les faibles, comment on les persuade de leur non-justification, voire de leur culpabilité.

L'homme a toujours adoré ce qui le minimise, ce qui l'inquiète, ce qui donne à quelque parti ou seigneur prise et droit sur lui.

C'est à la fois par masochisme et par volonté de puissance. Il aime l'idée du pouvoir (qu'il le subisse ou l'exerce).

Et l'idée de la liberté, de la solitude aux prises avec le monde (Robinson), il l'aime aussi et s'en exalte : il aime sa condition de « chasseur plutôt que gibier » , d'animal relativement puissant et habile, d'animal-l'un-des-mieux-doués. Dans sa relation avec le monde, il est *sportif.*

Les Fleurys, 22 août 1951

Ces étroits fuseaux, branches, fagots, chenets, barreaux,

student), holding a pebble in his hand, before the gravedigger holds the skull.

Les Fleurys, August 21, 1951

That *I* is another—there's a recent discovery that man has made about himself in order to make his life difficult and add to his worries.

Is this what you believe about yourself? You make me laugh. Let me explain to you who you are. You're the prey of history (Marxism). You're a bunch of complexes (Freud). You're a criminal, a libidinous viper, a *petit bourgeois* (Bolshevism). There's nothing you can do about it. You're guilty (all religions). You should hope for your own destruction (we'll take care of it if you don't). Autocriticism. Confession.

That's the new definition of the *problem* of "grace," of "destiny." There's *Terror* (and as well *"Terror in Literature"*).

That is how the weak are upset, how they're persuaded of their nonjustification, even of their culpability.

Man has always adored what diminishes him, what troubles him, what gives some party or lord a legal hold over him.

He does it simultaneously by masochism and a will to power. He likes the idea of power (whether he submits to it or wields it).

And the idea of liberty, of solitude in the midst of the world (Robinson), he likes that, too, and exalts in it: he likes his status of "hunter rather than prey," of being an animal relatively strong and clever, an animal, one-of-the-best-endowed. In his contacts with the world, he is a *sportsman*.

rampes, baguettes, bâtons, épées, pieux ou fusils de bronze, piquets, épieux : à quoi pouvaient-ils servir? Quelle était leur destination?

— Il est vrai qu'on était alors à l'époque des *oeuvres d'art*... Qu'en savons-nous? Peut-être ce n'était-il que des objets d'art?... *Peut-être n'étaient-ils que cela?*

— Bien différents pourtant, semble-t-il, de ceux qui caractérisent l'époque! (Je veux dire, des bibelots d'époque.)

— C'est peut-être qu'alors commençait l'époque de l'expression?

— Oui, cette curieuse époque où les artistes prétendaient encore faire des *oeuvres d'art* et cependant voulaient *s'exprimer*, hésitaient entre faire oeuvre d'art et s'exprimer... Prétendaient en somme imposer leur expression comme *objets d'art* — Dieu! quelle complication!... *Vendre*, au surplus, comme telle, cette curieuse salade! (Il est vrai pourtant que Giacometti s'occupait assez peu de cela.)

Dans quelle mesure pouvaient-ils prétendre à la vendre? Seulement dans celle où certains individus trouvaient là matière à contemplation, selon leur goût, ou leur besoin. A contemplation, à stupéfaction...

Ici, semble-t-il (ou plutôt *alors, en ce temps-là*), dans la mesure où ils avaient besoin de se faire une idée de l'*Homme*. (Ils n'adoraient plus aucun Dieu.) Ils s'adoraient, se plaignaient eux-mêmes comme misérables, se cherchaient, désiraient subsister (et d'abord se trouver). Chaque homme alors cherchait un homme, se cherchait, cherchait l'Homme : se délectait, se désespérait (comme un homme qui passe sa vie à se demander « comment suis-je? » ou « c'est donc moi? Est-il possible que ce soit moi? » devant un miroir, une collection de photos).

Les Fleurys, August 22, 1951

These narrow spindles, branches, faggots, andirons, bars, ramps, sticks, batons, swords, stakes or bronze rifles, pickets, boar-spears: what were they good for? What was their purpose?

—It is true that *works of art* were then in fashion. . . . And then? Perhaps they were only art objects? . . . *Perhaps only that?*

—Nevertheless, they seemed quite distinct from those that typified the period! (I mean, the trinkets of the period).

—Could it then have been the beginning of an expressionist period?

—Yes, that curious period when artists were still pretending to make *works of art* and yet were already anxious to *express themselves*, hesitating between making works of art and expressing themselves. . . . In fact, hoping to pass off their expression as *art objects*—God! How complicated! . . . And, above all, to *sell* this the way it was! (It is true, however, that Giacometti was little interested in that).

How did they expect to sell that? Only when certain individuals enjoyed contemplating that art, when it agreed with their taste, or their needs. Contemplation, stupefaction . . .

Right here, it seems (or rather *then, in that time*), to the extent they needed to provide themselves with an idea of *Man*. (They no longer adored God.) They adored themselves, commiserated over their fate, looked for themselves, hoped to subsist (and first of all, to find themselves). At that time, each man looked for a man, looked for himself, looked for *Man*: in delight, in despair (like a man who spends his life

Brimés au maximum, il est vrai, par l'époque. Brimés et magnifiés. Brimés parce que magnifiés. Élimés, laminés, mais d'autant plus exaltés et « coupants », tous moines de la Sainte Inquisition ! Tous à la fois bourreaux et juges, passés au four des crématoires, plus qu'à moitié grillés, ou « trempés ». D'autant plus durs. Marchant comme un seul homme. A l'appel des radios, sous la terreur des « partis ». Tous comme l'herbe des champs. Tous froment ou ivraie.

. . . .

Les Fleurys, vendredi 24 août 1951

Plusieurs choses à considérer à propos de Giacometti :

I

A. Le problème de l'existence authentique d'un artiste comme artiste. Cela nous intéresse actuellement parce que :

1) On nous dénie le droit de vivre ainsi. Idée du devoir social.

2) Critique surréaliste de l'activité artistique ou littéraire.

3) Impossibilité d'admettre le monde, l'ordre social. Nécessité de nous justifier dans le monde, d'avoir une vie qui nous plaise.

Nous avons beau être d'une génération pour laquelle le mot artiste est interdit, néanmoins ça existe.

a) Il a vécu dans une famille d'artistes, a commencé à peindre, dessiner, illustrer de très bonne heure, a été poussé dans cette direction par son père (peintre connu lui-même), envoyé à l'académie, a fait des études, etc., a eu un atelier, etc.

looking at himself in the mirror or going through an old collection of photographs and asking: "How am I?" or "Is that really me? Is it possible?").

He was bullied to the extreme by the times. Bullied and magnified. Bullied because he was magnified. Threadbare, laminated, but all the more exalted and "trenchant," all monks of the Holy Inquisition! All of them, both executioners and judges, victims of the crematoriums, more than half burned, or "drenched." All that much tougher. Walking as a single man. To radio appeals, the terror of the "parties." All like grass in the fields. All wheat or tares.

. . . .

Les Fleurys, Friday, August 24, 1951

Several things to keep in mind about Giacometti:

I

A. The problem of the authentic existence of an artist as artist. We are interested in this just now because:

1. We are denied the right to live this way. Theory of social duty.

2. Surrealist criticism of artistic or literary activity.

3. The impossibility of accepting the world, the social structure. The need to justify ourselves in the world, to lead a life that is pleasing to us.

Although we were born into a generation where the word artist was forbidden, nevertheless, it does exist.

a) He lived in a family of artists, started to paint, draw, illustrate when he was young, was encouraged in that direc-

Donc déterminé (à sculpter, dessiner et peindre) de la façon la plus courante, la plus commune.

b) En même temps, il le déclare lui-même :

1) Il était *sensible* (au lieu d'aller à l'école des Beaux-Arts à Genève, il allait peindre le lac, ou d'autres paysages).

2) Dès qu'il chercha à sculpter d'après nature, il n'en sortait plus (ce qui lui arriva chez Bourdelle, à la Grande Chaumière).

3) Il ne veut faire que ce qui l'affecte réellement. Il est saisi par le côté bête de l'activité artistique.

Façon de peindre ou de sculpter de *mémoire*. Ce à quoi ça l'amène. Autocritique : dessins; figures longues. — Objets abstraits valables comme sculptures.

B. Moment où tout cela se fond harmonieusement (est-ce trop dire? Sans doute! C'est le moment survenant si je puis dire « à l'ancienneté », où les études désespérées sont considérées comme succès relatifs). Et où la *nécessité* rejoint le *bonheur d'expression* : *l'art*.

II

C. *Objectivement, les productions de A. Giacometti* rendent compte de l'individu actuel. Le plus particulier rend le plus commun vivant.

tion by his father (also a well-known painter), sent to the academy, pursued his studies, and so on, had a studio, and so forth.

Therefore, determined (to sculpt, draw, and paint) in the most current, the most common manner.

b) At the same time, as he himself puts it:

1) He was *sensitive* (instead of going to the Ecole des Beaux-Arts in Geneva, he went to paint the lake, or other landscapes).

2) He reached an impasse as soon as he began sculpting live models (that is what happened when he studied with Bourdelle at the Grande Chaumière).

3) He only wants to do what really moves him. He is gripped by the naïve side of artistic activity.

Ways of painting and sculpting from *memory*. What that leads to. Autocriticism: drawings; elongated figures.— Abstract objects considered as sculptures.

B. The moment when all of that fuses harmoniously (is that too much to say? Unquestionably! It is the moment which finally attains "seniority," where hopeless studies are considered relative successes). And when *necessity* finds its most *perfect expression in art.*

II

C. *Objectively, A. Giacometti's productions* provide a true account of the contemporary individual. The most specific one makes the most ordinary one come alive.

BRAQUE
ou l'art moderne comme événement et plaisir

Quitter la proie pour l'ombre, je n'en ferai pas ma prouesse, et ce n'est pas de gaieté de coeur, certes non, que j'échangerais par exemple le plaisir que me donne l'oeuvre de Braque, contre celui, mêlé d'embêtement et d'ennui, d'échafauder à son propos quelque théorie.

Mais il ne s'agit pas de cela. Que me propose-t-on seulement? De justifier ici, c'est-à-dire à un grand public,[1] ce plaisir, l'intérêt que je porte à cette oeuvre, et mon désir enfin (tout cela est certain) de les voir partagés.

Eh bien! aux réalistes en politique dont je me flatte d'être l'élève et l'ami je rappellerai pour commencer, m'excusant d'avoir à le faire pour qu'ils m'en donnent acte d'abord, que Braque est tenu à juste titre l'un des plus importants parmi les peintres de l'école de Paris. Or, je m'excuse de le rappeler aussi, l'école de Paris dans le bouleversement actuel des civilisations, c'est un peu comme l'école italienne au moment de la Renaissance : un signe seulement peut-être, mais aussitôt si visible (par définition), et avec tant de bonheur, tant d'autorité formulé, qu'il risque d'être dans ce bouleversement au moins aussi actif que toute autre chose et d'en devenir (d'en être considéré plus tard) à tort ou à raison origine et centre.

Les peuples de ce monde, les guides des peuples de ce monde auraient intérêt à y venir voir. Cela les concerne directement. Cela peut avoir des suites de plusieurs siècles.

*

1. Écrit pour une feuille à grand tirage.

BRAQUE
or modern art as an event and a pleasure

I wouldn't let go the prey for the shadow as a test of my prowess, and it is not with a light heart, surely not, that I would exchange, for example, the pleasure that Braque's work gives me against the one, filled with difficulties and worries, of constructing a theory about him.

But it isn't a question of that. What have I been asked to do? To explain this pleasure, here, before a large audience,[1] this interest I find in his work, and finally my hope (all that is evident) of sharing it with others.

On with it! First, I would say to the political realists whom I count both as my masters and my friends (excusing myself for the need to do so, in order for them to be aware of it immediately), that Braque rightfully figures as one of the most important painters of the School of Paris. And, I'm sorry to bring this up, but the School of Paris in the present upheaval of civilizations, is rather like the Italian School at the time of the Renaissance: perhaps only a sign but immediately so visible (by definition), and with such success and such an unquestionable authority, that in this upheaval, rightly or wrongly, at least as active as anything else, it risks being considered (analyzed at a later date) as its origin and center.

The nations of the world, those who guide the nations of the world would do well to come and see it. This concerns them directly. This may have repercussions for centuries to come.

1. Written for a mass circulation newspaper (F. P.).

Peut-être un jour viendra-t-il où le public n'aura plus besoin qu'on attire son attention sur de tels événements, où il en éprouvera spontanément l'importance, parce qu'il ne sera plus réactionnaire en peinture (pour me limiter à cet art). Il y a deux façons d'être réactionnaire en art : la première est de ne pas y attacher d'importance, la seconde d'y attacher de l'importance mais aux oeuvres qui n'en ont pas. Je n'aimerais pas que mes amis se trompent ainsi. Le fait est que beaucoup se trompent, que le public est plutôt réactionnaire en art (je parle du public le plus avancé par ailleurs). Plusieurs bonnes raisons à cela sans doute. La principale, pour parler bref, doit être que le peuple a trop à faire (on m'entend). Qu'il y a un ordre des urgences, et qu'on ne peut se demander tout à la fois. Peut-être. J'ai dit que j'étais élève en réalisme, élève par choix et sûr de mes maîtres. Au surplus, quel découragement en concevrais-je? Cela n'empêche rien. Ne m'empêche nullement, par exemple, autant que je m'en crois capable, de me demander (à moi-même) tout à la fois...

J'entends (c'est un bourdonnement constant, mais je l'entends quand même), OUI j'entends bien que les oeuvres d'art doivent être d'abord pour me plaire, me divertir, m'exalter au besoin : CERTES. (Je mâche aussi mon foin de vérités premières.) MAIS — et de cela je me persuade tout seul, du moins en de certains chemins — il leur faut avant tout me CHANGER. Et donc d'abord me tendre, contracter : bouleverser un peu cette partie de moi-même qui n'a pas encore changé.

Je parle ici d'art moderne. Le goût, en fait d'art moderne, va alors consister en quoi? Sans doute à savoir reconnaître, parmi les raisons de surprise ou d'irritation que me donnent les oeuvres, celles qui sont, par quelque appel *au fond* de moi-même, efficientes et motivées. A savoir reconnaître aux *désagréments* ou *défauts* de telle oeuvre un tel support de

*

A day will come perhaps when the public's attention will no longer have to be called to such events, when it will spontaneously recognize their importance, because it will no longer have reactionary tastes in painting (to restrict myself to that art). There are two ways of being reactionary in art: the first is not to attribute any importance to it; the second to attribute importance to works that have none. I would not like my friends to err in either of these directions. The fact is many people do commit that error, the public being rather reactionary in art (I am thinking about those whose tastes are most advanced in other areas). No doubt there are good reasons for this. The major one, to be brief, is that people have too much to do (as I see it). That there is an order of priorities, and that not everything can be done at the same time. Perhaps. I said I was a student of realism, student by choice and sure of my masters. Furthermore, how could I possibly be discouraged by them? That doesn't rule out anything. As much as I believe myself capable of it, it doesn't rule out, for example, my asking myself (to myself) at the same time. . . .

I know (it is a constant buzzing, but I can still make it out), YES, I know well enough that works of art must first please me, distract me, even exalt me if needs be: all that is TRUE. (I also chew my batch of first principles.) BUT—and I arrived at my own conclusions on this, at least in certain areas—they must, before all other things, CHANGE me. And thus, first of all, stretch me and contract me: shake-up a bit that part of me that hasn't yet been changed.

I'm speaking about modern art. What then is taste in modern art? No doubt, it will consist in the ability to recognize, among the reasons for surprise and irritation that these works give me, those that are efficient and motivated in their

qualités (en somme à ces défauts même tant de qualité) que par la suite ils seront eux-mêmes jugés qualités.

L'homme est ainsi fait, et en particulier l'artiste (qui n'est qu'un homme comme les autres, un peu plus sensible peut-être et plus enragé d'expression) — tout d'ailleurs autour de lui change à chaque instant à tel point — qu'il ne peut faire preuve de ses *qualités* les plus constantes, passées comme futures s'entend, qu'en les réinventant chaque fois à partir de zéro (comme on dit), c'est-à-dire à partir de ses plus simples rapports d'individu à Société et d'homme à Nature, et (qui plus est) à propos de ses *défauts* les plus particuliers, à propos de sa révolte, de son inadaptation, et des grincements que provoque l'insertion dans la nature de sa personne, cette *nouveauté*.

Les créateurs (ceux que l'on nomme ainsi) sont ceux qui éprouvent à la fois beaucoup de difficulté à s'insérer dans le monde, et beaucoup de persévérance et de *pouvoir* à s'y insérer : ils font alors grincer l'assemblage, de façon qu'ils attirent l'attention sur eux, provoquent d'abord de l'agacement et de la colère, enfin déforment le tout de manière irrémédiable, si bien que le monde dès lors sera conformé selon eux. La satisfaction vient alors.

Quand je dis qu'il leur faut du pouvoir à s'y insérer, c'est que ce pouvoir seulement les distingue des utopistes ou des simples fous. Voyez les fous, par exemple. Malgré leur rage d'expression souvent, ils n'ont jamais réussi à changer le monde (notre vision du monde). Le monde a changé, mais eux c'est toujours la même chose, la même inadaptation sans pouvoir.

Mais les artistes (et les révolutionnaires) changent le monde. Ils changent la demeure humaine. Ils changent la nature, la société et l'homme lui-même. C'est, me dira-t-on, qu'ils vont, qu'ils *sont* dans le sens de l'évolution historique.

appeal to the *depth* of myself. In the ability to recognize in *what is disagreeable*, or in the *defects* of such a work, such a grounding of qualities (in point of fact, in its very defects so much quality) that, later, they too will be considered as so many qualities.

Man is made so, and the artist in particular (who is a man like any other, perhaps slightly more sensitive, and more fired by the need to communicate)—anyway everything changes around him at every instant to such a point—that he can only show his most constant qualities, past and future, let it be said, by reinventing them every time from scratch (as we say), that is, from the simplest relationship of the individual to Society and man to Nature, and (what's more), concerning his most particular *defects*, concerning his revolt, his alienation, and these creaking noises, this *novelty* that is created when his person is inserted into nature.

Creators (those who are called that) are those who feel simultaneously a great deal of difficulty in inserting themselves into the world, and a great deal of perseverance and *strength* in inserting themselves: at that moment, they make the structure creak, in a way that calls attention to themselves, provoke first of all an irritation, then anger, and finally deform the whole in an irremediable manner, to such an extent that from that moment on, the world will be shaped by them. Satisfaction then follows.

When I say they need strength to insert themselves in it, I mean that it is only this strength that tells them apart from utopists and madmen. Take madmen, for instance. Though they often have a furious need to communicate, they have never succeeded in changing the world (our vision of the world). The world has changed, but they have always remained the same. The same alienation without strength.

Sans doute. Ils sont cette évolution, son outil le plus perçant. Ouvrant des rainures telles que le monde y pénètre après eux.

En somme, qu'est-ce qu'un artiste? C'est quelqu'un qui n'explique *pas du tout* le monde, mais qui le change. Vous reconnaissez à peu près la formule? Très bien. N'y voyez de ma part aucun sacrilège. Voyez plutôt ce tableau. Ce tableau vous met fort en colère : il ne *représente* rien. Bien sûr, puisqu'il vous présente l'avenir. L'avenir de la nature, l'avenir de l'homme. Cela ne vous intéresse pas davantage? Plus que n'importe quelle représentation (ressemblante), théorie ou explication?

*

Braque maintenant a passé soixante ans et le monde a commencé d'entrer dans sa rainure.

D'autres, depuis, ont entrepris de faire grincer le monde a leur tour. Certains le feront grincer jusqu'à leur dernier souffle, continueront inlassablement à tarauder : ils perceront, ils aboutiront peut-être à plus profond. Ou peut-être à si profond, que l'homme n'entrera jamais dans leur rainure qu'agité d'une vibration exceptionnelle, comportant exécration, ironie. Avec Braque, il en est un peu autrement.

Avec lui, l'orifice, la libération sont aussitôt trouvés.

Peut-être en est-il ainsi seulement de certains chefs-d'oeuvre spécifiquement français. Je ne prétends pas qu'il s'agisse là d'une supériorité (ni d'une infériorité) : seulement d'une particularité, d'une différence. L'orifice, la libération y sont trouvés et en même temps quelque peu cachés, amortis, voilés : de telle façon qu'on ne ressente plus tellement la trouvaille, la hardiesse, que la satisfaction, l'harmonie. Le moteur est sous carter; rodé; il tourne (dès l'abord) au-dessous, semble-t-il, de sa puissance. A un régime (sans jeu de mots)

But artists (and revolutionaries) change the world. They change the human habitat. They change nature, society, and man himself. You'll say that's because they are going in the direction, that they *are* in the direction of historical evolution. No doubt. They are this evolution, its sharpest tool. Making such furrows that the world follows after them.

In the final analysis, what is an artist? Someone who in *no way* explains the world, but who changes it. Do you see the outline of the formula? Very well. I do not mean at all to be sacrilegious. Rather, take a look at this painting. This painting infuriates you: it does not *represent* anything. That's right, since it shows you the future. The future of nature, the future of man. Aren't you more interested in that? More than by any representation (likeness), theory, or explanation?

*

Braque is now over his sixtieth year and the world has begun to enter his furrow.

Others, since, have tried to make the world creak in their turn. Some will make it creak until their last breath, they will ceaselessly continue to tap: they will pierce, perhaps they will reach even farther down. Or perhaps so far down that man will never enter into this furrow except agitated by an exceptional vibration, comprising execration, irony. With Braque, things are rather different.

With him, both orifice and liberation are immediately found.

Perhaps this is only so for certain masterpieces specifically French. I do not suggest that this is a case of superiority (or of inferiority): only a particularity, a difference. The orifice, the liberation are both located and, at the same time,

où il ne *vibre* plus. Où il rend une musique (discrète) au dia-
pason de la nature, quelque chose comme le chant de la
toupie parfaite.

Et plus d'échafaudage, si prestigieux soit-il. Plus d'idées.
L'idée, dit Braque, est le *ber* du tableau. C'est-à-dire l'échafaudage d'où le bateau se libère, pour glisser à la mer. Point
de porte-à-faux. Surtout point de recherche du porte-à-faux.
Le tableau est fini quand il a chassé l'idée, qu'on est arrivé au
fatal. La tête libre.

*

Ce qui m'assure aussi bien de la profondeur où s'est livré
le combat, du niveau auquel la victoire est atteinte, la cause
gagnée, c'est le choix des sujets dans cette peinture.

Il s'agit des objets les plus communs, les plus habituels,
terre à terre. C'est à eux que nous devions nous réadapter.
Voilà qui rend bien compte de la profondeur de notre trouble.
Nous sommes de nouveau jetés nus, comme l'homme primitif, devant la nature. Les canons de la beauté grecque, les
charmes de la perspective, l'historiographie, les fêtes galantes, il n'en est vraiment plus question. Ni même de décora-
tion. Qu'aurions-nous à décorer? Notre demeure est détruite,
et nos palais, nos temples : dans notre esprit du moins; ils
nous dégoûtent. Et certes, cela ne veut pas dire que nous fassions fi des civilisations englouties. Comment pourrions-nous
ne pas en tenir compte? Mais nous sommes bien forcés de
jeter tout cela dans le même sac de sauvagerie. Sinon,
qu'aurions-nous à faire ici, je vous le demande...

Comment cela se fait-il? D'où vient? De la conscience
maintenant prise — enfin! Mieux vaut tard que jamais! — de
la conscience donc enfin prise — à la faveur de quelles désillusions, quels désastres! Mais aussi de quel espoir! — que

somewhat concealed, subdued, obscured: in such a way that one is no longer struck by the conceit, the boldness, but by the satisfaction, the harmony. The motor is encased; well broken-in; it seems that (from the beginning) it has operated below capacity. At a rate of speed (no pun intended)[2] where it no longer vibrates. Where it produces a (discreet) music in pitch with nature, somewhat like the song of the perfect top.

And no more scaffolding, however prestigious. No more ideas. The idea says Braque is the *launching dock* of the painting. That is, the scaffolding from which the boat frees itself to slide down into the sea. No overhangs. Especially no overhanging effects. The painting is finished when it has dismissed the idea, when the inevitable has been reached. Then there are no more thoughts.

*

The choice of subject matter in these paintings also reassures me of the depth where the struggle took place, the level at which the victory was reached, the cause won.

They are the most ordinary objects, the most common, down to earth. We should readapt ourselves to them. This indeed gives an accurate account of the depth of our difficulty. We are, once again, like primitive man, thrown naked into the world. The tenets of Greek beauty, the charm of perspective, historiography, *fêtes galantes*—all these things are no longer pertinent. Neither is decoration. What would we decorate? Our home is destroyed, and our palaces and our temples: at least, in our minds; we find them disgusting. This doesn't mean in any way that we despise those civilizations that have been swallowed up. How could we ignore

2. *Régime* is at once an allusion to a diet and to a motor (S. G.).

nous vivons seulement, depuis la nuit des temps — et quand finira la nuit? — *la préhistoire de l'homme.* Que l'homme est vraiment à venir. Que nous avons à le construire. Que l'individu, encore, n'existe pas à vrai dire, sinon comme désordre innommable et chaos, plus que la société, que la nature.

Innommable? Qu'est-ce à dire? Voilà que nous atteignons le point.

Car enfin nous voilà aux prises avec les casseroles, les brocs, les caisses de bois blanc, un outil, un caillou, une herbe, un poisson mort, un morceau de charbon.

Voilà des objets à qui nous demandons, car d'eux *nous savons l'obtenir*, qu'ils nous tirent hors de notre nuit, hors du vieil homme (et d'un soi-disant humanisme), pour nous révéler l'Homme, l'Ordre à venir.

Comme nous les avons choisis aussi éloignés que possible de l'ancien pittoresque, de l'ancien décor, voire de l'ancien langage, nous avons donc et n'avons plus dés lors qu'à les renommer, honnêtement, hors de tout anthropomorphisme, comme ils nous apparaissent chaque matin, à l'aube, *avant* la pétition de principe, avant le sempiternel lacis des explications par le soleil, avant le prétoire garni à sa dévotion et son apparition, sous un dais, nimbé d'un trémolo de folie.

Voilà le juste, le modeste propos de l'artiste moderne, voilà la nécessité où sa nature honnête le met. Voilà comment il travaille, parallèlement au savant et au militant politique, *comme eux avec passion dans une lumière froide.* Voilà comment il oeuvre, dans sa spécialité, pour le peuple. A lui forger les qualités de l'homme à venir. A aménager sa demeure : une nature dont il n'ait pas honte, dont il jouisse, à son avénement.

Mais pourtant, comme cette synthèse que constitue tout chef-d'oeuvre de l'art ne figure qu'un palier dans la dialectique, cela, malgré la satisfaction que nous en ressentons,

them? But we are really forced to throw all that into the same bag of savagery. If not, I ask you, what would we be doing here? . . .

How did all this come about? Where did it come from? From an understanding now reached—finally! Better late than never! —from an understanding finally reached—after so many disillusionments, so many disasters! But also with such expectations! —that we are only living *man's prehistory* since the night of time,—and when will night end? That one day man himself will truly come. That we have to build him. That the individual, even now, doesn't really exist except as an unnamable disorder and chaos, more so than society, more so than nature.

Unnamable? Meaning what? Now we're getting closer.

Because we are finally coming to grips with pans, jugs, white wooden boxes, a tool, a pebble, a herb, a dead fish, a piece of coal.

From such objects, because *we know we can obtain it* from them, we can ask that they take us out of our night, out of man's old forms (and out of a so-called humanism), to reveal Man to us, the Order that is to come.

Since we have chosen them as far away as possible from the old quaintness, the old setting, indeed, the old language, consequently, there is nothing more to do but to rename them honestly, untouched by any anthropomorphism, as they appear to us every morning, at dawn, *before* begging the question, before the never-ceasing entanglement of explanations offered by the sun, before the court adorned for its devotion, and its appearance, under a dais, nimbed with a tremolo of folly.

That is the modern artist's accurate and modest intention, that is where he finds himself, at one with the necessity of his honest nature. That is how he works, similar to a scien-

ne justifierait aucun son de cloche ou de buccin, aucun *Te Deum*, aucun cri de triomphe.

A notre homme, en tout cas, rien ne conviendrait moins.

... Une constatation seulement, sur le ton le plus simple ; sans grands mots.

Les Fleurys, mai 1947.

tist or a political activist. *Like them, passionately, and in a cold light.* That is the way, within his own speciality, he creates for the people. Forging for it qualities of the man to come. Furnishing his house: a nature that he will not be ashamed of, that he will rejoice in when he comes.

And yet, since this synthesis which constitutes all masterpieces of art only considers a single term of the dialectic, and despite the satisfaction that we feel, this would not justify any ringing of the bells, any trumpets, any *Te Deum*, any shouts of triumph.

In any case, for our man, nothing would be less appropriate.

... A single acknowledgment, on the simplest note; and no pompous words.

Les Fleurys May 1947
From *Le Peintre à l'étude, Tome premier*, pp. 511-518.

TEXTE SUR L'ÉLECTRICITÉ

Pour nous conformer au style de vie qui est le nôtre depuis que le courant électrique est à notre disposition, nous établirons le contact sans plus attendre et jetterons brusquement la lumière sur nos intentions.

Pourquoi nos gestes intellectuels après tout devraient-ils être si différents de ceux que nous avons pris l'habitude d'accomplir chaque jour dans la vie courante? Le premier hommage à l'électricité me paraît être de parler d'elle autrement que selon des formes académiques compassées, et bref d'en traiter intellectuellement comme nous en usons dans la vie pratique.

Quant à nos lecteurs, habitués eux aussi aux nouvelles façons de vivre, nous ne devons pas supposer *a priori* que nos manières les choquent. Et pourquoi souhaiterait-on entrer dans un livre comme dans je ne sais quel appartement obscur ou quel secret labyrinthe : à tâtons et tenu par la main, comme un enfant ou comme un infirme? Nous ne pouvons croire que notre lecteur désire être ainsi traité, et nous sommes persuadé au contraire qu'il nous saura gré de notre franchise.

Nous ne nous adressons pas non plus, du reste, à un lecteur éventuel ni indéterminé. Nous tenons précisément quelqu'un en face de nous, ou plutôt quelqu'un tient ce livre. Il l'a ouvert. Ses yeux courent maintenant sur ces lignes, et il commence probablement à désirer y saisir quelque chose, quelque chose de net, qui impressionne directement son esprit, et qu'il puisse aussi facilement conserver en mémoire : enfin quelque chose de déjà résolu, si je puis dire. Voici donc.

TEXT ON ELECTRICITY

To conform ourselves to a style of life which has been ours since the electrical current was placed at our disposal, we shall immediately establish contact and suddenly throw light on our intentions.

After all, why should our intellectual moves be so different from those that we are in the habit of executing everyday in our daily lives? The first homage to electricity seems to me to speak about it in terms other than formal academic ones, and, in brief, to treat it intellectually in the same way we use it on a practical level.

As for our readers, equally accustomed to these new ways of living, we should not suppose a priori that our ways will shock them. And why should anyone wish to enter a book as if it were some kind of dark apartment or secret labyrinth: feeling around, and held by the hand, like a child or an invalid? We cannot believe that our reader wants to be treated in this fashion, and we are convinced, on the contrary, that he will be grateful for our frankness.

Neither do we have in mind some future or vaguely defined reader. We are looking at someone, or rather, someone is looking at this book in his hands. He has opened it. His eyes are now running over these lines, and, in all probability, he is beginning to wish that he could grasp something, something clear, that immediately makes an impression on his mind, and that he could, just as easily, store in his memory: that is, something already resolved, if this can be said. Here goes.

Ce livre s'adresse aux architectes,[1] mais il a été conçu en deux livraisons, dont celle-ci est la première. L'une de l'autre, d'ailleurs, nettement séparées : pourquoi? Parce que la seconde, parfaitement technique, n'intéressera dans les architectes (ou dans ceux qui touchent d'assez près à cet art) que cette partie de leur esprit qui fonctionne professionnellement, pendant les heures de bureau ou de chantier. Tandis que cette première brochure, bien qu'elle ne doive d'aucune façon leur paraître inégale ou sans rapport avec la seconde (mais doive au contraire, dès l'abord comme à la longue, leur paraître heureusement la compléter), il faudrait pourtant qu'en eux elle puisse intéresser l'autre homme, je veux dire celui qui est encore un architecte, bien sûr, mais aussi un homme de loisir, un homme dont l'esprit et le goût sont ouverts à bien d'autres choses, un homme qui aime pouvoir laisser sur sa table — celle de son bureau ou celle de son salon — un beau livre, — qui aime le montrer à sa femme, aux amies de sa femme, à ses amis. Est-ce clair? Il me semble que c'est clair.

Maintenant, il faut être un peu plus franc encore et dire *pourquoi* nous offrons un tel livre aux architectes, à leurs femmes et à leurs amis. Car notre entreprise, on s'en doute, n'est pas — comment pourrait-elle être? — entièrement désintéressée.

Nous nous occupons d'électricité. Dans l'électricité, pour l'homme de la rue, il y a deux choses. D'une part, la production et le réseau de distribution (ce réseau, en France, actuellement à peu près complet). D'autre part, il y a les machines, les appareils, l'orchestre des appareils qui fonctionnent à l'électricité. Mais *entre eux*, si je puis dire, il y a les bâtiments

---

1. Fait sur la commande de la Compagnie d'Electricité pour accompagner une brochure plus technique destinée à convaincre les architectes d'avoir à songer à l'électrification de leurs édifices quand ils en conçoivent les plans.

Text on Electricity

This book is addressed to architects,[1] but it has been conceived in two installments. This is the first. Furthermore, the first one is distinct from the other. Why? Because the second one, wholly technical, will only interest that part of the architects' mind (or those who are closely associated with that art) that functions professionally during working hours in offices or on a construction site. Whereas this first brochure, although it shouldn't in any way appear to them to be unequal or without relationship to the second (but should, on the contrary, from the beginning, as in the long run, appear to them as happily complementing it), should, however, touch in them the other man, I mean the one who is still an architect, of course, but also a man of leisure, a man whose mind and taste are receptive to many other things, a man who would like to leave on his table—in his office or in the living room—a handsome book,—who would like to show it to his wife, to his wife's friends, to his own friends. Is that clear? It seems clear to me.

Now, I have to be even a bit more frank and explain *why* we are offering such a book to architects, their wives, and their friends. It is obvious (how could it be otherwise?) that our enterprise is not entirely without design.

Our business is with electricity. For the man in the street, there are two aspects to electricity. On the one hand, production and electrical mains (these mains are practically all built in France). On the other hand, there are the machines, the appliances, the orchestra of appliances that use electricity. But *among them*, if I can express it this way, there are the dwellings that contain these appliances; there are the homes and the offices of the men who use them. And since there are

1. Commissioned by the Electrical Company to accompany a more technical brochure meant to convince architects to think about putting in electricity in their buildings when they are drafting their plans (F. P.).

qui contiennent ces appareils, il y a les demeures et les ateliers des hommes qui les utilisent. Et, puisqu'il y a les bâtiments, il y a les architectes qui les construisent, et il y a aussi les clients, les femmes, les amis des architectes, qui leur commandent ces constructions, et généralement s'en remettent à eux, comme ils ont raison de le faire.

Or, et voilà qui *a priori* peut paraître étrange, mais qui a ses explications (nous en parlerons plus loin), il semble bien que certains architectes encore oublient parfois l'électricité. Je veux dire qu'il leur arrive de ne pas la prévoir — j'entends en première ligne : au même titre que l'air ou que le jour — dans le moment qu'ils établissent leurs plans. Cet ouvrage n'a qu'un but : c'est d'être assez je ne dis pas convaincant, mais plutôt inoubliable, pour qu'aucun de ses lecteurs, jamais, puisse oublier que l'électricité existe, que les appareils d'application existent, qu'il s'en trouve ou va s'en trouver (de plus en plus nombreux) dans chaque bâtiment, dans chaque demeure, et qu'il faut donc prévoir, au moment que l'on conçoit ce bâtiment, l'arrivée, la « circulation » et le débouché au maximum d'endroits possible, du ou des courants mis à la disposition de chacun. Est-ce clair? Je crois que c'est clair.

Et maintenant nous allons, sur ce livre et sur nos intentions, éteindre les plafonniers, allumer plutôt les lampes de bureau ou de chevet, et nous allons avoir un contact plus intime, une conversation plus familière, à voix un peu plus basse, si vous le voulez bien.

Et voyez ici déjà, entre parenthèses, comme il est plaisant de pouvoir ainsi varier instantanément les éclairages selon son état d'esprit, ou selon la mise en scène, l'atmosphère ou comme on dit l'ambiance que l'on veut créer.

Pourquoi donc maintenant cet aparté? Croyez-le si vous voulez le croire : par simple pudeur de ma part. En effet, il va

buildings, there are architects who build them, and there are also the clients, the wives, the friends of these architects who commission these constructions, and in general, confide in them, as they rightly should.

Now, and however curious this may appear in an a priori manner, but there are explanations for it (we shall speak about them later on), it seems that some architects still forget electricity at times. I mean, that some still do not account for it—that is, as being of an importance equal to that of either air or daylight—when they draft their plans. This work has only one aim: and that is to be—I do not say convincing—but rather unforgetable, so that not a single one, as readers, will ever forget that electricity exists, that appliances exist, that they can be found or will be found (in greater and greater numbers) in each building, in each house, and that, consequently, when plans are being conceived for a building, one must arrange for the outlets, the "circulation," and the availability at the maximum number of places, of one or more currents placed at everyone's disposal. Is that clear? I believe it is.

And now, we are going to turn off the ceiling lights on this book and on our intentions and instead, turn on the desk lamps or the bedside ones, and, with your permission, we are going to become more intimate, and have a more familiar conversation, in a slightly lower voice.

Isn't it already evident, in parenthesis, how pleasant it is thus to vary the lights instantaneously according to our state of mind, or according to the setting, the atmosphere or, as the saying goes, the ambiance that one wants to create?

Why should I, at this time, introduce this aside? Believe it or not, simply as a question of modesty on my part. Because I am going to speak about myself, about the person

être question de moi, de moi à qui l'on a demandé ce texte et confié le soin de vous séduire. Nous allons nous demander pourquoi. Toujours dans le même esprit de franchise, mais la franchise n'exclut pas, comme vous allez le voir, la modestie. Je veux dire, bien entendu, la modestie de part et d'autre... Ni la pudeur, qui prélude si agréablement à l'intimité.

Ainsi, l'on s'est donc adressé à un profane. Oui, un profane, il faut que je l'avoue. Mais un profane d'une certaine sorte. Bref, une certaine catégorie de techniciens (intelligents) ayant à s'adresser à une autre catégorie de techniciens (également intelligents) a choisi l'intermédiaire d'un troisième personnage, parfaitement profane en l'une et l'autre technique. Voilà qui pourrait donner lieu à de nombreuses réflexions. Je ne vous en épargnerai pas quelques-unes.

Il est vrai que ce profane est lui-même un technicien d'une autre technique. Laquelle? Celle du langage, tout simplement. Quand je dis tout simplement, c'est une façon de parler. Nous verrons cette simplicité tout à l'heure. Pour l'instant, ne compliquons pas les choses.

Il y a plusieurs sortes d'écrivains. Parmi ceux qui peuvent intéresser les techniciens dans leurs rapports avec un public quel qu'il soit, se trouvent les rédacteurs de publicité, les journalistes, les vulgarisateurs, puis les littérateurs proprement dits, c'est-à-dire ceux pour lesquels la perfection de l'ouvrage littéraire semble compter plus que toute autre chose, plus même que l'objet ou le contenu de cet ouvrage. Mais peut-être y a-t-il enfin une dernière sorte d'écrivains, pour lesquels entre en ligne de compte, au même titre que la perfection interne et la conditionnant, une certaine adéquation de leur ouvrage à son objet ou à son contenu. C'est parmi ces derniers que j'ai toujours désiré qu'on me range et sans doute y ai-je tant soit peu réussi puisque j'ai eu l'honneur d'être désigné.

who was asked to write this text and given the job of seducing you. We are going to ask ourselves why. Continuing in this same spirit of frankness, but frankness excludes neither diffidence...nor modesty, which so agreeably precedes intimacy, as you shall see, and diffidence on all sides, of course.

And so, a layman was called in. Yes, a layman, I must admit it. But a layman of a particular kind. In short, a certain category of (intelligent) technicians having to address themselves to another (equally intelligent) category of technicians, chose a third kind of person as an intermediary, a perfect layman in one and the other of the two techniques. This might give rise to a number of speculations. I will not spare you all of them.

It is true that this layman is himself a technician in another field. Which one? Language, quite simply. When I say quite simply, that is a manner of speaking. We shall attend to this simplicity in a moment. For the time being, let us not complicate matters.

There are several types of writers. Among those who might interest technicians in their contacts with a general audience, one finds public relations men, journalists, popularizers, then writers, strictly speaking, that is to say, those for whom the perfection of the literary work seems to count more than anything else, even more than the object or the content of the work itself. But perhaps there is still another type of writer, the one who is concerned not only with internal perfection, and that which determines it, but also with a particular relationship between the work, its object or its content. It is among this latter group that I have always wished to be placed, and undoubtedly I must have succeeded in some way since I have had the honor of being chosen.

Nevertheless, one should not hide the fact that choosing

Pourtant, il ne faut pas se le dissimuler, choisissant n'importe quel homme de l'art, on courait un risque. Lequel? Voici. Introduisant une troisième technique, on risquait un nouveau langage spécialisé. Car enfin, pourquoi les seuls techniciens du langage échapperaient-ils à la loi qui semble régir actuellement toutes les techniques? Pourquoi ne s'enfonceraient-ils pas, eux aussi, dans leur spécialité, dans leurs problèmes, laissant à quelque catégorie intermédiaire (disons par exemple les critiques) le soin de les présenter au public? Ne croit-on pas qu'ils puissent en sentir le besoin, et que ce besoin soit légitime, du fait qu'ils connaissent, eux aussi, beaucoup de difficultés dans leur technique : de difficultés, c'est-à-dire de satisfactions? On serait assez imprudent de ne pas le croire, et, j'ose le dire, assez malvenu.

Pourquoi cependant fallait-il courir ce risque, pourquoi était-il intelligent de le courir? Parce qu'à tout prendre *notre* langage est le seul auquel reste, dans la Tour de Babel des techniques, quelque chance d'être par tous et par toutes entendu. Ses matériaux, en effet, empruntés au bien commun de tous : la Parole, sont pour le moins autant que sensibles *intelligibles* : à condition d'être bien agencés.

Je ne suppose pas qu'on ait pu lire le passage précédent sans impatience, et pourtant il fallait y passer. Car nos trois techniques ont en commun quelque chose de noble, qu'il fallait que je fasse sentir : c'est qu'elles sont indispensables à toutes les autres. L'Architecture loge toutes les techniques. L'Électricité les éclaire et les anime. Et la Parole? Eh bien, la Parole (en un autre sens, il est vrai) les loge, les anime et les éclaire à la fois. Electriciens, ô mes profanes! vous l'aviez instinctivement compris.

A présent, il faut que j'avance, c'est-à-dire que je refuse d'avancer dans mon seul sens. Il faut que je dévie brusque-

any man of art involves a certain risk. Which one? Let us see. Introducing a third technique, one ran the risk of a new specialized language. Why, indeed, should technicians of language be the only ones to escape a law that now seems to apply to all other techniques? Why shouldn't they also not sink deeper and deeper into their specialty, into their problems, leaving to some intermediary category (let us say, critics, for example) the task of introducing them to the public? Do we believe they are incapable of recognizing that need, and couldn't that need, in turn, prove to be legitimate, since they also encounter many difficulties in their technique—difficulties, that is to say, satisfactions? One would be rather imprudent not to think so, and, I dare say, rather ill advised.

And yet, why did this risk have to be taken? Why was it an intelligent one to take? Because, all things considered, *our* language is the only one that has, in the Tower of Babel of techniques, some chance of being understood by one and all. Its materials, in fact, borrowed from the common good— Speech—are at least as *intelligible* as they are sensitive: on the condition of being well handled.

I doubt whether the previous paragraph could have been read without some impatience, and yet, it had to be written. Because our three techniques have something noble in common, that I had to clarify, and that is, they are all indispensable to all the others. Architecture houses all the techniques. Electricity sheds light on them and animates them. And Speech? Well, Speech (in another sense, it is true) houses them, animates them and sheds light on them, all at once. Electricians, o laymen! you had instinctively understood this.

And now I must go on, that is, I refuse to keep on going solely in my own direction. I must suddenly turn aside and dig in: I must go back to my plan.

ment et m'endigue : il faut que je revienne à mon plan.

Mon plan m'indique que je dois ici, à voix plus basse, encore plus basse, me donner pour ce qu'on nomme un poète. Qu'est-ce à dire? Eh bien, un profane, mais profane en toutes choses, systématiquement. Et justement, paradoxalement, parce qu'en toutes choses il détecte, hume et profane le sacré. Parce que, ravi de toutes choses, ou plutôt de chacune tour à tour, il n'a de cesse qu'en chacune il n'ait fait floculer sa ressource intime, pour en faire jouir ses lecteurs.

Vous voyez bien qu'il me fallait parler à voix basse. Intensément basse, cela s'entend.

J'abrège. Vous voici préparé. Ou peut-être seulement agacé. Désireux (en tout cas) qu'il se passe tout de suite autre chose... Et voici donc le moment de rallumer brusquement les plafonniers.

Rassurez-vous, c'est pour les réteindre aussitôt. Mais vous avez senti, n'est-ce pas, comme il est merveilleusement en notre pouvoir de jeter tantôt sur vous, sur moi, sur les lieux de l'évidence et de l'activité, forte, vive et impitoyable lumière, et tantôt de nous replonger dans la nuit. Et vous goûterez maintenant la nuit, et vous goûterez la poésie qui va s'en ensuivre, avec une tout autre violence, une tout autre volupté.

Un petit paragraphe ici (un petit instant, je vous prie) — à noter sur mon carnet personnel — pour demander à mon architecte de prévoir, dans la maison qu'il me bâtit, des interrupteurs près des fenêtres (et non seulement près des portes ou des lits), pour me permettre de mieux goûter la nuit.

Nous voici donc dans la nuit et voici la fenêtre ouverte. Que le temps, comme on dit, soit couvert, que l'obscurité soit sans faille et que nous devions alors, par exemple, nous attendre à quelque orage — ou que des myriades d'étoiles, au

According to my plan, at this moment, speaking in a lower voice, lower still, I must call myself a poet. What does that mean? Well, a layman, but lay in all things, systematically. That's right, and, in a paradoxical manner, because in all things he detects, inhales, and profanes the sacred. Because, charmed by all things, or rather, each one in its turn, he only rests satisfied when he has succeeded in showering down his intimate resources on them for the enjoyment of his readers.

Now you understand why I had to speak in a low voice, intensely low.

Let me cut this short. You are prepared. Or perhaps only bothered. Desirous (in any case) that something else occurs immediately. . . . And now, the moment has suddenly come to switch the ceiling lights back on.

Be reassured, I only did that to turn them off just as soon. But you felt, didn't you, how it is marvelously within our power to throw, alternately on you, on myself, within the locus of the evidence and activity, a strong, vivacious and pitiless light, and then to plunge us again into night. And you will now taste the night, and you will taste the poetry that will come from it, with a wholly different violence, a wholly different voluptuousness.

A short paragraph here (but a moment, if you please)— to remind myself in my personal notebook to ask my architect, in the house he is building for me, to put in light switches near the windows (and not just close to doors and beds) so that I can better savor the night.

Here we are, then, in the night, and here is the open window. Whether the sky is overcast, as the saying goes, whether the darkness is without a break, and we should, for example, expect a storm, or that myriad stars, on the contrary, appear

contraire, s'aperçoivent au firmament, notre sentiment fondamental est le même : nous sommes tout à coup remis en présence des forces naturelles, et de l'infini, spatial et temporel à la fois.

Ressentirions-nous d'abord l'infini spatial, l'astronomique, nous savons depuis quelque temps qu'il ne s'y agit que d'électricité. Notre science n'est pas ancienne, mais Henri Poincaré ayant produit sur ce sujet de belles et saisissantes formules, nous en sommes très intimement persuadés. Pourtant, laissons cela pour le moment, s'il vous plaît, et plongeons de préférence dans l'infini temporel : dans la Nuit des Temps.

La transition est facile, par l'intermédiaire par exemple de la notion d'années-lumière, et par l'idée (devenue un véritable cliché) que l'une de ces brillantes étoiles dont nous recevons la lumière pouvait être morte déjà à l'époque où les astronomes chaldéens observaient le même ciel, à l'époque où Thalès, étudiant dans les sanctuaires d'Égypte, connaissait déjà, par ailleurs, la propriété électrique de l'ambre jaune.

« Par ailleurs », ai-je dit, et pourquoi ai-je employé cette expression? Parce que tous les articles de dictionnaires concernant l'électricité, tous les manuels et toutes les histoires des sciences nous ont habitués à faire commencer l'électricité à Thalès et à l'ambre jaune — étant entendu qu'il faut attendre Gilbert, médecin de la reine Élisabeth, pour que la propriété électrique soit reconnue à l'ensemble des corps terrestres, et Franklin pour que la liaison soit opérée entre ces phénomènes et ceux de l'électricité atmosphérique.

Sans doute les meilleurs parmi ces manuels nous indiquent-ils (presque aussitôt) que certaines lois se rapportant à l'électricité atmosphérique semblent avoir été connues, bien avant Franklin, bien avant Thalès même, par certains prêtres ou initiés, tels que Moïse, Salomon, Numa et même par les

in the firmament, our basic feeling remains the same: we are placed, all of a sudden, and once again, in the presence of natural forces, and the infinite—spatial and temporal at the same time.

If we were, first of all, going to feel spatial infinity, the astronomical one, we now know that it is only a matter of electricity. Our knowledge is not very old but Henri Poincaré having written on this subject beautiful and striking formulas, we are now thoroughly persuaded. However, with your permission, let us put that aside for the moment, and let us rather plunge into temporal infinity, into the Night of Time.

The transition is easy, operating, for example, through the intermediary of the notion of light years, and through the idea (now a true cliché) that one of those brilliant stars emitting light, might have been dead at the time the Chaldean astronomers were observing the same sky, at the time when Thales, a student in the Egyptian sanctuaries, had already discovered, through other sources, the electrical properties of yellow amber.

"Through other sources," I have said, and why did I put it that way? Because, all the entries in dictionaries dealing with electricity, all the manuals and all the histories of sciences have accustomed us to mark the beginning of electricity with Thales, and with yellow amber—it being understood that one had to wait for Gilbert, Queen Elizabeth's physician, for electrical properties to be attributed to all terrestrial bodies, and Franklin, who established the relationship between these phenomena and those of atmospheric electricity.

Of course, the best among these manuals tell us (almost immediately) that certain laws pertaining to atmospheric electricity seem to have been known well before Franklin, even before Thales himself, by certain priests or initiates,

Gaulois. N'importe : on commence toujours par Thalès, et dans Thalès par l'ambre jaune, et il est toujours professé qu'aucune liaison n'avait été faite, avant le XVIIe ou le XVIIIe siècle, entre le phénomène de la foudre et celui de l'attraction de particules légères par les bâtons d'ambre frottés.

Pourtant, j'avoue qu'ici quelque chose me trouble et me porte irrésistiblement à douter. Étant, comme je le suis (comme tout le monde), sensible à la grande et pour ainsi dire supérieure beauté des choses de l'ancienne Égypte, de l'ancien Orient, de l'ancienne Grèce — et quand je dis des choses, je n'entends pas seulement la sculpture ou l'architecture, mais encore les fables et les constructions de l'esprit (par exemple la géométrie grecque) —, je n'accepte pas facilement l'idée qu'en fait de connaissance scientifique, l'on ait été alors très inférieur à nous. Je suis un peu gêné d'avoir à accepter l'idée d'une supériorité quelconque de l'homme moderne sur l'homme de ces époques. Instinctivement, je récuse cette prétention. Puis, autre chose encore vient recouper mon intuition. La voici.

Tous nos dictionnaires et manuels précités disent aussi que les phénomènes en question ont été nommés électriques parce que le succin ou ambre jaune se nommait en grec Électron. Bien! Et rien en cela que de plausible. Mais ce qui me paraît plus étonnant, c'est qu'on ne cherche nullement à savoir *pourquoi* l'ambre jaune avait été nommé *justement* Électron. Pardonnez-moi, mais je suis, quant à moi, plus curieux. Sans doute parce que les mots, fait bizarre, intéressent les poètes plus encore (c'est sensible) que les faiseurs de dictionnaires. Et peut-être parce que tout le passé de la sensibilité et de la connaissance m'y semble inclus.

Si bien que, naturellement, je rapproche (à mon tour) Électron d'Électre, celle de la mythologie des anciens Grecs. Et je vais aussitôt à Électre, et je vais aux origines d'Électre.

such as Moses, Solomon, Numa, and even the Gauls. It doesn't matter: everything always begins with Thales, and in Thales, with yellow amber, and it is always claimed that no relationship had ever been made, before the seventeenth or eighteenth centuries, between the phenomenon of thunder and the attraction of light particles by sticks of amber that had been rubbed.

Nevertheless, I must admit, that here I am disturbed by something that irresistibly leads me to doubt. Being, as I am (as is everyone) sensitive to the great, and so to speak, superior beauty of the things of ancient Egypt, of the ancient East, of ancient Greece—and when I say things, I do not only mean sculpture or architecture but fables and mental constructs (Greek geometry, for example)—I cannot easily accept the idea that in the area of scientific knowledge, they were considerably inferior to us. I am slightly embarrassed when I have to accept the idea that modern man is in any way superior to the man of those epochs. Instinctively, I challenge that claim. Then, other things come to confirm my intuition. Here they are.

All the dictionaries and manuals that I have already mentioned also say that the phenomena in question were given the name electricity because succin or' yellow amber was called Electron in Greek. Well! all that is quite plausible. But I am surprised that no one wants to know *why* yellow amber had been *specifically* called Electron. Forgive me, but as for myself, my curiosity goes further. No doubt because words, and this is an odd fact, interest poets even more (that's apparent) than those who compile dictionaries. And that may be because I can find in them all past sensitivity and knowledge.

To such an extent that I readily associate (in my turn) Electron with Electra, the one in ancient Greek mythology.

Fille d'Atlas, dont on sait par ailleurs qu'il portait le *ciel* sur ses épaules. Et donc petite-fille de Japet, et nièce de Prométhée (ravisseur du *feu*). Soeur par ailleurs de Cadmos (dont notons entre parenthèses primo que Thalès descendait de lui, et secundo qu'il représentait en Grèce centrale ce que Danaos représentait à Argos, c'est-à-dire l'influence égyptienne). L'une des Pléiades, et donc elle s'était *suicidée*, comme elles se suicidèrent toutes, par désespoir de la mort de leurs soeurs, les Hyades, dans le nom collectif desquelles il y a *la pluie*, et qui elles-mêmes se suicidèrent à la mort de leur père Atlas. Enfin, parmi les Danaïdes, car elle est aussi l'une de celles-ci, pourquoi ne serait-elle la même qu'Hypermnestre, seule à n'avoir pas tué son époux, Lyncée, lequel était doué d'une *vue si perçante qu'elle traversait même les murailles?* En tout cas, ce fut elle qui apporta le Palladium à Troie, mais « apporta » qu'est à dire? puisque nous savons que cette idole *tomba du ciel* près de la tente d'Ilos.

Voilà donc qui était Électre. Si l'on veut bien noter encore que Thalès, ne se bornant nullement aux propriétés de l'ambre jaune, sut par ailleurs se rendre célèbre en prédisant l'éclipse solaire de 610 avant Jésus-Christ, je voudrais bien qu'on me dise en vertu de quel décret, faisant fi de tous ces indices, on lui refuserait, à lui et à nos ancêtres des anciennes civilisations de la Màditerranée, d'avoir connu le rapport de l'ambre et de la foudre, at d'avoir eu quelque idée, aussi juste que la nôtre, de ce que nous appelons (à leur suite) Électricité.

J'ai cité tout à l'heure les noms d'autres personnages, en particulier celui de Moïse, dont il ne semble pas tout à fait absurde de supposer qu'ils aient pu être initiés à certains de ces phénomènes, s'ils semblent en avoir usé seulement pour accroître leur prestige. Il paraît que le fameux Tabernacle des Juifs, l'Arche Sainte construite par Moïse, étant donné sa

And I immediately go to Electra, and I go back to the origins of Electra.

Daughter of Atlas, about whom we know, moreover, that he carried *heaven* on his shoulders. And thus, granddaughter of Japet, and niece of Prometheus (ravisher of *fire*). Also sister of Cadmos (and let us note in parenthesis, *primo*, that Thales himself descended from him, and, *secundo*, that he represented, in central Greece, what Danaos represented in Argos, that is, Egyptian influences). One of the Pleiads, and therefore, a *suicide*, as they had all committed suicide, in despair over the death of their sisters, the Hyades, in whose collective name the word *rain* can be found, and who, in turn, committed suicide when their father Atlas died. And finally, among the Danaids, because she is also related to them, why shouldn't she be the same as Hypermenstra, the only one not to have killed her husband, Lynceus, he who had the gift of such *piercing sight that it could even go through fortified walls?* In any case, it was she who brought the Palladium to Troy, but what do we mean by "brought"? since we know that the idol *fell from the sky* near Ilos's tent.

So much for Electra's ancestry. Furthermore, if indeed Thales, in refusing to limit himself to the properties of yellow amber, knew through some other sources, how to make himself famous in predicting the solar eclipse of the year 610 before Jesus Christ, I would like someone to tell me, by virtue of what decree disregarding all these indices, one could not accept that he (and all our ancestors of those ancient Mediterranean civilizations) knew about the relationship between amber and thunder, and had some vague idea, as correct as ours, of what we call (after them) Electricity?

A moment ago, I specifically mentioned Moses and the names of other persons whom it does not seem absolutely absurd to assume that they might have been initiated to cer-

description comme elle figure au chapitre XXV du livre de l'Exode, pourrait être considérée comme un très savant condensateur. Faite, selon les ordres du Seigneur, en bois de sétim (isolant) recouvert sur ses deux faces, intérieure et extérieure, de feuilles d'or (conductrices), surmontée encore d'une couronne d'or destinée peut-être, grâce au classique « pouvoir des pointes », à provoquer la charge spontanée de l'appareil dans le champ atmosphérique, lequel, dans ces régions sèches, peut atteindre paraît-il jusqu'à des centaines de volts à un ou deux mètres du sol, — il n'est pas étonnant que cette Arche Sainte, toute prête à foudroyer les impies, ait pu être approchée sans danger seulement par les grands prêtres, tels Moïse et Aaron, dont l'Écriture nous apprend par ailleurs qu'ils portaient des vêtements « entièrement tissés de fils d'or et ornés de chaînes d'or traînant jusqu'aux talons ». Comme l'ajoute le patient commentateur auquel nous empruntons cette hypothèse, cette ingénieuse « mise à la terre » leur permettait de décharger le condensateur sans dommage pour leur personne.

Dans le même ordre d'idées, et dans la même religion, on sait encore[2] que le Temple de Jérusalem nous est décrit par l'historien Josèphe comme hérissé de baguettes pointues en or, tandis qu'un érudit allemand fait remarquer que, durant une existence de mille années, ce Temple ne fut pas frappé une fois par la foudre. Il suffit de supposer, comme le font allégrement nos esprits forts, que ces pointes aient été reliées au sol par des conduites métalliques, destinées par exemple à l'écoulement des eaux, pour créditer Salomon d'une *science* dont certaines données de l'Écriture laissent penser d'ailleurs qu'elle ne le cédait pas à celle de Moïse.

Inutile d'ajouter, car chacun le sait,[3] que Moïse sortait

2. Collection : « *Que sais-je?* », passim.
3. Collection : « *Que sais-je?* », passim.

tain of these phenomena, even though they may have only used them to increase their own prestige. It would seem that the famous Tabernacle of the Jews, the Holy Vessel, built by Moses, given its description as it figures in Chapter XXV of the Book of Exodus, might be considered as a very clever condenser. Built, according to the Lord's commandments, of shittin wood (insulating), covered on both its sides, interior and exterior, of gold leaves (conductors), further topped by a gold crown, destined, perhaps, thanks to the classic "power of the points," to provoke a spontaneous charge of the machine in the atmospheric field, which, in those dry regions can, it is said, reach up to hundreds of volts, two to four feet off the ground—it is not surprising that this Holy Vessel, always ready to strike down the impious, could only have been approached without danger by the great priests such as Moses or Aaron, about whom, we are told, elsewhere in the Scriptures, that their clothes were "entirely woven of gold threads and decorated with gold chains that hung down to their heels." The patient commentator, from whom we have borrowed this hypothesis, adds that this clever "grounding" allowed them to discharge the condenser without harming their persons.

Following this same trend of thought, and in the same religion, one also knows[2] that the historian Josephus describes the Temple of Jerusalem as being wholly surrounded by gold-tipped rods, while a German scholar observed that, during a period of a thousand years, the Temple was not even struck once by lightning. One merely has to conjecture, as our strong minds do without hesitation, that these rods had been anchored to the ground by metallic conductors, destined, for example, to drain water, in order to credit Solomon with a

2. Collection *"Que sais-je?"* passim.

d'Égypte, où il vécut entre le XVIe et le XVe siècle avant notre ère.

Mais Lucain, dans sa *Pharsale*, consacre quelques vers à un aruspice d'Étrurie, nommé Aruns, qui, vivant à la même époque, savait rassembler les feux épars de la foudre pour les engouffrer dans la terre avec un bruit sinistre. *Datque locis numen :* il consacre ainsi les lieux.

Beaucoup plus tard, Numa, l'un des premiers rois de Rome, connaissait le moyen d'invoquer le feu de Jupiter. Et je me suis laissé dire, chez l'un des meilleurs sculpteurs de notre temps, qu'il existait sous le Capitole une grotte ouverte où l'on exposait les nouvelles statues de bronze des Dieux, afin qu'au cours d'un de ces orages, si fréquents à Rome vers les cinq heures du soir, elles aient la chance que la foudre un beau jour les consacre, au risque d'en fondre quelque partie : ainsi, en quelque façon les signant.

Je ne sais si mes lecteurs auront goûté comme vraiment poétique tout ce qui vient, dans les lignes précédentes, d'être rappelé. Certains pourront, injustement je le crois, y mépriser un goût décadent pour l'archéologie, et d'autres, tout aussi injustement, juger au contraire que c'est là, en effet, que la poésie se trouve, et même qu'elle se trouve exclusivement là, mais à la condition cependant que la forme ancienne y soit maintenue. Pour moi, je ne suis de l'avis ni des uns ni des autres, et sachant pourquoi je m'y plais, j'espère le faire mieux entendre par la suite.

Quoi qu'il en soit, tout a bien changé depuis lors et une autre conception de l'homme a prévalu, ainsi que de ses rapports avec l'univers. Pas plus que nous ne l'avons fait pour la civilisation ou le magma des civilisations précédentes, nous ne traiterons exhaustivement de celle-ci, bien que cela soit,

knowledge that, certain comments from the Scriptures seem to indicate, in fact, was not second to Moses'.

Needless to add, because everyone knows it,[3] that Moses left Egypt, where he lived, between the sixteenth and fifteenth century before our era.

But Lucan, in his *Pharsalia*, devotes a few lines to a haruspex from Etruria by the name of Aruns, who, living at the same time, knew how to bring together the scattered fires of thunder and bury them in the ground with a sinister noise. *Datque locis numen:* thus he consecrated sites.

Much later, Numa, one of the first kings of Rome, knew how to invoke Jupiter's fire. And I was informed, by one of the best sculptors of our time, that an open grotto existed beneath the Capitol where new bronze statues of the Gods were exposed, so that during one of the storms, so frequent in Rome around five o'clock in the afternoon, they might be lucky enough one day to be consecrated by thunder, at the risk of melting some part of them, thus, in a way, being signed by it.

I do not know if my readers will appreciate as truly poetic all that has just been recalled in the preceding lines. A few might, unjustly, disdain it as a decadent taste for archaeology; others, equally unjustly, might judge, on the contrary, that it is exactly here, in fact, that poetry is to be found, and even, that it is exclusively here that it is found but on the condition that it be written according to ancient forms. As for me, I share neither the first nor the second view, and knowing why I take pleasure in it, I hope to shed some light on this later on.

3. Ibid.

en quelque façon plus méritoire, car, pour celle-ci, *nous le pourrions.*

Restons donc dans la nuit quelques instants encore, mais reprenons ici conscience de nous-même et de l'instant même, cet instant de l'éternité que nous vivons. Rassemblons avec nous, dans cette espèce de songe, les connaissances les plus récentes que nous possédions. Rappelons-nous tout ce que nous avons pu lire hier soir. Et que ce ne soit plus, en ce moment, qui songe, le connaisseur (un peu) des anciennes civilisations, mais celui aussi bien qui connaît quelque chose d'Einstein et de Poincaré, de Planck et de Broglie, de Bohr et de Heisenberg.

Comment vais-je alors considérer le spectacle que la nuit offre à mes yeux? Certes, il me semble en comprendre confusément quelque chose, et une certaine représentation en figure globalement dans mon esprit. Par exemple, j'ai été profondément marqué par la très-frappante image, proposée par Henri Poincaré, qui, rapprochant les deux infinis, nous fait concevoir l'atome comme un système solaire et ses électrons libres comme des comètes. Et certes je n'ignore plus que les phénomènes électriques s'interprètent maintenant à partir de la constitution même de la matière. Enfin, bien que je craigne instinctivement de reconnaître là comme un nouvel exemple de cette Illusion de Totalité récemment dégagée par un illustre logicien de mes amis, je veux bien concéder pour un moment que tout ne soit que charges électriques, champs électriques, etc.

Bien. Certes, j'ai retenu aussi et la loi de Planck, pas si difficile à « encaisser » qu'on pourrait la croire, et le principe d'incertitude, et la relativité de l'Espace et du Temps, et la notion de l'Espace courbe, voire l'hypothèse de l'extension indéfinie de l'univers.

Be that as it may, much has really changed since then, and another concept of man has prevailed, as well as a new concept of his relationship to the universe. Just as we did not discuss civilization, or the magma of preceding civilizations, we will not treat this one exhaustively, although in some ways, this would be more meritorious, since *we could do it* for this one.

Let us remain in the night a while longer but let us once again become aware of ourselves, and of the very instant, this instant of eternity through which we are living. Let us gather together, in this type of musing, the most recent knowledge that we possess. Let us remember all that we were able to read last night. And let it no longer be at this moment of musing the (slight) expert in ancient civilizations but someone who is acquainted with Einstein and Poincaré, Planck and de Broglie, Bohr and Heisenberg.

How should I then consider the spectacle that night offers to my eyes? In ways that are yet unclear, I do understand some things about it; and in my mind I do have certain general notions concerning it. For example, I was deeply impressed by the very striking image, suggested by Henri Poincaré, who, bringing the two infinities closer together, made us conceive of the atom as a solar system and its free electrons as comets. And, indeed, I am no longer ignorant of the fact that electrical phenomena are now interpreted on the basis of the constitution of matter itself. And though I am loathe to consider it as a new example of that Illusion of Totality recently brought to light by an illustrious logician friend of mine, I am willing to concede for a moment that everything is an electrical charge, an electrical field, etc.

So far so good. Neither have I forgotten Planck's law, not as difficult to "accept" as one might imagine, nor the prin-

Mais, en fin de compte, s'il faut que je le dise, eh bien, c'est la ressemblance de cette figure du monde avec celle que nous ont présentée Thalès ou Démocrite qui me frappe, plutôt que sa nouveauté.

Lorsque je regarde, par exemple, un schéma de la course des électrons libres, de leurs imprévisibles zigzags et de leur lent entraînement concomitant dans ce que nous appelons un courant électrique, je ne vois là rien qui ne me rappelle, compte tenu de la notion de quantum d'action et du principe d'incertitude — qui ne font que le confirmer —, le fameux *clinamen* de Démocrite et d'Épicure, appliqué aux corpuscules qu'ils avaient fort bien conçus.

Et certes j'admire que Planck ait pu calculer la constante « h », j'admire le « progrès » des mathématiques, comme j'admirais déjà, je vous prie de le croire, les calculs un peu plus anciens qui furent confirmés par la découverte, un jour, de Neptune à la place où on l'attendait. Mais comment ne me souviendrait-il aussitôt que Thalès a bien pu prédire l'éclipse de 610 avant notre ère, et comment m'empêcherais-je de me demander si par hasard il ne l'aurait pas calculée, et si les moyens de calculer cela ne se trouvaient pas justement dans les sanctuaires d'Égypte?

Et puis, je relis Lucrèce et je me dis qu'on n'a jamais rien écrit de plus beau; que rien de ce qu'il a avancé, dans aucun ordre, ne me paraît avoir été sérieusement démenti, mais au contraire plutôt confirmé. Et je sais bien qu'on a pu me le décrire comme un anxieux et un fou, et prétendre, car cela arrangeait quelques-uns, qu'il se serait à la fin suicidé. Mais puisque nous sommes toujours sur notre balcon, l'électricité éteinte, et que le ciel nocturne est devant nos yeux, je peux aussi prétendre, me rappelant Électre, qu'il s'agit là d'un comportement divin; et constater qu'il a été, lui aussi, comme il avait été fait d'Électre et de ses soeurs, placé parmi les astres,

ciple of uncertainty, and the relativity of Space and Time, and the notion of curved Space, that is, the hypothesis of the indefinite extension of the universe.

But, in the final analysis, if I must admit it, it is the resemblance of that figure of the world with the one that had been presented to us by Thales and Democritus that impresses me, rather than its novelty.

When I look, for example, at a model of the path followed by free electrons, their unpredictable zigzags and their slow incorporation into what we call an electrical current, there is nothing there that does not remind me, given the quantum notion of action and of the principle of uncertainty (which only confirms it), of the famous *clinamen* of Democritus and Epicurus, applied to the corpuscles that they had so clearly understood.

And, of course, I admire Planck for having calculated the "h" constant; and I admire the "progress" in mathematics, as I had already admired, I ask you to believe it, the slightly older calculations that were confirmed one day by the discovery of Neptune at the very place it had been expected. But then, how could I forget that Thales had predicted the eclipse of the year 610 before our era, and how could I stop wondering, if by chance, he might not have calculated it, and if the means to do so had not precisely been there in those Egyptian sanctuaries?

And then, I reread Lucretius and I said to myself that nothing as beautiful has ever been written; that nothing that he had put forth, in any discipline, seemed to me to have been seriously questioned, but that, rather, everything he said had been confirmed. And I know that he has been described as an anxious person, and as a madman, and some people have claimed (and that would suit them) that he eventually committed suicide. But since we are still on our balcony, with the

quoique seulement dans la mémoire des hommes, où sa lumière non plus ne s'est pas éteinte.

Enfin, considérant les conséquences, pour l'esprit, des dernières hypothèses, qui ne peuvent plus nous être communiquées que par les hautes mathématiques, et semblent plonger les physiciens, ou du moins les philosophes à leur suite, dans un touchant vertige, sinon (et je les en félicite) dans le moindre repentir, — il me semble apercevoir, quoique confusément encore, quelque raison de ce que je ne m'expliquais pas jusqu'ici.

Notez que nous n'avons pas encore rallumé. Je pressens que ce va être bientôt, mais il me faut profiter, quelques instants encore, de l'ombre et des possibilités de « constructions », au sens psychiatrique, qu'elle contient ; des monstrueuses abstractions qu'elle permet.

Nous voici donc revenus, dirai-je, à un temps tout pareil à celui des Cyclopes, bien au delà de la Grèce classique, bien au delà de Thalès et d'Euclide, et presque au temps du Chaos. Les grandes déesses à nouveau sont assises, suscitées par l'homme sans doute, mais il ne les conçoit qu'avec terreur. Elles s'appellent Angström, Année-Lumière, Noyau, Fréquence, Onde, Énergie, Fonction-Psi, Incertitude. Elles aussi, comme les divinités sumériennes, stagnent dans une formidable inertie mais leur approche donne le vertige. Et sur leurs tabliers sont inscrites les formules, en écriture abstraite, en hautes maths.

Aucun hymne, en langage commun, ne saurait s'élever jusqu'à elles. Il n'atteindrait pas leurs genoux. Et c'est aussi pourquoi nous ne saurions en entendre aucun (c'est un fait), ni non plus songer à en composer un qui vaille.

Nos formes de penser, nos figures de rhétorique, en effet datent d'Euclide : ellipses, hyperboles, paraboles sont *aussi*

lights out, looking at the nocturnal sky, I can also maintain, remembering Electra, that one might find in it an example of divine behavior; and further observe, as it had happened to Electra and her sisters, that he too had been placed among the stars, except that this had only occurred in the memory of man, where his light has not yet diminished.

And now, considering the consequences on the mind of these last hypotheses, incomprehensible to us except through the most advanced mathematics, and that seem to plunge physicists, or at least the philosophers in their wake, into a touching dizziness, if not (and I congratulate them on it) into the slightest repentance—I am beginning to see, although still indistinctly, a few reasons that had prevented me from explaining them up to now.

Note that we still haven't turned the lights back on. I have a feeling that this will soon occur but I must benefit a little longer from the darkness and, in a psychiatric sense, the possibilities of "constructions" that it contains; the monstrous abstractions that it allows.

Here, I would say, we are back at a time very similar to that of the Cyclopes, far beyond classical Greece, far beyond Thales and Euclid, and almost at the time of Chaos. The great goddesses are sitting, once again, undoubtedly conjured up by man, but he is terror stricken when he imagines them. They are called Angström, Light-Year, Nucleus, Frequency, Wave, Energy, Psi-Function, Uncertainty. Like the Summerian divinities, they too stagnate in a fantastic inertia but approaching them makes one dizzy. And on their aprons, written in abstract script, formulas are inscribed in advanced math.

No hymn, in everyday language, could ever reach them. It would not even reach their knees. And that is why we can-

des figures de cette géométrie. Que voulez-vous que nous fassions? Eh bien, sans doute ce que nous faisons, nous artistes, nous poètes, lorsque nous travaillons bien. Et je ne dis pas, pour moi, que ce soit aujourd'hui. Sûrement non. C'est quand nous nous enfonçons, nous aussi, dans notre matière : les sons significatifs. Sans souci des formes anciennes et les refondant dans la masse, comme on fait des vieilles statues, pour en faire des canons, des balles... puis quand il le faut, à nouveau des Colonnes, selon les exigences du Temps.

Ainsi formerons-nous un jour peut-être les nouvelles Figures, qui nous permettront de nous confier à la Parole pour parcourir l'Espace courbe, l'Espace non-euclidien.

Bien. Tout cela a quelque allure. Nous nous sommes fait aussi gros qu'un boeuf. A la faveur de la nuit sans limites, nous avons gonflé nos baudruches. Et si, jusqu'à présent, nous n'étions pas un poète, je crois que nous le sommes devenu. Il me faut avouer qu'en somme il y a quelque agrément. Mais enfin, je ne puis m'empêcher d'une remarque, me connaissant comme je me connais : à savoir que si je me suis payé cette fantaisie, c'est que je savais pouvoir l'abolir en un instant. Pour cela, que suffit-il de faire? Eh bien, d'éclairer. tout à coup.

Sans délai, dans le monde visible, me voici rétabli sur pieds. Et comme j'avais mieux goûté la nuit en supprimant le crépuscule, mieux que l'aube lente et sanglante je goûte la brusque aurore de la raison.

Aussitôt, à la lumière des ampoules, m'apparaissent plusieurs démentis éclatants à ce que la nuit me fit construire.

Tout d'abord, la différence évidente entre les profanes que nous sommes et ceux des anciennes religions. Puis, que les progrès de la science sont prouvés autrement que par des formules.

not hear any of them (that is a fact), nor be tempted to compose a fitting one.

Our forms of thought, our rhetorical figures, actually date from Euclid: ellipses, hyperboles, paraboles, are *also* figures of that geometry. What would you want us to do? Well, exactly what we are doing, we artists, we poets, when we work well. And I do not pretend, in my case, that this has just happened. Assuredly not. It happens when we too dig into our matter: into meaningful sounds. Heedless of ancient forms and melting them back into a mass, as it is done with old statues, in order to make cannons out of them, ammunition...and, when necessary, new columns according to the demands of the Times.

Thus, we may perhaps, one day, create new Figures that will allow us to put our trust in the Word, in order to traverse curved Space, non-Euclidean Space.

Not bad at all. We have become as fat as a bull. Under cover of the limitless night, we have blown up our gold-beater's skin. And, if we hadn't been a poet, as of that moment, I think now we have become one. I must admit there is something agreeable about all that. But to tell the truth, knowing myself as I do, if I have indulged in this fantasy, it was only because I knew how to suppress it instantaneously. What did I have to do? Well, suddenly switch the lights back on.

And here I am, without delay, back on my feet in the visible world. And as I had better savored the night, by eliminating dusk, so to the slow and sanguine dawn, I prefer the rush of morning reason.

At that instant, in the glare of the electric bulbs, I see how wrong I had been about several things that the night had led me to construct.

First of all, the evident difference between the laymen

En effet, sur les genoux des colossales déesses, sont grimpées des myriades d'étudiants et de techniciens, de savants et de bricoleurs, enfin des gamins de tous âges, désinvoltes ou minutieux, imprudents ou précautionneux, taciturnes ou bruyants. Et ils n'y ont pas seulement inscrit leurs grimoires : ils y ont placé mille machines, mille appareils merveilleux.

Cela nous vaut, il faut bien le dire, de temps à autre quelque désagrément : court-circuit ou bombe atomique. Mais nous le prendrons comme il faut : indulgemment, avec philosophie. Nous nous occupons, à la vérité, d'autre chose et nous savons parfaitement choisir ce qui nous convient, dans le magasin qui, quelques années plus tard, en résulte. Dès que cela est bien « au point », nous l'adoptons.

Nous en sommes aux machines à laver, au magnétophone et au rasoir électrique. Pourquoi pas? Nous aurions tort de nous en priver. Non, nous ne serons pas les derniers à nous en servir. Pas les premiers, mais pas les derniers : ce qui est plus sensé qu'on ne pense.

J'ai l'air de plaisanter, et peut-être que je scandalise, mais je demande qu'on me l'accorde : tel est l'état d'esprit général. Les électriciens l'ont bien compris, ayant constaté par exemple que, pour les seuls besoins domestiques, la consommation d'électricité double pratiquement tous les dix ans. Ou encore, que le développement de la seule télévision dans les seuls États-Unis d'Amérique, a fait s'accroître la consommation d'une quantité égale à celle exigée par l'ensemble des besoins en France, tant industriels que privés. Oui, y compris toutes nos grandes usines et l'électrification de nos réseaux de transport!

Ainsi, les électriciens l'ont compris, et peut-être serait-il temps que les architectes le comprennent. Pourtant, j'ai parlé de modestie réciproque, et il me faut revenir sur moi-même.

De l'électricité, telle qu'actuellement à la sensibilité de

that we are and those of ancient religions. And then, that scientific progress does not have to be proven by formulas.

Look at the way myriad students, and technicians, scholars and handymen, as well as youngsters of all ages— easygoing or scrupulous, careless or cautious, taciturn or boisterous—have climbed on the knees of those colossal goddesses. And there, they have not only scribbled all over them but have placed a thousand machines on them, a thousand marvelous appliances.

Admittedly, at times, this can be rather unpleasant: a short-circuit or an atomic bomb. But we shall take it in stride, with indulgence, philosophically. To tell the truth, other things concern us, and we know exactly what we need in the store that one day will be built. As soon as it is "tested," we adopt it.

We have now adopted washing machines, tape recorders, and electric razors. Why not? We would be foolish to get along without them. However, we will neither be the last ones to use them, nor the first, definitely not the last—which makes more sense than one suspects.

I seem to be joking, and perhaps this is scandalous, but let me have my say—that's how people think in general. Electricians have understood this well. They have observed, for example, that just for domestic needs, electrical consumption has practically doubled every ten years. Or that the development of television, in the United States alone, has raised the consumption to a quantity equal to that required by the combined needs of France, both industrial and private. Yes, including all our large factories, and the electrification of our transport systems!

Electricians have understood this. Isn't it about time architects understood it, too? However, I spoke about reciprocal modesty, and so I must once again speak about myself.

l'homme elle se propose, aucun grand texte, aucune grande chose dans l'ordre poétique, après tout, n'est sortie non plus. Ce retard, chez les architectes comme les poètes, ne tiendrait-il pas aux mêmes causes? Les architectes, comme les poètes, sont des artistes. En tant que tels, ils voient les choses dans l'éternité plus que dans le temporel. Pratiquement, ils se défient de la mode. Je parle des meilleurs d'entre eux.

Est-ce que la rapidité même des progrès de la science n'inciterait pas les architectes, comme les poètes, à une certaine résistance quant à leur adhésion *profonde*, à leur affiliation, à leur « branchement »?

Il me souvient fort bien de ce qui se passa, lors de ma première enfance — j'avais alors sept ou huit ans — quand fut accomplie la modernisation, quant à l'éclairage, de la grande maison que nous habitions dans un faubourg d'Avignon. La « suspension » de la salle à manger était équipée de la classique grosse lampe à pétrole. On modifia cette lampe, pour lui adapter un manchon « Auer », et une lumière beaucoup plus blanche et brillante en rayonna : c'était le « gaz ». Mais deux ans s'étaient à peine écoulés, que les ouvriers revinrent. L'on arracha ici et là des tuyaux de plomb, ailleurs on les écrasa. Et ce fut l'électricité. On plaça des interrupteurs, et dès lors, la suspension ne fut plus jamais abaissée ni remontée. Mais ces arrachements, ces écrasements, à vrai dire, je ne les ai jamais oubliés.

Tout le monde a une anecdote de ce genre en mémoire, et cela m'a paru assez inquiétant pour que je n'hésite pas à traverser Paris, afin d'interroger, dans les laboratoires de la rue Lord-Byron, un de mes amis qui s'y occupe exclusivement de la nouvelle forme d'énergie à la mode, je veux dire de l'énergie nucléaire. Et je lui ai demandé si l'on devait penser qu'on arracherait bientôt les fils électriques, si l'on délogerait les compteurs, pour installer, à leur place, quelque cyclotron

The way that man presently feels about electricity has not yet produced any major work, any major poetic work. Couldn't this lag, among architects and poets, be due to the same causes? Architects like poets are artists. As such, they see things in eternity rather than in the temporal. For all intents and purposes, they are wary of fashion. I speak of the best of them.

Wouldn't the very speed of the progress of science prompt architects, like poets, to a certain resistance insofar as their *deep* commitment, their affiliation, their "connection" is concerned?

I am here reminded of what happened when I was quite young—seven or eight years old—and lighting was modernized in our large house in the suburbs of Avignon. The "hanging lamp" in the dining room was equipped with a classic heavy oil-burning lamp. This lamp was modified so that an "Auer" gas outlet could be fitted on it; as a result, there was a much whiter and more brilliant light—that was "gas." But two years had hardly elapsed when the workers were back. Here and there, lead pipes were ripped out, elsewhere, they were crushed. And thus came electricity. Switches were installed, and from that time on, the hanging lamp was never lowered or raised again. But, to tell the truth, I have never forgotten all that ripping and crushing.

Everyone can remember an anecdote of this kind, and I was sufficiently troubled by this to cross the whole of Paris in order to question, in the laboratories of the rue Lord Byron, a friend of mine who was solely concerned with the new form of fashionable energy, I mean, nuclear energy. And I asked him whether electrical wiring would soon be ripped out, if the counters would be taken away, in order to install some cyclotron in their place, in a house or on a floor. Well, believe me, I left reassured. I had only needed a single com-

d'immeuble ou d'étage. Eh bien, vous pouvez m'en croire, j'en suis sorti rassuré. Il y avait suffi d'une remarque, dont il me semble que je l'avais faite déjà; à savoir que pour désintégrer la matière, l'électricité est encore nécessaire, et qu'il est bien utile d'être branché.

Sortant de là, je fus dans la rue ébloui par toutes sortes de lumières, et je me rendis chez une duchesse de ma connaissance, qui me fit dîner aux bougies.

Si bien qu'une nouvelle évidence se fit bientôt jour dans mon esprit. C'est que l'électricité est une définitive merveille, non seulement parce qu'elle conditionne notre conquête de l'avenir, mais parce qu'elle ne nous empêche en aucune manière de goûter les plaisirs du passé, et peut-être nous les rend plus sensibles.

Il y avait trente-six personnes chez notre duchesse, aviateurs, chirurgiens, metteurs en scène, mais je ne voyais plus rien d'eux, à vrai dire, sinon leur auréole d'électricité. Je voyais ces projecteurs à faisceaux serrés, braqués pour les uns sur un nuage afin d'en mesurer la hauteur, pour les autres sur un organe malade ou sur une table d'opération, pour d'autres encore sur telles parties d'une scène qu'il s'agit à tel instant d'éclairer. Et je me dis que je pouvais aussi braquer ces faisceaux sur le fronton de tel monument pour en faire surgir comme jamais auparavant quelque détail, ou les prier, dans l'écrin des frondaisons nocturnes, de m'offrir le diamant de son volume d'ensemble. Je me dis que je pouvais grâce à eux éblouir un assaillant ou fasciner une proie. Et encore, contemplateur des choses, doubler, multiplier par eux mon attention. Enfin la diriger à ma guise, et provoquer les scandales ou les surprises, les stupeurs ou les grimaces parfois nécessaires à la révélation d'une vérité. Ces jeux, me dis-je, sont à ma volonté, comme ils sont à l'infini.

ment, and it seemed to me that I had already made it, and that was that electricity was still necessary to disintegrate matter and connections were still useful.

Out in the street once more, I was stunned by all sorts of lights. I then went to the home of a duchess friend of mine where I dined by candlelight.

Because of this, I soon became aware of a new fact. Electricity is a lasting marvel, not only because it determines our conquest of the future but because it does not, in any way, stop us from appreciating the pleasures of the past, and perhaps makes us more sensitive to them.

There were thirty-six guests at our duchess': pilots, surgeons, stage directors, but frankly speaking, I could no longer see them except for their halo of electricity. I saw those projectors with their pinpoint beams aimed, some of them, on a cloud in order to measure its distance, others on a sick organ or an operating table, and still others, on that part of a scene that had to be lit up at a specific moment. And I said to myself that I too could aim those beams on the pediment of a monument in order to bring out, as never before, a particular detail, or to beg them, in the jeweled nocturnal foliations, to give me the diamond of their concerted volume. I said to myself that thanks to them, I could dazzle an assailant or fascinate a prey. And, further, as a contemplator of things, use them to double or multiply my observations. Finally, to direct it at will and provoke scandals or surprises, amazement or those grimaces that sometime accompany the revelation of a truth. These games, I said to myself, depend on my will, and they are endless.

Coming back home in a mental state you can imagine, I felt simultaneously spurred on by emulation, an imperious

Rentré chez moi dans l'état d'esprit qu'on devine, je sentais à la fois, piqué par l'émulation, un impérieux besoin de m'asseoir à ma table pour écrire enfin un hymne valable à l'Électricité, mais aussi, parce que telles sont les contradictions de la nature, un besoin non moins impérieux de fraîcheur, de silence et de recueillement dans la nuit.

Si bien qu'éteignant les lumières je me remis au balcon.

Où en étais-je resté, me disais-je, de mes déesses et de leurs genoux? Mais aussitôt toutes choses se mêlèrent et je vis ces déesses assises sur les montagnes près de la Truyère, ou dans les souterrains de Brommat. J'entendis crouler les trente tonnes d'eau par seconde de Marèges. J'évoquai les millions de volts, les transformateurs géants, et je n'oubliai pas *le danger;* et il ne me parut pas trop difficile de me lancer à partir de là dans mon hymne, enfin dans une certaine poésie. Vous savez,[4] ces princesses hindoues, ces intouchables, qu'il suffisait d'effleurer pour mourir? Bien. J'aime assez ça.

L'électricité, certes, est une princesse, et qu'elle ait le teint du cuivre ne me déplaît pas. Exact. Mais pourtant les yeux bleus, s'il vous plaît, ou plutôt un certain reflet bleu, à fleur de sa peau de cuivre. Très bien. Cela marche même avec ce que nous savons, que la molécule de cuivre ionisée est bleue, tandis qu'à l'état neutre elle était rouge.

Mais pourtant, cette princesse est aussi une domestique : comment vais-je arranger ça?

C'est ici, je m'en rends compte, qu'il va me falloir rallumer.

Oui, que j'approche la main de l'interrupteur, instantanément la solution est trouvée.

Il suffit de saisir entre le pouce et l'index la petite oreille

4. Collection: *Que sais-je?*, passim.

need to sit down at my desk and finally write a worthy hymn to Electricity, but also, and such are the contradictions in nature, a need, no less imperious, for coolness, for silence and meditation in the night.

So much so that, switching off the lights, I went out on the balcony again.

I asked myself where I had left my goddesses and their knees? But right away, all things mingled and I saw these goddesses sitting on mountains near Truyère, or in the caverns of Brommat. I heard the thirty tons of water per second tumbling down at Marèges. I imagined the millions of volts, the giant transformers, and I did not forget the *danger;* and as of that moment, it no longer seemed impossible for me to begin writing my hymn, writing a certain type of poetry. Did you know[4] that men died the moment they so much as touched those Hindu princesses, those untouchables? Well, I find that rather to my liking.

Electricity is indeed a princess, and the fact that she has a copper complexion does not displease me. Exactly. Nevertheless, would you believe it, she has blue eyes, or rather, a particular blue reflection on the surface of her copper skin. Very well. That even agrees with what we know—that ionized copper molecules are blue, whereas in their neutral states they are red.

But this princess is also a maid: how will I explain that?

I realize that here I will have to turn the lights back on.

Yes, I've only to put my hand near the switch and the solution is instantaneously found.

One only has to grasp between the thumb and the index the little cold ear of this child when, on the spot, stripping off

4. Ibid.

froide de cet enfant, pour qu'aussitôt, déchirant sa robe de soie qui se placarde, les ailes étendues, aux murs et au pluf-fond, une éblouissante personne, sa mère, — est-ce notre princesse hindoue, en est-ce mille, sont-ce mille esclaves qui se précipitent toutes nues à notre service?

Quel ennoblissement, quel plaisir procure une telle domesticité!

Quel luxe d'être servi par cette grande figure méta-physique, vêtue de soie bruissante et frémissante, et d'ailleurs nue, coiffée d'aigrettes, parée de rivières de diamants! Pour-tant si agile, si zélée!

Ah! *zélée* m'oblige à renvoyer toutes ces métaphores et à leur préférer celle de la libellule, et en effet, tournant le com-mutateur, il m'a paru parfois que l'abord de cette éblouissante personne était un peu frémissant, même commotionnant.

Elle attire puis repousse. Il n'y a en elle pas la moindre familiarité.

L'on dit de la meilleure domestique que c'est une perle, mais celle-ci n'est-elle pas un diamant, toutes les mines de dia-mants du monde? Non, car certes, cela est tout aussi cristal-lin, étincelant, mais c'est beaucoup plus fluide : il faut y ajou-ter cette qualité.

Toutes les rivières, donc, toutes les rivières rapides et oxygénées du monde! Toutes les rivières à truites, avec les truites qui fuient dedans!

Ainsi, vêtue comme une maharanée, en grande toilette du soir, mais nue aussi, étincelante et parée, — ah! je ne vivrai plus que la nuit, pour le plaisir d'être servi par elle! — soudaine, élégante, fière, magnétique : c'est une domestique qui a le caractère d'une princesse. Ses origines sont des plus nobles, et elle ne dégénère jamais.

On me dit qu'elle me sert comme elle sert tout le monde,

its showy silk dress, its wings spread out, on the walls and on the ceiling—there is a dazzling person, its mother. Is it our Hindu princess, a thousand of them, a thousand naked slaves that rush forward to serve us?

What nobility, what pleasure such domesticity procures!

What a luxury to be served by this great metaphysical figure, clothed in rustling and shimmering silks, and naked besides, coiffed with aigrettes, adorned with rivers of diamonds! Yet so agile! so zealous!

Ah! *zealous* forces me to reject all those metaphors and choose instead the firefly, and, in fact, turning on the switch, it seemed to me at times that the approach of this stunning person was a bit fearful, even shocking.

She attracts then repels. She does not allow the slightest familiarity.

One says of the best maids that they are pearls, but this one, is she not a diamond, all the diamond mines in the world? Not quite, for all that is also crystalline, sparkling and also much more fluid—that quality must be added.

All the rivers, then, all the rapid and oxygenated rivers of the world! All the trout rivers, with trouts fleeing below!

Thus, clothed like a maharani, in evening clothes, but naked also, sparkling and bejeweled—ah! I would only live at night for the pleasure of being served by her! Brusk, elegant, proud, magnetic: a maid with a princess' character. Her origins are of the noblest, and she never degenerates.

I am told that she serves me the way she does everyone, and that any peasant can afford her. To tell the truth, she is a prostitute, but what do I care since she never loses her distinction, since she keeps her distance as a matter of principle.

She isn't a part, in any way, of what she lights. Wind or

et que le moindre paysan peut se l'offrir. En effet, c'est une prostituée, mais que m'importe, puisque jamais elle ne perd rien de sa distinction, de son éloignement par principe.

Elle ne participe nullement à ce qu'elle éclaire. Le vent ou l'orgie peuvent souffler. Elle ne titube ni ne cille. Et ni son corps, ni son âme ne s'en trouvent agités.

Viendrait-on à la toucher, l'intouchable ne vous mord pas, comme le faisait la flamme, cette sauvage! Elle vous le rappelle par un frémissement, ou vous tue.

Disposant dans son appartement d'une telle ressource, d'un tel empressement à servir et d'une telle discrétion à la fois, comment ne voudrait-on la soumettre à mille épreuves, inventer mille jouets, mille instruments à lui offrir? Ne serait-ce que pour la varier et en jouir. De ces instruments de son zèle, je me ferais bien collectionneur. Mieux, inventeur. Qui plus est, elle vous en suggère...

A partir de là, je rêvai beaucoup. J'inventai mille appareils... mais enfin : ne se pourra-t-il un jour, me dis-je, que *tout*, non seulement de l'actualité universelle, mais de l'intemporalité (voyez déjà le planetarium) soit automatiquement enregistré — je ne songe pas seulement au visuel — pour devenir à plaisir sensible, pour peu qu'ils le veuillent, à tous ceux qui n'en auraient pas la perception directe?

Songeant à cela, je fixais stupidement mon ampoule, dont l'impassibilité brusquement me saisit. Je craignis aussitôt de m'être laissé entraîner en quelque excessif lyrisme, ou dans la fameuse illusion de totalité. Je devins très mécontent de mon hymne, et si je l'avais écrit, je l'aurais alors déchiré.

Finalement, me dis-je, car je me sentais fatigué, je crois que l'électricité a agi sur la poésie et l'art plutôt négativement. Son influence, nous l'éprouvons dans une modification générale du goût. Je veux dire qu'elle a contribué à faire préférer la

orgy may blow: she neither staggers nor blinks. And neither her body nor her soul is ever perturbed.

Were one to touch her, the untouchable does not bite back like the flame, that savage! As a reminder, she jolts you or kills you.

Having such resources in one's apartment, such an eagerness to serve and such a discretion at the same time, how wouldn't one want to make it go through a thousand tests, invent a thousand toys for it, offer her a thousand instruments? If only to make her change and rejoice in that. I would readily become a collector of the instruments of her zeal. Better still, an inventor. What's more, she suggests some to you. . . .

With that in mind, I began dreaming a lot. I invented a thousand appliances. . . . But, finally, I said to myself, the day will come when *everything*, not only pertaining to universal actuality but to intemporality (the planetarium is a good example) will automatically be recorded, in order to become (I am not only thinking about the visual) a perceptible pleasure, even if they don't want it, for all those who would not have experienced it directly.

Thinking about that, I stared dumbly at my bulb whose impassibility suddenly struck me. I was immediately afraid that I had allowed myself to be carried away by some lyrical excess, or by that well-known illusion of totality. I became very dissatisfied with my hymn and, had I written it, I would then have torn it up.

In the end, I said to myself, because I was tired, I think that electricity has acted in a rather negative manner on poetry and art. We experience its influence in a general modification of taste. I mean to say that it has contributed in making us prefer clarity to the penumbra, perhaps pure colors to

clarté à la pénombre, peut-être les couleurs pures aux couleurs nuancées, peut-être la rapidité aux lentes manières et peut-être un certain cynisme à l'effusion.

Tout cela a joué, dans tous les arts, en faveur d'une certaine rhétorique : celle de l'étincelle jaillissant entre deux pôles opposés, séparés par un hiatus dans l'expression. Seule la suppression du lien logique permettant l'éclatement de l'étincelle.

Poésie et électricité s'accumulant dès lors et restant insoupçonnables jusqu'à l'éclair, voilà qui marche avec l'esthétique des *quanta*. Et bien sûr qu'aucun hymne ou discours dans le style soutenu n'est plus possible, quand triomphe, en physique, le discontinu.

Tel est l'état de fait qui doit être bien observé des architectes, car on ne saurait revenir en arrière : il s'agit d'une modification irréversible du goût.

... Maintenant, ce que je me demande, c'est si je ne me moque pas de moi, et du lecteur. En effet, tant d'affirmations en tous sens, si contradictoires... Il est tard. Prenons un miroir. Face à mon visage, une forte lampe... Un penseur, le doigt sur la tempe? Ou un bouffon qui se grime? Mais les deux ensemble sans doute : un vieil homme, qui a compris.

Là-dessus, je me mis à rire, me sentant tout rajeuni. Je me levai, et tournant sur moi-même, je me fis un *nouveau* discours, reprenant le ton du début.

Il ne me semble pas que nous ayons, dans tout ce qui précède, manqué de montrer, bien qu'à notre façon seulement (et comment aurions-nous pu, sans devenir inauthentique et perdre alors toute vertu de persuasion, faire autrement?), montrer, dis-je, l'importance de l'électricité dans

subdued ones, perhaps speed to casual manners, and perhaps a degree of cynicism to effusion.

All that has had a part, in all the arts, in shaping a certain type of rhetoric: one marked by a spark leaping between two opposite poles, separated by a hiatus in the expression. Only the elimination of the logical link allowing the spark to flash.

Poetry and electricity accumulating from that moment on, and remaining unknown until the lightning: that seems to go hand in hand with quanta aesthetics. And, of course, how could anyone write a hymn or a speech in the sustained manner, after the discontinuous has triumphed in physics?

Such is the state of things that must be taken into account by architects, because there is no turning back: taste has now been irreversibly modified.

. . . Now, I ask myself if I haven't been fooling both myself and the reader. All those affirmations, in all directions, so contradictory. . . . It is late. Let us take a mirror. In front of my face, a powerful lamp. . . . A thinker, finger on the temple? Or a clown, putting on his make-up? Why, both of course—an old man who has understood.

At that point, I started to laugh, feeling young again. I rose, and pirouetting, spoke to myself once more, taking up the tone of the beginning.

It seems to me that we have indeed shown in everything that we've just said, although in our own way (and how could we have done otherwise, without becoming inauthentic and losing all our capacity of persuasion), shown, I say, the importance of electricity in dwellings, the function or rather the functions of the greatest importance that it per-

l'habitation, le rôle ou plutôt les rôles de premier plan qu'elle y joue, et encore l'ennoblissement qu'elle apporte à la vie domestique.

L'homme n'en demeure pas moins, bien sûr, le protagoniste. Un nouvel homme dit-on, et je suis en partie d'accord. En effet, un homme renouvelé : rajeuni, plus propre, plus lisse, plus libre (comme on dit d'une roue libre) et en somme, plus *détaché*. Je n'ose, et pourtant sans doute le devrais-je, dire un homme mieux différencié.

Oui, ce que je voudrais démontrer pour finir, c'est qu'un tel homme est d'autant plus valable que sa transformation s'opère dans le sens de sa nature profonde, je veux dire de ce qui a toujours fait, parmi les êtres du monde, sa différence.

Je parle de différence, qu'on le note, me gardant de prononcer le mot de supériorité. Et je prie qu'on attache à cette nuance la valeur qu'à mon avis elle mérite. Que ceux auxquels l'idée d'une supériorité est nécessaire, qui en ont besoin pour vivre et déjà pour tenir debout, que ceux-ci se l'attribuent par surcroît, rien, dans ce que je viens de dire, ni non plus dans ce que je vais dire, ne saurait les en empêcher. Quant à moi, l'idée de ma différence me suffit, et le plus important me paraît être d'accepter, de bien connaître et d'aimer enfin sa différence, de la vouloir. Elle seule, à mon avis, suffit bien à nous justifier ; à faire de nous, dans l'ordre et l'harmonie du monde, ou si l'on préfère des termes moins laudatifs, dans la machine, dans l'horlogerie du monde, un rouage parfaitement indispensable. Engrené, certes, parmi les autres, mais aussi important qu'aucun d'eux et donc sans sujet de souffrir d'aucun complexe (d'infériorité ou de non-justification). Je dirais même que l'orgueil de la supériorité, voilà ce qui me semblerait non seulement un peu ridicule, mais aussi un peu dangereux. Peut-être, après tout, n'est-il pas bon pour la santé d'un rouage, qu'il se figure être le

forms, and further, the mark of nobility that it brings to life in the home.

To be sure, man still remains the protagonist. A new man, it is said, and I am partially in agreement with that. In fact, a renewed man: younger, cleaner, smoother, freer (as one says of a disengaged wheel) and, on the whole, more *detached*. I dare not, and yet I should say, a man better differentiated.

What I would really like to show, in conclusion, is that such a man is all the more valuable in that this transformation operates in accordance with his true nature, that is, with that part which has always been responsible for his difference among beings in the world.

I speak of difference, purposely eliminating, as one can see, the word superiority. And I hope that this nuance will be given its proper due. As for those to whom the idea of superiority is necessary, who need it in order to live, and even to stand up, let them be free to adopt it, since there is nothing in what I have just said, neither in what I am about to say that can stop them from doing it. As for me, the idea of my difference is sufficient, and the most important seems to me to accept, to be familiar with, and, finally, to live one's difference, to want it. In my opinion, it alone suffices to justify us; to make of us, in the order and the harmony of the world, or if one prefers less laudatory terms, in the machine, in the clockwork of the world, a perfectly indispensable gear. Connected to others but as important as any of them, and thus, without any need to suffer any complex (inferiority or nonjustification). I would even say that a sense of vanity in one's superiority would seem to me to be not only slightly ridiculous but even slightly dangerous. After all it may not be a good thing for a gear to consider itself the principal gear. It might then run away, spin at too fast a rate, wearing and

rouage principal? Peut-être risque-t-il alors de s'emballer, de tourner à un régime trop rapide, usant et fatigant pour lui? Enfin, nous les connaissons, n'est-ce pas? ces dépressions qui suivent les exaltations? Pourquoi nous mettrions-nous en ce cas? Pourquoi risquerions-nous, chantant trop fort notre supériorité et notre gloire, de devoir un jour déchanter, nous placer trop bas, nous jeter dans le sentiment de notre impuissance; et descendre, un peu trop vite sans doute, l'escalier des caves... (vers les tabous!) Mais enfin que chacun choisisse. Cela ne change rien à ce que je vais dire.

Qu'on y voie, en effet, une supériorité ou seulement une différence, *sa* différence, il semble bien que, de tout temps, la nature de l'homme ait été de pouvoir, grâce à certaines facultés (que l'on a nommées d'*esprit*), évoluer, s'adapter et se perfectionner, en restant néanmoins simple et nu. Plus exactement encore, de pouvoir fabriquer des outils, des armes, des cuirasses, des instruments de détection, de combat, d'appréhension, de déplacement, des façons de rendre ses aliments plus faciles à digérer : enfin une infinité d'appareils, de plus en plus nombreux, variés et perfectionnés, *mais tous entièrement distincts de sa personne.*

Quand je dis qu'il a su s'adapter, voyez par exemple les autres espèces, mettons un mammifère (nous trouverions la même chose chez les poissons, les reptiles ou les oiseaux). Un porc doit-il vivre dans les forêts, il lui faut *devenir* tout à fait autre, que ses défenses s'allongent, etc. Qu'un cheval doive se nourrir dans une région où il y a moins d'herbe à brouter que de feuilles haut placées sur les arbres ou de régimes de bananes ou de dattes, et le voilà obligé de *perdre* beaucoup des qualités du cheval afin de devenir girafe. Ailleurs, mais je n'en finirais pas... Eh bien, remarquons que l'homme peut être amené à vivre sous telle ou telle latitude, il n'aura besoin de perdre aucune de ses qualités. Il inventera les outils et les

tiring itself. We're familiar with that, aren't we? Those depressions that follow exaltations! Why should we put ourselves in such a situation? Why would we want to risk, singing too loudly our own superiority and our glory, see ourselves forced to stop singing one day, demean ourselves, wallow in our feeling of helplessness; and, take off a bit too rapidly down the stairs that lead to the cellar . . . (toward taboos!) In the end, you've got to choose for yourself. That will not affect what I have to say.

Whether, in fact, one considers it as a superiority or simply as a difference, *his* difference, it seems clear that throughout history, man's nature has been able, thanks to certain faculties (pertaining to the *mind*) to evolve, to adapt, and to perfect himself, all the while, staying simple and naked. More to the point, capable of making tools, weapons, armor, instruments for detection, for war, for transportation; capturing devices; making his food easier to digest: truly an endless series of appliances, increasingly numerous, varied, and perfected, but *all of them absolutely free of his person.*

Isn't it evident that he has managed to adapt himself in comparison to other species, and let us say to mammals (the same thing holds true for fish, reptiles, or birds). If a pig has to live in the forest, it must completely *change* itself; its tusks must grow, etc. If a horse must feed itself in a region where there is less grass to eat than leaves, bananas, or dates placed on a high branch, then it is *forced* to lose many qualities of the horse in order to become a giraffe. Elsewhere . . . but then I would never finish. . . . Let us just conclude that man can be forced to live under this or that latitude; he will not be forced to lose any of his qualities. He will invent the tools and the weapons appropriate to his new condition in the world, and to the dangers or the resources inherent to it.

armes convenant à sa nouvelle situation dans le monde et aux dangers ou aux ressources que cette situation comporte.

Et quand je dis qu'il a su perfectionner son outillage, le plus simple est de le comparer à ces arthropodes, dont l'observation d'ailleurs, pour l'invention des meilleurs appareils, n'est sans doute pas inutile. Voyez par exemple homards ou crevettes. N'est-il pas merveilleux d'admirer leurs cuirasses et leurs appareils d'estime et de détection, de combat et d'appréhension? Et pourtant! Sans doute n'est-il pas très commode de ne pouvoir jamais quitter sa cuirasse, ni aucune de ses armes, ni aucun de ses appareils, et de toujours devoir vivre avec cet attirail sur le dos. Que dis-je! non seulement sur le dos, mais intimement mêlé à sa chair, et donc à son psychisme, et donc vous faisant devenir entièrement autre, vous faisant devenir cuirassé, périscope, etc. Voilà qui peut être assez gênant quant à une vue un peu claire, une allure un peu dégagée, légère, une domination quelconque de la situation. On peut dire, dans tous les sens que ce mot comporte, y compris le sens argotique, que *ce qui devint* le homard s'est trouvé, par la Nature, et en somme comme en détail, monstrueusement *refait*.

Voilà l'avatar, qui, par merveille, se trouve à l'homme épargné. Qu'est-ce que l'homme? C'est un homard qui pourrait laisser sa carapace au vestiaire, son périscope, et ses étaux, et ses cannes à pêche. Une araignée qui pourrait ranger son filet dans un hangar, et le réparer du bout des doigts, au lieu de devoir l'abandonner pour en tisser un autre, que dis-je, pour en baver un à nouveau. L'on imagine quelle infinité d'exemples je pourrais trouver dans la nature pour faire suite à ceux-là. N'insistons pas. Je pense que le point est acquis. D'ailleurs, il n'y a qu'à regarder le premier venu parmi nous. Sortant de son avion ou de sa voiture, qu'il laisse au garage,

And when I say that he has managed to perfect his equipment, the easiest thing to do is to compare him to those arthropods which, by the way, it would not be a waste of time to observe, in order to invent better appliances. Look at lobsters or shrimp for example. Isn't it marvelous to admire their armor, their reckoning and detecting systems, their combat and capturing devices? And yet! how very inconvenient it must be never to leave one's armor, or any of one's weapons, or any of one's devices and always live with that equipment on one's back! What am I saying! Not only on one's back but intimately part of one's flesh, and thus of one's psyche, and, therefore, forcing one to become wholly different, a destroyer, for example, or a periscope, etc. How awkward, if one wanted a better vision, and a rather free and easy walk, a degree of control over the situation! One might say, in all the various meanings implied in the word, including the slang meaning, that, *what became* a lobster, was monstrously *refashioned* by Nature, both in its general and in its specific aspects.

Man has been spared such transformations! What is man? A lobster that can check its shell in the cloakroom, its periscope, its hand-vices, its fishing rods. A spider that could put its web in a hangar and repair it with the tips of its fingers, instead of having to abandon it in order to weave another, or more exactly, to slaver out a new one. One can imagine how many examples I could find in nature to add to these. The point has been made. I think you've understood. Besides, all you've got to do is look at the first arrival. Stepping out of his plane or his car which he leaves in the garage, dressed in his suit which he leaves in the bathroom, he appears to us just as he was on the first day: as naked, naked as a worm, as pink, as integrally clean and free as possible.

habillé de ses vêtements, qu'il laisse dans sa salle de bains, le voilà comme au premier jour : aussi nu, nu comme un ver, aussi rose, aussi intégralement propre et libre que possible. Je ne connais guère, non, sinon les anges, je ne connais guère d'animal plus nu.

Mais attention! Vous n'aurez pas manqué de le remarquer, architectes, j'ai fait intervenir à chaque instant la notion de vestiaire, celle de hangar, d'atelier, de placard. C'est qu'en effet, avec des outils que l'on peut quitter, il faut bien quelque endroit pour les ranger, et lorsqu'on reste nu, quelque maison, caverne ou palace, pour s'y abriter au besoin. Et c'est ainsi que l'homme, dès les premiers temps, a dû se loger, non seulement pour établir le nid de sa compagne et de sa progéniture, mais pour ranger ses membres détachables et pouvoir les retrouver au besoin. Certes, l'on a connu, l'on connaît encore des populations humaines nomades, mais elles se font suivre généralement de chariots, et il faut bien reconnaître que la tendance n'est pas dans cette direction-là. J'ai vu ainsi, autour de la Méditerranée, les bateaux des pêcheurs diminuer, pendant que leurs installations à terre devenaient chaque année plus conséquentes.

Il se trouve encore, — c'est ici que je fais intervenir dans mon raisonnement un troisième terme — il se trouve que l'homme a pensé bientôt se dispenser de fournir lui-même tout ou partie de la force nécessaire au fonctionnement de ces appareils, c'est-à-dire de ses membres ou de ses organes séparés. Et il s'est ingénié à utiliser à cette fin, soit (en restant encore à la force musculaire) des animaux domptés et domestiqués à cet effet (boeufs, rennes ou chevaux); soit, constatant l'impétuosité des vents ou des eaux (et toujours en restant au domaine mécanique) à utiliser leur énergie pour faire

With the exception of angels, I do not know of any animal that is as naked.

Wait a minute! I'm sure that none of you architects have overlooked the fact that I have constantly brought into play the notion of cloakroom, hangar, workshop, closet. That is because, when one has tools, there must necessarily be a place to put them; and when one is naked, there must be some house, some cavern or palace to provide needed shelter. And that is the reason why man, from the beginning, has had to find shelter, not only to nestle his companion and his off-springs but to put his detachable members in a place where he could find them again when he needed them. True, there have been, and there still are nomadic populations, but they are generally followed by carts—and after all, it must be admitted that the future does not lie in that direction. I myself have seen, in the Mediterranean region, fishing boats decline in number while fishermen's installations on shore have become, year by year, more important.

It also appears—and here I introduce a third element in my argument—it further appears that man no longer wanted to provide all or part of the necessary power needed to assure the functioning of these appliances, that is to say, of his members or independent organs. To that end, he ingeniously used either (keeping to muscular power) animals trained or domesticated for this purpose (cattle, deer, or horses); or, observing the impetuosity of wind and water (and always keeping to the mechanical level), utilizing their energy to make hís mills go round, and even his elevators. He then discovered the resources of the elasticity of metals and springs, and from that, the movements of the clock. Since then, he has gone a little farther still. The kinetic energy of gas and steam has

tourner ses meules, et jusqu'à ses ascenseurs. Il a découvert ensuite les ressources de l'élasticité des métaux, ressorts, et de là les mouvements d'horlogerie. Mais il est depuis lors allé un peu plus loin encore. L'énergie cinétique des gaz et des vapeurs lui a fourni plusieurs nouvelles sortes de machines. Enfin il a réussi à capter l'énergie électrique, et si bien imaginé ses applications, si bien constaté sa puissance, que maintenant ses principaux appareils sont confiés à cette forme de l'énergie qui, comme il est naturel, à chaque instant lui en suggère d'autres. A tel point que, chose curieuse, ce n'est pas chez les nations les plus retardataires et qui commencent seulement à s'équiper, que les besoins en énergie électrique croissent le plus vite, mais bien chez les nations déjà les plus habituées à cette technique, parce qu'elles en subissent le charme, et pour ainsi dire la persuasion.

Je ne reviendrai pas sur les avantages merveilleux des appareils animés de cette façon ; il me semble en avoir assez dit. Je voulais seulement, en ce dernier chapitre, montrer que leur trouvaille et leur constant développement sont dans l'ordre exact de la différence caractéristique, enfin du *perpétuel* de l'homme. J'ai dit que l'homme était un animal à membres et organes séparés, qu'il pouvait quitter et reprendre, et dont il ne voulait pas s'empêtrer. Il donnera donc toujours la préférence à ce qu'il peut commander à distance, et du geste le plus facile. Eh bien, l'électricité à cet égard n'a pas sa pareille, puisque c'est la force qui se transmet le plus vite, le plus intégralement et par les conduites les moins encombrantes, les plus fines et presque les plus imperceptibles qui soient. Mais il faut évidemment qu'elle « débouche », commodément, à notre disposition.

Il me semble qu'à partir de là, la conclusion est facile, puisque j'en ai réuni tous les éléments.

provided him with many new types of machines. Ultimately, he succeeded in mastering electrical energy and he was able to foresee, to such an extent, the ways it was going to be applied, to such an extent observe its power, that now, his major appliances use this form of energy. They in turn naturally suggest others at every moment. Curiously enough, this is true to such an extent that the need for electricity does not increase as fast in the most underdeveloped nations that are just beginning to equip themselves, as it does among those nations that are already the most accustomed to its use because they have fallen under the spell and, one might even say, that they have been converted to it.

I will not insist on the marvelous advantages of appliances that work in this way; I think I have said enough about that. In this final chapter I only wanted to show that their discovery and their constant development fit perfectly well in the order of the differential characteristic, in fact, in what is *perpetual* in man. I said that man was an animal with independent members and organs that he could leave or take up again, and in which he did not want to entangle himself. He will, therefore, always prefer to command from a distance, and in the least complicated manner. Well, electricity has no peer in this regard, since it is the power that is transmitted the fastest, with the least loss, and through the least cumbersome wires, the thinnest and probably the least visible ones. But obviously it must have a readily accessible "outlet."

From this point forward, it seems to me that the conclusion is evident since I have brought all the elements together.

You have guessed it, dear architects, those appliances man has invented must be attached not to himself, thank God, but to his dwelling. These appliances are now electric.

Vous l'avez compris, chers architectes, c'est à sa demeure, Dieu merci, et non à lui-même, que doivent être attachés les appareils que l'homme sait s'inventer. Or ces appareils sont devenus électriques. Concluez.

Si vous voulez que l'homme, sans déroger à son *détachement* merveilleux, jouisse de tous ces outils et instruments qu'il s'est fabriqué et ne soit pas embarrassé par leur multiplication même, eh bien, puisque c'est par l'usage de l'électricité qu'il a commencé de se dépêtrer, et que ses appareils de proche en proche sont devenus électriques, concluez.

Si vous voulez contribuer à ce qu'il redevienne l'ange tout rose et tout nu qui fut déposé ici-bas par la Nature, et qu'enfin plus jamais il n'en démorde, en dépit des songes métaphysiques les plus orgueilleux ou de regret de l'état de nature qui lui vient parfois, — mais il n'aura plus rien à regretter et ici tous les pessimistes auront tort;

Si vous voulez qu'il soit l'ange et l'athlète, à la fois nu et armé, spirituel et puissant, innocent et malicieux, désinvolte et songeur, ami de l'orgue et du cirque, enfin l'Ariel shakespearien qu'il est;

C'est facile. En lui construisant ses demeures, et au moment même de les concevoir, songez à l'électricité. Tous les réseaux de distribution sont prévus. Tous les instruments de la symphonie sont en place. Que dis-je tous? Il en viendra s'ajouter mille autres. Prévoyez seulement dans nos demeures le chemin à plaisir de tout cela.

Aidez-nous à refaire de lui cet Ariel.

Nous comptons sur vous.

Ainsi soit-il.

Mais je songe que je m'adresse à des techniciens, qui se défient peut-être un peu du lyrisme et ne goûteront qu'à demi

Conclude for yourselves.

If you want man to remain true to his marvelous *detach-ment*, and enjoy all of those tools and instruments that he has made without being hampered by their proliferation, well, since he began to free himself by using electricity, and since all appliances have become, step by step, electric, conclude for yourselves.

If you want to contribute to his becoming that angel, all pink and naked that was put here by Nature, and who, in the end, will never change again, despite the proudest meta-physical musings, or the nostalgia he feels at times for the state of nature—but he will no longer have anything to regret, and on this point all the pessimists will be in error;

If you want him to be that angel and athlete, both naked and armed, witty and strong, innocent and malicious, airy and dreamy, friend of the organ and of the circus, in a nut-shell, the Shakespearian Ariel that he is;

The answer is easy. Build him his dwellings, and at the very moment of conceiving them, think about electricity. All the electrical mains have been foreseen. All the symphonic instruments are in place. What am I saying, all? A thousand others will be added on. All you have to do is provide for the path of such pleasures in our dwellings.

Help us make him again that Ariel.

We are counting on you.

So be it.

But I realize that I am speaking to technicians who are perhaps slightly suspicious of this lyricism and will not really appreciate this prayer assimilating them to the gods. Conse-quently, I will find another way of ending, rather like the way I began.

une prière qui les assimile à des dieux. J'en finirai donc autrement, et plutôt comme j'ai commencé.

Ouvrant mon dossier, dans une vive lumière, j'en ai défini les intentions. Pour le clore dans la même lumière, il me faut résumer ce que j'ai dit.

Il me semble avoir montré que l'électricité a ses titres de noblesse, et, sans doute, de royauté; oui, des parchemins très anciens.

Il me semble avoir détruit l'argument qu'elle puisse être détrônée.

J'ai montré de plusieurs façons qu'elle nous permet de conquérir l'avenir tout en nous faisant mieux goûter le passé.

Démontré aussi qu'elle a bouleversé sans doute nos façons de vivre et modifié d'une manière irréversible nos goûts,

Mais en nous replaçant dans notre véritable état de nature, si bien qu'aucun moraliste ne saurait lui rien reprocher.

Enfin peut-être, chemin faisant, ai-je élucidé les raisons du retard, quant à l'Électricité, des poètes (et des architectes aussi bien).

Ces raisons sont de la nature des ombres. Sans doute suffisait-il de les éclairer pour qu'elles se dissipent...

Ainsi soit-il.

I had opened my folder in a bright light to define my intent. To close my folder, in the same light, I must sum up what I have said.

I think I have shown that electricity has its titles of nobility, and even of royalty: yes, its deeds are very ancient.

I think I have dashed all hope that it might be dethroned.

I have shown in several ways that it gives us a chance to conquer the future, while allowing us to better appreciate the past.

Also shown that it has unquestionably upset our ways of living and modified, in an irreversible manner, our tastes.

But it has done so by placing us once again in our true state of nature, in such a way that no moralist could ever find fault with it.

Finally perhaps, and in the process, I have explained why, as to electricity, poets (and architects as well) have lagged behind.

These reasons are inherent in the nature of shadows. All that was needed, I dare say, was to throw some light on them in order to disperse them . . . .

So be it.

From *Le Grand Recueil,* pp. 145-182.

ARDENS ORGANUM
(Extraits du *Malherbe*)

Dans la mesure où Malherbe dédaignait la Littérature, tout en lui assignant des règles on ne peut plus strictes, il est très proche de nous.

. . . .

C'est une littérature sans illusions.

Une activité décidée et prise de haut, pour des raisons éthiques fort précises, et peut-être en désespoir de toute illusion éthique, philosophique ou religieuse.

. . . .

Ainsi, le goût le plus difficile et le plus avancé trouve son compte à contempler Malherbe, et je ne dis pas s'y satisfait, mais s'en peut servir de tremplin, et s'y exalte.

. . . .

Peut-être un jour s'apercevra-t-on, peut-être deviendra-t-il clair que la principale qualité d'une oeuvre de langage, qu'il s'agisse de prose ou de vers, de philosophie ou de poésie (comme aussi bien de technique ou de journalisme) lui vient du goût qu'elle révèle quant au choix et à la mise en place des valeurs verbales (mots ou syllabes) qui la constituent.

Enfin des *sons significatifs* dont elle est faite, (lesquels se trouvent encore — depuis l'invention de l'écriture et plus encore depuis celle de l'imprimerie — être sensibles *à l'oeil.*)

Quand je dis la qualité principale, je veux dire celle qui assure l'effet le plus certain et le plus durable à la fois sur les sens et sur l'esprit de l'homme.

Quand je parle du goût qu'elle révèle, c'est que ce choix et cette mise en place sont commandés non du tout unique-

ARDENS ORGANUM
(Selections from *Malherbe*)

Malherbe is very close to us to the extent that he disdained Literature, all the while assigning to it the strictest possible rules.

. . . .

His is a literature without illusions.

An activity settled upon and at the highest level of the writer's vision for very specific ethical reasons, and perhaps in despair of all ethical, philosophical, and religious illusions.

. . . .

In this manner, the most demanding and the most advanced taste is rewarded when it contemplates Malherbe, and I do not say that it finds satisfaction in it but that it can use it as a springboard, and exalts in it.

. . . .

Perhaps one day it will become apparent, perhaps it will become clear that the principal quality of a written work, whether prose or verse, philosophy or poetry (technical subjects or journalism) comes from the taste that it reveals insofar as the choice and the disposition of verbal values (words or syllables) that constitute it.

And, of course, the *meaningful sounds* that compose it (that, furthermore—since the invention of writing and much more so since the invention of printing—make an impression on the *eye*).

When I speak of the principal quality, I mean that one which assures the most certain and the most durable effect both on the senses and on the mind.

215

ment par la raison, mais par le goût, par les sens, par une sorte d'instinct antérieur à ce goût même.

Mais comme aussi, dans les oeuvres de langage, la *signification* a une importance fort grande — aussi bien quant au besoin qui les conditionne, à la nécessité qui est à leur origine que quant à la possibilité d'accueil, d' « accord » qu'elles supposent et attendent de la part du lecteur ou de l'auditeur — c'est pourquoi le goût dont je viens de parler (goût physique, goût des oreilles et des yeux, des valeurs tonales et formelles) ne s'exercera-t-il pour ainsi dire que par des *censures.* C'est-à-dire qu'*étant donné ce qui est à dire* (à faire entendre, à communiquer) *l'écrivain refusera de le dire autrement que d'une certaine façon* (selon telle allure, tel timbre, etc.) *qui est justement celle que lui impose son goût, celui de ses sens.*

Il s'agit en somme ici d'un surcroît d'exigence, et donc, naturellement, si cette exigence est satisfaite, d'un surcroît de satisfaction et de volupté.

Qui est sensible à ce genre de valeurs, est un lecteur pour la poésie.

*

Ainsi comment faire le portrait d'un auteur, si ce n'est en y intégrant les traits de caractère décelables dans le *goût* qui dans sa création le conduit, secrètement, le détermine?

Sans doute, quand, tournés comme nous le sommes de préférence vers l'avenir, nous nous retournons avec amour et admiration vers un grand écrivain du passé, de ce passé *contre* lequel nous écrivons, en faveur de ce qu'il n'a pas su dire encore (du monde muet);

Sans doute pouvons-nous bien être les jouets de quelque illusion, attribuant à je ne sais quelle domination de caractère (supériorité de caractère) ce qui n'était peut-être que le fait de

When I speak of the taste it reveals, I mean that this choice and this order are not all solely formed by reason, but by taste, by the senses, by a sort of instinct anterior even to that taste.

Further, since *meaning* is very important in works that use language—as much in regard to the needs that condition them, the necessity that is at their origin, as well as the way they will be received, the "understanding" that it supposes and expects on the part of the reader or the listener—that is why, in speaking about taste (physical taste, ear and eye taste, formal and tonal values), it can only function, so to speak, through what it *eliminates.* That is to say, *given what must be expressed* (heard, communicated), *the writer will only express it in a particular manner* (according to a particular cadence, a tonal pitch, etc.) *which is precisely the one his taste and his senses dictate.*

We are here essentially concerned with greater expectations, and thus, naturally, if these expectations are met, with a greater satisfaction and voluptuousness.

Anyone sensitive to such values is a reader of poetry.

*

If this is so, how are we to draw the portrait of an author if not by including within it those character traits, discernible in his *taste*, which lead him in his creation, and determine his choices?

Although our preferences tend to the future, we turn back with love and admiration to a great writer of the past, this past *against* which we write, opting for what it had yet to learn how to articulate (of the silent world).

We may also well be the subject of some illusion, attributing to who knows what domination of character (superi-

l'époque et lui en venait naturellement et sans mérite.

Mais pourtant, il faut bien reconnaître que la même époque a vu nombre d'autres artistes, que nous ne pouvons créditer des mêmes supériorités, et nombre où se remarquent les défauts que notre héros évite, les manques qu'il ne connaît pas.

Lorsqu'il s'agit d'un maître dans la simplicité et la rigueur, c'est une autre façon de parler qui convient, et par exemple, nous parlerons alors des défauts, non qu'il évite, mais qu'il dissout dans ses qualités, et en somme dont il est capable, plutôt donc mauvaises qualités que défauts.

Ce qui fait la merveilleuse puissance, solidité, indestructibilité de Malherbe, c'est qu'il semble avoir eu le secret *d'un alliage.*

Il arrive à fondre toutes les qualités, bonnes ou mauvaises, même les plus contraires à ce qu'on appelle le classicisme, par exemple, les plus baroques, les plus précieuses aussi, celles dont se contentent, par faiblesse de nature (de tempérament) d'autres écrivains de son époque;

Il arrive, dis-je, à les fondre dans la superbe et simple pierre de taille dont sont faites ses oeuvres.

Il en est ainsi de tous les grands, les plus grands auteurs. *Tout y est*, même s'ils choisissent un ton particulier. On a l'impression que c'est *par excès* de génie (générosité de création), de capacité qu'ils deviennent simples, par une qualité supplémentaire à l'excès des autres, — sachant fondre en eux toutes les complications et les charmes de l'imperfection.

Par exemple, peuvent *encore* aimer Malherbe ceux qui sont à ce point blasés de la littérature et des beaux-arts en général qu'ils n'aiment plus que « les peintures idiotes ».

Supposons ainsi que nous en soyons au point où est parvenu Rimbaud quand il écrit : j'aimais les peintures idiotes... Il est bien certain que nous ne pourrons plus aimer les

ority of character) what may only have been at that time current practice which, therefore, came to him naturally and
without any merit.

And yet, it is evident that, in the same period, there were
a number of other artists who cannot be credited with the
same superiority, and a number who exhibited flaws that our
hero avoided, weaknesses that he did not know.

When we consider a master of simplicity and severity,
we must adopt another way of talking and, for example, we
should consider speaking about his flaws, not those that he
avoided but those that he dissolved in his qualities and those
that he mastered, so that they became like inferior qualities
rather than flaws.

What accounts for the marvelous strength, solidity,
indestructability of Malherbe is that he seems to have found
the secret for *alloying*.

He succeeded in fusing all the qualities, good or bad,
even those most opposed to what we call classicism, and for
example, the most baroque ones, as well as the most
"precious" ones, those that satisfied other writers of his time
because of a weakness of character (or nature).

I say that he succeeded in fusing them in the superb and
simple freestone out of which his works are carved.

This is so with all of the great, all of the greatest authors.
Everything is present, even when they select a particular
tone. One has the impression that it is by an *excess* of genius
(generosity of creation), of capacity, that they become simple, by a quality above and beyond the others—knowing
how to fuse in themselves all the complications and the
charms of imperfection.

Malherbe, for example, can *still* be loved by those who
are so blasé about literature, and the fine arts in general, that
they can only love "idiotic paintings."

« grandes » oeuvres, les « grandes » peintures que dans la mesure où elles comportent *de surcroît* les qualités des peintures idiotes, dans la mesure où elles nous permettent de les aimer *comme* peintures idiotes.

L'oeuvre des grands esprits est ainsi telle, qu'elle peut plaire encore aux esprits sans illusions.

*

Lien (*confusion*, au sens noble) du moral, du contingent et de la poésie (de la littérature) dans Malherbe.

D'où la *nécessité* de son lyrisme, et sa hauteur.

Ses besoins les plus contingents, les plus particuliers (les plus authentiques du point de vue marxiste) sont résolus en proverbes des plus nécessaires ; ce sont des maximes, des expressions vitales, aussi indispensables à son équilibre que les chants du rossignol, pour ne pas tomber de la branche.

Proverbes du plus haut-lieu, le lieu spécifique de l'espèce humaine, qui est une espèce parolière.

Il chante *pour* vivre.

Voilà pourquoi il est sur le Parnasse.

Musique pythagoricienne (?)

Le plus admirable est que ce ne sont pas des formules abstraites ; elles participent de la géométrie, des nombres, mais il s'agit de nombres *concrets*. Il s'agit de paroles, non de chiffres. Il s'agit des nombres concrets du Verbe, qui ont rapport aux Choses. Il s'agit de la nomination de choses du monde sensible, en *nombres sensibles*.

> Bien que de mes vertus je te croie la plus proche
> Décède aux lieux communs, tu es faite pour eux.

Bien marquer la différence entre les nombres de la géométrie, de la mathématique, — et ceux du Verbe, du Monde

Let us suppose we are now where Rimbaud was when he wrote: "I loved idiotic paintings...." It is obvious we will no longer be able to love "great" works, "great" paintings, except insofar as they *also* contain those qualities found in idiotic paintings, insofar as they allow us to love them *as* idiotic paintings.

The works of the greatest minds are such that they can still please individuals who have no more illusions.

*

A connection (*confusion*, in the noble sense) between the moral, the contingent, and the poetic (the literary) in Malherbe.

Therefore, the *necessity* for his lyricism and his loftiness.

His most contingent needs, the most specific ones (the most authentic, according to a Marxist point of view) are resolved in the most necessary proverbs; maxims, fundamental expressions, as indispensable to his equilibrium as the songs of the nightingale are to its ability to remain on the branch.

Proverbs of the highest level, the specific level of mankind, which is a speaking kind.

He sings *in order to* live.

That is why he is on Parnassus.

Pythagorian music (?)

What is most admirable is that they are not abstract formulas; they draw from geometry, from numbers, but *concrete* numbers. Words and not figures. The concrete numbers of the Verb, those that pertain to Things. The nomination of things belonging to the sensitive world, in *sensitive numbers.*

> Although I find you to be the closest to my virtues
> Die in the commonplaces you are made for.

221

sensible. Les uns ne sont que des divisions quantitatives de l'Unité ; les autres des espèces de la Pluralité, des variétés de la vie. Des harmoniques ou divisions *qualitatives* de l'Unité.

Elles signifient la vie, la variété. Elles exigent moins de l'esprit et risquent donc moins de partager ses erreurs.

La Poésie est alors la *science* la plus parfaite, non la Mathématique, ni la Musique. Tout ceci, senti intuitivement par moi, est encore trop confus, il me faudra y revenir et essayer de préciser. Différence de la musique verbale et de l'autre. Il s'agit ici d'un concert de vocables, de sons *significatifs*. Où la signification (c'est-à-dire, qu'on le veuille ou non, le rapport aux choses du monde extérieur, et leur évocation précise) entre pour une part (une assez importante part).

*

Breton pourrait dire, à mon sens, que Malherbe est « surréaliste de la raison ». En effet, il pousse la raison à un point... ! La Raison à haut prix. Au plus haut prix.

Folle enchère à la raison. La raison absurde.

Sainte-Beuve déjà trouvait que Malherbe « exagérait ».

Arland, à propos de Malherbe et de moi, déclare que « cette raison, dans sa folle rigueur, est peut-être un mode (le plus imprévu) de la poésie ».

Oui, c'est la poésie du « certainement ».

C'est le langage absolu. Le dictionnaire en ordre de fonctionnement.

La Parole parle. L'articulation du « Oui ». Le développement articulé de la syllabe nécessairement magique du OUI. De l'affirmation nécessaire au Verbe, lequel implique profération, donc prétention à la communication et naïveté foncière.

Mark well the difference between geometrical and mathematical numbers—and those of the Verb, of the sensitive World. The first are only quantitative divisions of Unity; the others, kinds of Plurality, varieties of life. Harmonics or *qualitative* divisions of Unity.

They signify life, variety. They are less demanding of the mind and are thus less prone to make its mistakes.

Poetry, rather than Mathematics or Music is then the most perfect *science.* I have felt all of this intuitively, and it still remains unclear; I will have to come back to it and try to make it more precise. Difference between verbal music and the other kind. Here, it is a concert of words, of *meaningful* sounds. Where the meaning (that is, whether one wants to or not, the relationship to the things of the exterior world, and their specific evocation) plays a part (a rather important part).

*

As I see it, Breton could have said that Malherbe's "reason was surrealistic." As a matter of fact, he drives reason to a point...! Reason at a high value. At the highest value.

Irresponsible bid for reason. Absurd reason.

Sainte-Beuve already thought Malherbe "exaggerated."

Arland declared about Malherbe and myself that "this reason, in its excessive demands, is perhaps a way (the least expected) for poetry."

Yes, it is a poetry of "certainty."

It is absolute language. The dictionary in working order.

Speech talking. The articulation of the "Yes." The articulated development of the necessarily magical syllable: YES. From the necessary affirmation to the Verb, which implies a

Langage absolu. Raison absurde. Résonnance dans le vide.

Rien à dire *égale* Tout à dire.

Ce qui résonne par sa seule forme.

Musique en forme d'orgue.

Résonnera à tout propos.

*

I. — Malherbe doit être considéré d'un point de vue supérieur à celui des historiens d'habitude.

Ce livre, si je l'achevais cette année, porterait la date de 1955. Pour son auteur la vie commence à peine. Pourtant, elle dure depuis un demi-siècle. Pour son objet, depuis huit fois autant seulement. Malherbe naquit en effet en 1555. C'était donc hier. Voilà ce que nous ne pourrons plus oublier.

Malherbe est né en Normandie. Si 1555 était hier, c'était donc avant-hier en 1055. Nous ne trouvons là, et alors, que Lanfranc, cet italien, né à Pavie, homme de lettres et coadjuteur de Guillaume le Conquérant en Angleterre, abbé de Bec et archevêque de Cantorbery. De cette époque date aussi la fondation, à Caen, de l'Abbaye aux Hommes.

Cent ans après, ce fut Wace ; et cent ans avant Malherbe, Formigny. Cent ans après Malherbe, Corneille. Cent ans avant nous, Flaubert. Nous ne pouvons guère nous assurer d'autre chose, sinon de l'Abbaye aux Hommes, et de la Fondation de l'Université de Caen et du Parlement de Normandie.

*

Pour ce qui est de ce qu'on appellera plus tard *La France* dans l'Histoire Générale et Universelle des Civilisations, ou,

clear delivery, consequently, a claim to communicate and a fundamental naïveté.

Absolute language. Absurd reason. Resonance in the void.

Nothing to say *equals* Everything to say.

Resonating solely due to its form.

Music in the shape of an organ.

Will resonate on any subject.

*

I.—Malherbe must be considered from a point of view superior to the professional historians'.

If I were to finish this book now, it would be copyrighted 1955. Life has just begun for its author. And yet, it has lasted for half a century. For the subject of his book, only eight times as much. Malherbe, in fact, was born in 1555. Just yesterday. This is what we can no longer forget.

Malherbe was born in Normandy. If 1555 was yesterday, 1055 was the day before. The only other man we can find at that time was Lanfranc, an Italian born in Pavia, man of letters, coadjutor of William the Conqueror in England, abbot of Bec, and archbishop of Canterbury. The founding of the Men's Monastery in Caen also dates from that time.

A hundred years later—Wace; and Formigny one hundred years before Malherbe. Corneille one hundred years after Malherbe. Flaubert one hundred years before us. There's nothing else we can be sure of except the Men's Monastery, the founding of the University of Caen and the Parliament of Normandy.

*

si l'on veut, dans la Caractéristique Universelle, nous manquons, certes, encore un peu de recul. La France, en effet, dure encore et n'a pas dit son dernier mot. Pourtant cette *valeur*, la France, y a sa place déjà bien marquée. Et peut-être a-t-elle déjà connu son apogée.

C'est de ce point de vue, supérieur à celui des historiens d'habitude, que Malherbe peut, avec le plus de profit, être considéré, qu'il prend toute sa valeur, sa stature.

(Un paragraphe sur le fait que son nom ne pourrait être omis par aucune histoire de la littérature française, même réduite au minimum. Et même par aucune histoire de France, du jour où l'on se rendra compte qu'à lui seul il vaut une institution comme l'Académie française, et qu'il fut un ministre d'Henri IV (puis de Richelieu), au même titre que Sully par exemple).

*

II. — Pourquoi il est cependant le plus discuté de nos grands auteurs. Parce que c'est un monument abrupt. Comme les murailles de Chaldée ou d'Égypte. Poésie de pierre grise abrupte. Raison abrupte.

Nous circulons à son pied. Nous n'avons pas le recul nécessaire. Nous avons le nez dessus.

Même, c'est une importance *encore supérieure*, qui lui vaut notre incompréhension. Car il se dresse à une hauteur telle qu'il rejoint au zénith les oeuvres supérieures de tous les horizons, de toutes les autres civilisations, de tous les horizons civilisés.

Quand les pétroles de Rouen flambèrent, en 1940, les énormes colonnes de fumées et de flammes (la flamme à l'intérieur de la colonne de fumée) qui montaient de chaque « bac » s'élevèrent avec une telle force ascensionnelle, d'un tel

As for what will later be called *France* in the General and Universal History of Civilizations or, if one prefers, in the Universal Characteristic, we still lack the necessary perspective. France, in fact, is still in existence, and has yet to speak its final word. Nevertheless, France as a *value* has already succeeded in marking its place. And perhaps it has already passed its highest point.

It is from this point of view, superior to the professional historian's, that Malherbe can be most profitably considered; that he takes on his true value, his stature.

(A paragraph to explain that his name could not be omitted from any history of French literature, even were it to be reduced to a minimum. And not even from any history of France, from the moment one realizes that, all by himself, he is worth an institution like the French Academy, and that he was one of Henri IV's ministers (later, Richelieu's), as Sully had been, for example.)

*

II.—Why is he still, nevertheless, the most controversial of our great writers? Because he is a blunt monument. Like the fortified walls of Chaldea or those in Egypt. A gray and blunt stone of a poet. Blunt reason.

We circle at his feet. We are not far enough. Our noses are right on it.

But we can't understand him for *an even more* important reason. For he rises to such a height that at the zenith he joins the superior works of all horizons, of all other civilizations, of all civilized horizons.

When the oil burned in Rouen, in 1940, the enormous columns of smoke and flames (the flames within the columns of smoke) rose from each "tank" with such an upward thrust,

élan, avec une telle fougue, qu'elles me parurent se rejoindre au zénith.

Ainsi en est-il des oeuvres les plus importantes de chaque civilisation. Ainsi en est-il de celle de Malherbe, et voilà une figure assez neuve peut-être pour le Parnasse (ou le Panthéon Universel).

(En quoi cette image n'est pas tellement inadéquate (celle de la tour de feu) : la parole en un sens s'élève comme la fumée, mais elle n'est touchante, impressionnante, que dans la mesure où des flammes sont sensibles en son centre. La parole douée de force ascensionnelle, ardente, fougueuse, et qui monte tout droit malgré le mouvement baroque, hélicoï- dal des flammes, et qui donne l'impression d'une haute tour, qui nous porte irrésistiblement, d'un seul coup, dès les pre- miers mots, à un niveau supérieur. Penser aussi aux tuyaux d'orgue, aux grandes orgues, aux cheminées, par où passe le souffle, l'animation, et qui vibrent et produisent des ondes, contagieusement entendues, ressenties fort loin. En un sens les strophes de poèmes dans la page ressemblent à des tron- çons de tuyaux ou de tours ou de cheminées. L'esprit y cir- cule, évolue un peu à la façon des flammes, s'élevant en spi- rales à l'intérieur. (Ne pas insister, c'est presque un lieu com- mun). (Ce qui n'est pas du lieu commun, c'est de donner de l'importance à la colonne de *fumées* (c'est aussi de conserver son importance au fait qui me saisit si fort à Rouen, à savoir que ces colonnes, bien que parfaitement verticales, se rejoi- gnaient au zénith). (Il faut donner toute sa force à la *couleur* du phénomène, ces formidables colonnes *noires* dans un ciel de mai, sans nuages) (et presque sans vent, du moins au sol. On sait que le phénomène fut aperçu dans toute une région de la France, et se répandit jusqu'à Paris. Nous l'aperçûmes, quant à nous, d'Alençon, où nous nous trouvâmes au petit

such a drive, with so much spirit, that they seemed to me to be joining at the zenith.

So is it with the most important works of each civilization. So is it with Malherbe's work, and here is perhaps quite a new figure to include on Parnassus (or in the Universal Pantheon).

(Why this image is not so inadequate (the one about the tower of fire): words, in a sense, rise like smoke, but they are only touching, impressive, insofar as one can feel the flames at the center. Words endowed with an upward thrust, blazing, spirited, and rising straight up despite the baroque, helicoidal movements of the flames, and that look like a high tower, which carry us irresistibly, at one go, from the very first utterances, to a superior level. Imagine, if you can, organ pipes, great organs, chimneys through which breathing passes, a sense of life, and that vibrate and produce waves, contagiously heard, and felt at a great distance. In a way, the stanzas of a poem on a page resemble pieces of pipes or towers or chimneys. The mind moves within them; evolves rather like flames, rising in spirals from the inside. (This shouldn't be stressed: it's almost a cliché.) (What is not a cliché, however, is to recognize the importance of the columns of *smoke*) (it is also a way of recognizing the importance of the fact that I so strongly experienced in Rouen, that is, that those columns, although perfectly vertical, met at the zenith). (One must emphasize the extraordinary *color* of the phenomenon, those tremendous *black* columns in a cloudless May sky) (and almost windless, at sea level. We know that this phenomenon was seen throughout a region of France and as far away as Paris. We ourselves caught sight of it in Alençon, where we found ourselves in the early morning hours of the following day). (Wasn't it,

matin du jour suivant). (Après tout, il s'agissait, ici encore, en un sens, par hasard, d'un phénomène normand...)

Quoi qu'il en soit, me revient ici à l'esprit ce que dit un auteur à propos de Malherbe, « qu'il s'élève au-dessus de la poésie habituelle parce qu'il rejoint la métrique latine des longues et des brèves. » Son ambition, me semble-t-il (je l'ai dit) est d'opérer la confusion de la raison et de la *réson*. Ou si l'on veut, du raisonnement et du résonnement.

Il ne s'agit plus ici ni de baroquisme, ni de romantisme, ni de classicisme, (ni de pré-classicisme). Surtout, il ne s'agit plus d'opinions ni d'idées. Il ne s'agit que du Verbe (le Verbe français) et de sa rigueur et force ascensionnelle, la plus magnifique qui ait jamais été; pourquoi dis-je rigueur? parce qu'il ne se produit aucune dispersion selon les horizontales, tout est dirigé (droites et courbes, flèches et volutes), très énergiquement et très constamment vers le haut.

L'on peut dire encore que c'est le dictionnaire français dans toute son épaisseur, qui flambe. C'est le dictionnaire français mis en ordre de fonctionnement, saisi par le feu, par l'esprit. Qui fonctionne autant, *au moins autant*, qu'il signifie.

De la caisse de résonnance du verbe français, de la lyre française elle-même.

Et voilà pourquoi c'est seulement depuis Lautréamont et le surréalisme qu'on commence à pouvoir le comprendre.

Il trépigne comme la Pythie. Comme les grands génies.

« A la fin, c'est trop de silence ! » Il piaffe d'impatience.

C'est de cette supériorité altière, et agressive (comme prométhéenne), qu'il tient cet air de défi éternel, de provocation qui le rend odieux aux petits esprits, Dieu merci ! et lui vaut sa vie, sa réacidification perpétuelle.

Quant à nous, nous savons bien que c'est le « calme

after all, and by chance, once again, a Norman phenomenon . . .)

Be that as it may, I'm reminded of something that an
author said about Malherbe: "That he rises above traditional
poetry because he applies the longs and the shorts of Latin
metrics." His ambition, it seems to me (I have said it), was to
bring about a confusion of reason and *reson*. Or stated differently, of reasoning and resonance.

We're no longer dealing here with the Baroque, romanti-
cism, classicism (or preclassicism). And especially no longer
with opinions or ideas. We're only dealing here with the Verb
(the French Verb), and with its rigor and upward thrust, the
most magnificent there ever was; why do I say rigor? Because there are no horizontal dispersions; all is directed (the
upright letters, the curved ones, the dips, the whirls), very
energetically and very uniformly toward the top.

It can further be said that it is the French dictionary, in
all of its volume, which is ablaze. It is the French dictionary,
put into working order, seized by fire, by the mind. That
functions as much, *at least as much*, as it signifies.

The sound-box of the French verb, the French lyre itself.

And that is why we have just begun to understand this
since Lautréamont and surrealism.

He prances like Pythia. Like all great geniuses.

"Enough! There's too much silence!" He stamps impa-
tiently.

It is because of this haughty and aggressive superiority
(Promethean) that he has about him an air of eternal defiance, of provocation, that makes him, thank God! odious to
little minds, and accounts for his life, his perpetual reacidifi-
cation.

As for us, we know very well that we could not tolerate

olympien » qui nous serait intolérable, car ce calme n'est que celui de la suie qui retombe.

Nous préferons cet orgueil, cette joie terrible.

Tel est le côté Malherbe, mauvaise herbe.

Il faut bien par quelque côté rejoindre les bêtes, la bêtise ! Ici, c'est par le défi *absurde* porté incessamment à la prétendue intelligence.

Quant à la rigueur, dire que la violence du désir (*parfaitement furieux*) (dit-il) jointe à l'impossibilité de l'objet suffi(sen)t bien à la produire.

Ce sont tout à la fois *la violence du désir* et *la hauteur* (l'éloignement extraordinaire, l'altitude *impossible*) *de l'objet* qui maintiennent la parole *en forme*. Beaucoup plus encore que les contraintes techniques (voilà où je ne suis pas tout à fait d'accord avec Valéry et la théorie classiciste traditionnelle). Il suffit de vouloir très fort atteindre un objet lointain (et précis) (impossible et précis) pour prendre le plus court chemin, la ligne droite, pour *prendre* aussi et garder *la forme* d'une flèche, la plus profilée, comme on dit, la plus tendue, la moins dispersée selon les horizontales, la plus ramassée, ceci à l'intérieur d'un espace respirable (d'un vide animé). Naturellement aussi la plus vibrante. Comme dans les fusées stratosphériques, le désir doit s'y relancer lui-même à chaque instant, la strophe ne doit pas être trop courte (la préférée sera le dizain) de façon à contenir sa provision de relances et à pouvoir les développer (quoique toujours dans la même direction, *vers le but*). Pour se garder en forme. La violence même de nos intuitions nous maintient en forme. *Non les règles.*

Réfléchir encore sur le rapport de mes torsades de fumées, contenant flammes à l'intérieur, avec le caducée d'Hermès. D'une façon générale avec l'hermétisme, qui ne doit pourtant pas être premier mais second, la fumée étant

this "Olympian calm" since it is only the calm of falling soot.
We prefer this pride, this terrible joy.

That's Malherbe's malediction.[1]

In one way or another, we've got to meet up again with
dumb creatures, with dumbness! Here, it is by perpetually
holding up *absurd* defiance to our so-called intelligence.

As for rigor, it's the violence of desire (*perfectly furious*)
(says he) joined to the impossibility of the object that is sufficient to produce it.

It is at once the *violence of desire* and the *loftiness* (the
extraordinary aloofness, the *unattainable* altitude) *of the
object* that keeps the words *in shape*. Much more so than
technical constraints (on this point, I'm not fully in agreement with Valéry and traditional classical theory). If one
truly wishes to reach a distant (and specific) object (unattainable and specific), one only has to desire it with sufficient
ardor in order to take the shortest way, the straightest line, to
take and also to keep the *shape* of the arrow, the most
streamlined, as the saying goes, the tautest, the least dis-
persed along horizontals, the most compact, and this, within
the confines of a breathing space (of an animated void). And,
of course, the most vibrant one. Like rockets in outer space,
desire must, out of itself, leap anew at each instant; the
stanza should not be too short (ten lines are preferable) so as
to contain its stock of renewed bursts and the possibility of
developing them (although always in the same direction,
toward the goal). To keep in shape. The very violence of our
intuition keeps us in shape. *Rules do not.*

Look further into the relationship between my coils of
smoke, with the flames inside, and Hermes' caduceus; in general, with hermeticism, which should never be first but sec-

1. Untranslatable pun based on the spelling: *mauvaise herbe* meaning
bad grass (S. G.).

évidemment produite par la flamme — et non le contraire. La fumée étant le résidu corporel qui brûle quand il est saisi par l'esprit. Mais il faut *qu'il y ait* du résidu corporel et c'est la fumée qui le signifie, qui signifie qu'il *y avait* du corps, que la flamme a brûlé *quelque chose*, qu'une assomption (ou consomption) s'est produite. Et une métamorphose.

Que la flamme à l'intérieur de la colonne de fumées, c'est encore l'épée du matador cachée dans la muleta. C'est encore l'épée d'Hamlet jouant dans le rideau (colonne torse) derrière lequel est Polonius.

Chaque strophe de Malherbe (beaucoup mieux que n'importe quelle maxime de philosophe (serait-ce Héraclite), c'est à la fois la flèche et la forge qui l'a produite. On entend le sifflement de la flèche, on la voit vibrer au coeur de la cible, et, *dans le même instant*, résonne sur l'enclume le marteau du forgeron antérieur. Ainsi, à la fois la *cadence* et le *rythme*. A la fois le commencement, les développements et la fin. L'évidence de l'harmonie (de la musique) *et* la certitude qu'il n'y aurait pas de musique s'il n'y avait pas d'instrument ; qu'en Epire y aurait-il eu de vent, il n'y aurait pas eu d'oracles s'il n'y avait pas eu de chênes et de feuillages (de frondaisons).

Déni de l'abstraction et justification de la Parole. Déni de la mathématique et justification de la poésie (prise en ce sens).

Il faut du désir, donc un objet, un objet sensible, un objet de sensations, pour qu'il y ait départ et persistance de la parole.

« Véritable Condillac du vers, dit Taine de Malherbe, etc... »

Les paroles ce sont évidemment la fumée, résidu du corps-du-désir qui a brûlé. *Ce qui* fulgure à l'intérieur, par instants seulement entrevisible (entr'aperçu) : voilà la justification ou plutôt la *raison* (indicible) du phénomène.

234

ond, smoke obviously being produced by the flame—and not the reverse. Smoke being the corporeal residue which burns when it is grasped by the mind. But a corporeal residue *must exist*, and smoke is its indication, an indication that *there was* a body, that the flames did consume *something*, that an assumption (or a consumption) did occur. And a metamorphosis.

Furthermore, that the flame within the columns of smoke is the matador's sword concealed in his muleta. It is also Hamlet's sword playing with the curtain (twisted column) with Polonius behind it.

Each of Malherbe's stanza (much better than any philosophers' sayings—even Heraclitus's), is simultaneously the arrow and the forge that produced it. One hears the whistling of the arrow, one sees it vibrate in the bull's eye, and *at that very instant*, one also hears resonating the blacksmith's first hammer blow on the anvil. Thus, at the same time, *cadence* and *rhythm*. At the same time, the beginning, the developments, and the conclusion. The evidence of harmony (of music) *and* the certainty that there would be no music without instruments; that in Epirus, even had there been wind, there would have been no oracles had there been no oaks and leaves (foliations).

Denial of abstraction and justification of the Word. Denial of mathematics and justification of poetry (understood in this manner).

There must be desire, therefore an object, a sensitive object, a sensual object, to assure a beginning and a continuity of speech.

According to Taine, "Malherbe was the true Condillac of poetry..."

Words are obviously smoke, a residue of the body-of-desire that has burned. *What* flashes inside, only half-visible

235

*

De même que — toute modestie et tout orgueil transcendés — nous devons nous résoudre (je ne dis pas nous résigner) à nous concevoir comme partie, élément ou rouage non privilégié de ce grand Corps Physique que nous nommons Nature ou Monde extérieur ;

De même ne devons-nous concevoir nos écrits que comme partie, élément ou rouage de cette horloge, ou comme branchette ou feuille de ce grand arbre — également physique — que l'on nomme la Langue ou la Littérature française.

Ce n'est pas que, tout comme un autre, nous n'essayions incessamment d'en sortir.

Mais nous devons constater aussi que nous n'en sortîmes, ni sortirons probablement, jamais.

Tel est le rapport de *croître* à *croire*, comme il se devait bien que nous nous l'explicitions un jour : nous voyons bien quelles intermittences de la conscience et de l'inconscience, quelles alternances de la naïveté et de l'expérience, de l'intelligence et de la foi nous sont nécessaires. Nous voyons bien aussi que notre nature est telle, notre tempérament tel, que nous ne nous endormirons jamais, ne nous reposerons jamais (quiétisme) en l'une ou l'autre de ces attitudes... Du moins, tant que nous continuerons à croître.

Voici aussi pourquoi nous préférons — et de loin ! — *croître* à *croire* : à cause de cette lettre de plus, le *T*, qui exprime la poussée de la cime, la poussée du tronc vers le haut, vers l'avenir. Nous n'aimons croire que dans la mesure où cela nous aide à croître ; nous détesterions croire dans la mesure où ce ne serait plus que croître amputé de son *T*, et dès lors tonsuré, ou châtré, ou reclus dans l'inaction physique, dans l'euphorie trompeuse de la satisfaction et du repos.

(half-seen) at times: there's the justification or rather, the (inexpressible) *reason* for the phenomenon.

*

In the same way—rising above all modesty and all pride —we must resolve (I do not say resign ourselves) to consider ourselves as a part, an element, or nonprivileged piece of machinery in the great Physical Body that we call Nature or the exterior World.

In the same way, we must consider our writing as a part, an element or a piece of machinery of that clock, or of a small branch, or a leaf of that great tree—also physical—that we call Language or French Literature.

That's not to say that, like everyone else, we are not constantly trying to get out of it.

But we must also acknowledge that we have not gotten out of it, and that probably, we will never do so.

The relationship between *flourish* and *faith*[2] is such that we knew we had to explain it someday. We recognize that for us the following are necessities: the intermittences of the conscious and the unconscious, the alternation between naïveté and experience, intelligence and faith. We also recognize that our nature is such, our temperament such, that we shall never fall asleep, never rest (quietism) in either one or the other of these two attitudes.... At least, as long as we continue to flourish.

That is also the reason why we prefer—and by far! — *flourish* to *faith:* because of that extra letter, the L, which expresses the upward thrust of the summit, the upward thrust of the trunk toward the sky, toward the future. We only have

2. Untranslatable pun based on the spelling: *croître/croire* (S. G.).

Ainsi, nos « Moments Critiques », ou « Proêmes », nous ne les concevons que comme ressortissant à la fois à l'une et l'autre de ces disciplines, et ce sont aussi nos « Moments Lyriques ». C'est ainsi que nous comprenons fort bien, à partir de là, que Lautréamont ait pu intituler *Poésies* ses réflexions ou maximes morales ou méthodologiques. Voilà encore pourquoi, notre oeuvre entière, nous pourrions (nous avons sérieusement songé à) l'intituler : « *Pratiques* ».

Ainsi, sans doute, de l'une à l'autre de ces nécessités, de ces urgences momentanées, n'aurons-nous *jamais de repos*.

Mais ainsi, aussi bien, nous sommes-nous, une fois pour toutes (et je ne dis pas que ce soit par résolution, car il en fut toujours ainsi, dès l'origine), une fois pour toutes, dis-je, établi dans le *perpétuel*.

*

Pour ce qui est de notre appartenance à la Langue et Littérature françaises, naturellement nous leur appartenons *en cime*, en plein ciel, face à l'avenir, à l'inconnu, à la nuit. Comme sa plus haute feuille (ou fleur ; en réalité plutôt feuille que fleur, nous le voyons bien — et nous pourrions expliquer pourquoi) ; enfin, en quelque façon j'y reviens, comme sa cime (du grec *cuma*, pousse extrême), ou sa proue.

A cela, nous ne pouvons *mais*, si (par ailleurs) nous en sommes fiers, absurdement fiers.

Mais nous sommes prêts à en convenir aussi : toutes les feuilles sorties ces derniers jours, c'est-à-dire tous les textes, imprimés ou publiés, participent aussi de cette même qualité. Nous aimerions seulement, il nous suffirait que toutes en soient aussi conscientes, et aussi fières.

Quant à ce livre même, ce présent livre, bien qu'il concerne racines et tronc dudit arbre nommé Langue et Littéra-

faith to the extent that it allows us to flourish; we would hate faith were it to become flourish amputated of its L and as of that moment, tonsured or castrated, or condemned to physical inaction, and fall into the deceptive euphoria of satisfaction and rest.

Thus, we see our "Critical Moments" or "Proems" as depending both, one and the other, on these disciplines; they are also our "Lyrical Moments."

That is the reason why we are truly able to understand how Lautréamont could entitle *Poems*, his thoughts or moral and methodological maxims. And that is also why (and we seriously entertained the idea) we might have entitled our complete works, *"Practices."*

And that is why, going from one to the other of these necessities, these momentary emergencies, we shall never be in a *state of rest.*

But that also explains why, once and for all (and I do not say that this came about through a resolution, because it was always like this, from the very beginning), I repeat, once and for all, we have established ourselves in the *perpetual.*

*

As for our place in Language and in French Literature, of course, we belong to them *at the summit*, in the open sky, facing the future, the unknown, the night. Like its highest leaf (or flower; rather more leaf than flower, that's clear— and we could explain it), but in the end, in whatever way, I always come back to it, as its summit (from the Greek *cuma*, outermost growth), or its prow.

We cannot add anything to that *but* (in other respects) we are proud of it, proud to the point of absurdity.

But we are also ready to agree that all the leaves that

239

ture françaises (puisqu'il concerne Malherbe), eh bien, il n'en est pas moins, lui aussi, qu'une feuille seulement, toute neuve, extrême, essayée, risquée — ce printemps — et destinée peut-être à en être tôt arrachée, à subir quelque chute ou catastrophe dans l'oubli, par hasard ou par l'effet de quelque tourmente contingente de l'atmosphère. Certes, nous n'ignorons pas cela, nous n'ignorons nullement le nombre de possibles sacrifiés chaque printemps.

Voilà, pour être honnête, ce que nous devions dire d'abord.

L'on voit la différence de notre prétention, de notre projet existentiel avec celui des écrivains, professeurs, historiens, critiques, voire poètes d'habitude. Nous sommes à la fois beaucoup plus prétentieux, en ce que nous n'ignorons pas que nous sommes la cime, la feuille suprême de la Littérature française, mais beaucoup plus humble aussi, pour ce que nous ne nourrissons point trop d'illusions sur le nombre de chances que nous avons de nous transformer en fleur, fruit, et graines, ou du moins en branchette, branche puis branche charpentière, plutôt que d'être arraché par le vent et d'aller pourrir par terre ici ou là, plus ou moins loin du pied sacré du père.

Il s'agit à la fois d'une prétention et d'un manque d'illusions, l'une sur l'autre réagissant pour augmenter, et peut-être — je veux le croire — *assurer* nos chances.

*

J'ai dit que ce livre concernait tronc et racines de l'arbre. Oui, et donc *ce* qui a été un jour, à un moment donné de l'histoire, dans la même situation que nous connaissons aujourd'-hui, celle de cime, de feuille extrême, risquée.

have recently come out, that is to say, all the texts, printed or published, equally partake of that same quality. We would be most pleased and satisfied if all of them might be as aware of it, as proud of it.

As for this book, this present book, although it deals with the roots and the trunk of a tree called Language and French Literature (since it deals with Malherbe), well, it too is still but a single leaf, all new, extreme, tested, ventured—this spring— and soon destined perhaps to be cut down, without our knowing it, and thrown to the ground, or stricken by some catastrophe, by chance, or the effect of some storm dependent upon the weather. We are obviously not unaware of that, the only thing we do not know is the number of possible victims that fall each spring.

In all honesty, that's what we had to say right off.

The difference is evident between our pretension, our existential project, and those of writers, professors, historians, critics, including professional poets. We are at once much more pretentious, since we know we are at the summit, the supreme leaf of French Literature, and much more humble, since we do not harbor any illusions on the number of chances that we have to transform ourselves into flowers, fruits, and grains, or at least, into a branchlet, branch, then the central branch, rather than being broken by the wind and finding ourselves rotting on the ground, here and there, more or less far away from the sacred foot of the father.

Therefore, it is simultaneously a pretension and an absence of all illusions, the one and the other interacting to increase and perhaps—I want to believe it—*to assure* our chances.

*

On voit dès lors comment nous *le* considérerons. Avec quelle fraternité; aussi quelle vénération. A la fois comme notre *cause* et notre exemple; notre origine et notre prison, et encore, nous devons le vouloir, notre *destin* (l'image de notre *meilleur* destin). Notre cause et notre destin (du moins devons-nous le vouloir).

Aussi comme notre plateforme, notre tremplin, rampe de départ (de *V2*).

On voit aussi quelle sorte de travail, la cime, se retournant (assez étrangement, et peut-être antinaturellement) pour considérer son tronc, son pied, peut avoir à y faire : un travail de désencombrement, de bêchage, de binage, de déblaiement.

En particulier, peut-être avons-nous à balayer, arracher de notre pied, toutes les études, gloses, etc... qui l'étoufferaient bientôt, empêcheraient l'arbre de respirer, de s'élever plus haut, qui *nous* empêcheraient de faire notre devoir face au ciel, face à l'avenir, — et peut-être empêcheraient l'arbre (considéré objectivement) de croître encore, puisque nous ne pensons pas — nous ne pouvons penser — qu'il ait dit son dernier mot.

*

Pour prétentieuse (prétentieuse, par définition : comme l'est, comme *doit l'être* une chose en train de naître, de croître, afin de parvenir au jour) — pour prétentieuse donc que puisse, lecteur, t'apparaître la première proposition de ce livre, celle-ci même, dont les mots que tu es en train de lire font déjà effectivement partie, — je ne t'épargnerai pas de la lire jusqu'au bout, car elle me semble adéquate à son objet et à son (à mon) projet, à la fois. Cette proposition, qui ne con-

I said that this book dealt with the trunk and the root of the tree. Yes, and consequently, *what* once was, at a given moment in history, in a situation similar to ours today, the summit, the outermost leaf, ventured.

It is immediately evident how we would consider *it*. With what fraternity, also with what veneration. At the same time, our *cause* and our example; our origin and our prison, and further, and we must surely want it, as our *destiny* (the portrayal of our *best* destiny). Our cause and our destiny (at least, we must want it).

Also as our platform, our springboard, our launching pad (for a V-2 rocket).

One can also appreciate what kind of task the summit must perform when it looks down (rather strangely, and perhaps contrary to nature) in order to observe its trunk, its foot: a task involving clearing, spading, hoeing, removal.

And perhaps, first of all, we should sweep away, rip out from under foot, all studies, glosses, etc., that would soon stifle it, that would stop the tree from breathing, from rising higher, that would stop *us* from performing our task, facing the sky, facing the future—and might perhaps stop the tree (considered objectively) from flourishing further, since we do not believe—we cannot believe—that it has spoken its last word.

*

However pretentious (pretentious, by definition: as a thing is, *must be* at birth, as it flourishes, in order to see the light) however pretentious, therefore, this first proposal of the book may appear to you, reader, these very words that you are in the process of reading already belong to it—I will

cerne encore que ce livre, la voici : ce livre même, comme tu le tiens entre tes mains, venant de l'ouvrir et parcours présentement la *ni*ème ligne de son texte, qu'est-ce donc? Sinon l'un des bouquets terminaux, l'une des cimes, ouvertes dans le ciel présent, vers l'avenir, de ce glorieux, de ce vétuste mais vivant encore grand arbre qu'est la Langue et Littérature françaises.

. . . .

Mais voici plutôt, — à un niveau supérieur encore — comment nous pourrions débuter :

Résolution de notre projet existentiel :

Pour commencer par la première proposition de ce livre, dont les mots que tu te trouves en train de lire font déjà effectivement partie, voici, me semble-t-il, que je t'en ai déjà infligé l'évidence : puisque tu me lis, cher lecteur, donc je suis; puisque tu nous lis (mon livre et moi), cher lecteur, donc nous sommes (Toi, lui et moi).

Profitant de la stupéfaction où elle te plonge, pour considérer cette révélation dans sa *valeur*, c'est-à-dire par rapport à celles dont tu as coutume et dont elle te tire, *primo*, puisque tu continues à nous lire, c'est donc que le langage français, à l'heure qu'il est, fonctionne encore, que l'accord sur ces signes continue; *secundo*, par rapport à l'axiome cartésien : « Je pense, donc je suis » , une nouvelle conception s'est fait jour : « Puisque tu nous lis, donc nous sommes » , suivi de : « L'accord sur ces signes continue. » Nous constatons objectivement notre accord sur ces signes, qui donc existaient antérieurement à nous et nous n'existons qu'en fonction d'eux. Au commencement donc était le Verbe. *Tertio :* cette modification depuis Descartes de l'esprit de notre nation est significative, et il n'est pas inutile de nous en être explicitement rendu compte, puisqu'elle indique le chemin parcouru

not spare you the reading of it to the end, for it seems to me to be adequate both to its object and to its (to my) project. This proposal, that so far only concerns this book, here it is —this very book, as you are holding it in your hands, having just opened it, and presently reading the *nth* line of the text, what can it be? If not one of the terminal bouquets, one of the summits, open in the present sky to the future, of this glorious, this decaying, yet still living, this great tree that is Language and French Literature.

. . . .

This is how we might—on a more elevated plane—begin this section:

Resolution of our existential project:

To begin with the first proposal of this book, whose words you are in the process of reading, that are already here actually a part of it; but I think that I have already inflicted the evidence on you: since you are reading me, dear reader, therefore I am; since you are reading us (my book and myself), dear reader, therefore we are (You, it, and I).

Taking advantage of the amazement into which this plunges you, let us consider this revelation on its own *terms*, that is, in relationship to those values that you are in the habit of acknowledging, and out of which you are pulled; *primo*, since you continue to read us it is a proof that the French language still works at the present time, that the agreement concerning these signs still persists; and *secundo*, in relationship to Descartes's axiom: "I think therefore I am," a new idea has just been suggested: "Since you are reading us, therefore we are," followed by: "The agreement on these signs still persists." We can thus objectively acknowledge our agreement about those signs that existed before us, and upon which our existence depends. Thus, in the beginning, was the

depuis qu'était cime *ce* qui est devenu tronc, et que la présente cime a pris à tâche de considérer.

Mais il n'est pas difficile de démontrer que *Malherbe*, quelques années à peine avant Descartes, *fut cime*, en train de devenir tronc lorsque Descartes apparut.

*

Pour nous, comme pour Malherbe, ce qui nous intéresse, on le voit, ce n'est donc pas tellement la *Poésie* (au sens où l'on entend généralement ce mot) que la *Parole*.

Quoi, la *Parole*? Eh bien, ce phénomène mystérieux — mystérieux dans son origine : les *raisons* de parler et d'écrire ; mystérieux aussi dans ses effets : l'accord qui se fait grâce à lui, la communication qui se réalise, le pouvoir temporel et intemporel qu'il procure.

Et certes, si l'on veut nommer *Poésie* celle qui ne concerne que ce phénomène mystérieux et adorable, la *Parole* ; qui la manifeste à la fois et la pratique, et la cultive ; qui ne s'occupe enfin que de son mystère, de son autorité et de son culte, alors c'est en effet la *Poésie* qui nous intéresse.

Pourquoi préférons-nous finalement Malherbe à Descartes? Parce qu'au « Je pense, donc je suis », à la réflexion de l'être sur l'être et au prône de la raison, nous préférons la Raison en Acte, le « Je parle et tu m'entends, donc nous sommes » : le Faire ce que l'on Dit.

Plutôt qu'une oeuvre devant s'intituler comme celle de Valéry : Charmes ou Poèmes, nous tentons une oeuvre dont le titre puisse être : Actes ou Textes.

*

Verb. *Tertio*, since Descartes, this has significantly modified the mind of this nation, and consequently, it was not without value for us to have become aware of it, since it indicates the distance covered from *what* was then the summit and is now the trunk, and that the present summit has now decided to consider.

But it is not difficult to show that *Malherbe*, just a few years before Descartes, *was the summit* in the process of becoming trunk when Descartes appeared.

*

Consequently, for us as well as for Malherbe, what is of interest is not so much *Poetry* (the way this is generally understood), but the *Word*.

What? The *Word*? Yes, this mysterious phenomenon—mysterious in its origins: the *reasons* why one speaks and writes; mysterious also in its effects: the agreement that is produced thanks to it, the communication that is assured, the temporal and the intemporal power that it procures.

And if one *wants* to give the name of *Poetry* only to the *Word*, that mysterious and adorable phenomenon that expresses it, and at the same time practices it and cultivates it, and which is solely preoccupied by its own mystery, its own authority and its own cult, then indeed we are interested in *Poetry*.

In the final analysis, why do we prefer Malherbe to Descartes? Because to his "I think therefore I am," to the meditation about Man on Man, to his homily on reason, we prefer Reason in Action, the "I speak and you understand me, therefore we are": The "Doing what one Says."

RAISON ET RESON CHEZ MALHERBE.

Malherbe ne raisonne pas, à beaucoup près, autant qu'il ne résonne. Il fait vibrer la raison. « Qu'en dis-tu, ma raison ? »

Il s'agit chez lui d'un véritable « surréalisme » de la raison (dès lors à mieux nommer *réson*). Voilà le mot très simple que nous n'avions pas trouvé encore quand nous avons intitulé l'un de nos textes (paru dans le « Surréalisme A.S.D.L.R. ») *les Plus-que-Raisons*. Et pourtant nous l'avions conçu bien auparavant, cf. la dernière strophe du « *Jeune Arbre* » : « Parle ! Parle contre le vent Auteur d'un fort résonnement. » (C'est ce que j'appelle à présent la *Raison-à-plus-haut-prix*, ou le *Paradis des Raisons Adverses*) (A la vérité, il ne s'agit pas, chez Malherbe, des raisons *adverses* : telle est ma différence).

Cette confusion, ou coordination sublime, entre Raison et Réson, résulte de (ou s'obtient par) la tension au maximum de la lyre. Le style concerté. Le concert de vocables.

Malherbe a ôté plusieurs cordes à la lyre, et d'autant plus tendu celles qu'il conserva.

Ce classicisme-là, le seul qu'il soit de notre goût d'admettre ou de prôner, n'est que la corde la plus tendue du baroque.

Ronsard et son école avaient ajouté je ne sais combien de cordes à la vielle de nos anciens poètes : cordes et rubans hellénistiques.

Après Malherbe, durant le XVIIe siècle, la corde se détend à nouveau. Elle se détend dès la « Satisfaction ». Dès (d'autre part) que l'on *part* des règles, au lieu d'y aboutir.

Cette vibration de la corde la plus tendue, c'est exactement ce tremblement passionné, ce *tremblement de certitude*

Rather than a work that might be entitled like Valéry's, Charms or Poems, we are trying to write a work whose title might be: Acts or Texts.

*

REASON AND RESON IN MALHERBE

All things considered, Malherbe does not reason as much as he resonates. He makes reason vibrate: "What say you to that, my reason?"

In his case, it was really "surrealistic" reason (henceforth, better referred to as *reson*). That is the very simple word we hadn't yet found when we entitled one of our texts (published in "Surréalisme A.S.D.L.R.") *These-More-Than-Reasons*. And yet, we had thought of it much earlier, see the last stanza of the "Young Tree": "Speak! Speak against the wind, Author of a mighty resonance." (That's what I now call *Reason-at-Its-Highest-Reach* or the *Paradise of Adverse Reasons*.) (Strictly speaking, for Malherbe it was not a question of *adverse* reasons: this is where I differ from him.)

This confusion or sublime coordination between Reason and *Reson* results from (or is reached by) a maximum tension of the lyre. The concerted style. The concert of vocables.

Malherbe removed several strings from the lyre, all the tighter those that he retained.

This brand of classicism, the only one that our taste finds both acceptable and worthy of praise, is but the tightest string of the Baroque.

Ronsard and his school added who knows how many strings to the fiddle of our ancient poets: Hellenistic strings and ribbons.

que P. jugeait odieux chez moi, lorsque je venais de lui apporter mes « Proêmes ».

C'est le ton affirmatif du Verbe, tout à fait nécessaire pour qu'il « porte ». C'est le OUI du Soleil, le OUI de Racine, le OUI de Mallarmé; c'est le ton *résolu*, celui de ce que j'ai appelé la « résolution humaine », celui de la résolution stoïque : « à tout prix la santé, la réjouissance et la joie ». C'est enfin la seule justification de la Parole (prose ou poésie), une fois franchies toutes les raisons de se taire. C'est la décision de parler.

Allons-nous écouter les conseils des concierges ou des malades, des complexés de la littérature? On nous fatigue et décourage en nous vantant incessamment les mérites de la modestie.

Il s'agit, disais-je à propos de Mallarmé, de la massue cloutée d'expressions-fixes, permettant d'asséner le coup-par-supériorité; de la massue non-signifiante. Eh bien : rien de plus « beau », de plus méritoire, de plus difficile que de parvenir à porter ce coup à l'aide d'expressions signifiantes, valables sur le plan et au niveau de la communication, ou du discours, ou de la raison.

Cette vibration de la corde tendue, ce tremblement (à la fois de désir et de certitude) *comporte* nécessairement le sentiment de la victoire, de la conquête *possible*, donc d'un pouvoir, donc d'une supériorité relative (non tellement relative à son objet, mais relative à ses autres prétendants, si l'on y songe), donc l'orgueil. L'orgueil convient aux poètes, dit (à peu près) Ménage, car il est un effet de leur enthousiasme.

D'où, pour les petits esprits, son caractère odieux, antipathique... et, pour les esprits forts, le caractère réjouissant, exaltant d'un tel précédent, d'un tel exemple. Malherbe est sans doute un des seuls poètes qui aient donné lieu à tant d'inimitiés qu'un livre ait pu être consacré à cette passion

After Malherbe, in the course of the seventeenth century, the string is loosened again. It relaxes as soon as "Satisfaction" is attained. As soon as (on the other hand) one *begins* with the rules instead of ending with them.

When I gave my "Proems" to P, it was exactly this passionate trembling, this vibration of the tightest string, this *trembling of certitude*, that he found odious in my work.

It is absolutely necessary for the Verb to have its affirmative tone in order for it to be "understood." It is the Sun's YES, Racine's YES, Mallarmé's YES; it is the *resolute* tone, the one that comes from what I have called "man's resolution," the Stoics' resolution: "at all costs, health, pleasure, and joy." Finally, it is the only justification for Writing (prose or poetry), once all the reasons to remain silent have been cleared away. It is the decision to speak.

Are we going to heed the advice of the *concierges* or the sick, the neurotics of literature? We are worn out and discouraged by having the merits of modesty incessantly pointed out to us.

As I was saying about Mallarmé, we are dealing with a bludgeon fitted out with nailheaded expressions that allows one to deliver the master stroke of superiority; of the nonsignifying bludgeon. Well! there is nothing more "beautiful," more worthy, tougher than to strike back with the aid of meaningful expressions, valid on the level and in the area of communication, or discourse, or reason.

This vibration of the taut string, this trembling (both of desire and certitude) necessarily *carries* the sense of victory, of the *possible* conquest, consequently of a power, consequently of a relative superiority (not so much relative to its object, but relative to the other possibilities, if one thinks about them), consequently of pride. Pride fits poets, so says (more or less) Menagius, for it is an effect of their enthusiasm.

(« l'Antipathie contre Malherbe », par Dejob).

Donc, odieux mais enthousiasmant à la fois. Enthousiasmant et mécanisant à la fois. Comme un ressort tendu entraîne des mécanismes. Et je n'emploie pas sans référence une telle expression. (Ici la citation de Pellisson à propos de l'effet produit sur le jeune La Fontaine par la révélation de Malherbe. Citation aussi de Baudelaire : « de longues extases »).[1]

Mais l'antipathie elle-même... Je ne suis pas loin de croire que là réside la meilleure garantie de la vie éternelle de ces textes (leur caractère provocant, au meilleur sens du terme).

Fûts d'arbre (ou de colonne) et *fut*, passé simple de l'Etre (à la troisième personne du singulier): voilà qui, dans la Réson, signifie certainement quelque chose.

Et ainsi des allitérations et assonances, qui viennent, dans le bonheur et l'autorité d'expression, confirmer la signification. Le rythme, n'en parlons pas : c'est trop évident.

*

NOUVEAU PLAN

I. — Qu'on ne nous croie pas devenu *passéiste* pource

---

1. Voici la citation de Pellisson (Histoire de l'Académie Française, 1652) : « Il (La Fontaine) étudia sous des maîtres de campagne, qui ne lui enseignèrent que du latin, et il avait déjà vingt-deux ans, qu'il ne se portait encore à rien, lorsqu'un officier, qui était à Château-Thierry en quartier d'hiver, lut devant lui par occasion, et avec emphase, cette ode de Malherbe : « *Que direz-vous, races futures...* » Il écouta cette ode avec des transports mécaniques de joie, d'admiration et d'étonnement. [...] Il se mit aussitôt à lire Malherbe et s'y attacha de telle sorte, qu'après avoir passé les nuits à l'apprendre par coeur, il allait de jour le déclamer dans les bois. » Quant à la phrase de Baudelaire, elle est assez connue, nous ne la citerons pas.

That is why little minds consider it odious and disagreeable...and strong minds are heartened and exulted by the idea of such a precedent, of such an example. Malherbe is probably one of the few poets who has given rise to so much enmity that a book was devoted to this passion (*Aversion for Malherbe* by Dejob).

Therefore, odious but inspiring at the same time. Inspiring and mechanizing at the same time. As pieces of machinery respond to a taut string. And I do not use this expression without proper references. (Pellisson's quote made on the effect that Malherbe produced on the young La Fontaine when he first read him is cited below; also Baudelaire's quote: "Long ecstasies").[3]

But as for aversion...I would go as far as to say that the best guarantee for the eternal life of those texts depends on that reaction (their provocative character, in the best sense of the word).

Bole of the tree (or of the column) and *be*,[4] the imperative of Being (second person, singular): that certainly has something to do with *Reson*.

Similarly for alliterations and assonances that, along with a perfectly harmonious expression, come to confirm the meaning. As for rhythm—let's not even mention it: it's too evident.

3. Pellisson's quote: "He (La Fontaine) studied under country masters who only taught him Latin, and he was already twenty-two years old, and had yet to do something when an officer in winter quarters in Château-Thierry read him, by chance, and in an emphatic manner, Malherbe's ode: *"What will you say, peoples of the future..."* He listened to this ode with mechanical transports of joy, admiration and surprise.... He immediately began reading Malherbe and found him so extraordinary that, after having spent nights learning him by heart, he went about during the day declaiming him through the wood" (*Histoire de l'Académie française* [1652]). As for Baudelaire's sentence, it is too well known and we shall not quote it.
4. Untranslatable pun based on the spelling: *fût/fut* (S. G.).

que nous nous plaisons à Malherbe. Non, nous n'oublions pas l'avenir.

Parabole de l'arbre (la feuille, la pousse extrême vénérant le tronc).

II. — Raison et réson chez Malherbe.

III. — Actualité de ce comportement. Polémique contre les humilistes et réactionnaires (et révolutionnaires) de divers poil.

*

MYSTÈRES DE LA CRÉATION VERBALE.

Aux moments où l'*inspiration* est pressante, urgente et où la *corde sensible* est trouvée (corde unique), celle-ci ressemble aussi à un *thalweg* qui exprime alors tout un bassin, voire le monde-entier : tout va à la rivière, tout y afflue, tout lui apporte de l'eau. (Cf. le dernier morceau (de bravoure) de *La Seine*).

Il semble que le monde entier s'organise en sa faveur, les tiroirs du vocabulaire et des associations s'ouvrent, tout y dévale... Et de fait, il n'y a qu'à peine à modifier chaque élément offert (qui s'offre) ou entraperçu, pour qu'en effet il y rentre, et aide à confirmer, à enrichir la preuve, à apporter des arguments supplémentaires etc...

La *Vérité* alors *jubile*.

C'est l'afflux des spermatozoïdes dans la fente féminine ouverte et accueillante, en état de rut, en état de vide (celui dont la Nature a horreur et où tout se précipite, pour le combler). Rapport phonétique entre *viduité* et *évidence*.

Cela est tellement sensible chez Shakespeare, par ex.

NEW PLAN

I.—Let no one think we have become enamored of the past because of our interest in Malherbe. No, we have not forgotten the future.

Parable of the tree (the leaf, the outermost growth venerating the trunk).

II.—Reason and *reson* in Malherbe.

III.—The actuality of this comportment. Polemic against the Uriah Heeps and the reactionaries (and the revolutionaries) of various shadings.

*

MYSTERIES OF VERBAL CREATION

At moments when *inspiration* is pressing, urgent, and when the *sensitive string* has been found (the single string), one that also resembles a *thalweg* which then expresses a whole basin, indeed, the whole world: then everything goes toward the river, everything flows into it, everything carries water to it. (See the last [bravura] section of the *Seine*).

It seems the whole world organizes itself in its favor: drawers of words and associations are opened, everything empties into it . . . . And as a result, there is hardly any need to modify each element offered (that offers itself) or perceived, in order to assure that it contributes and helps to confirm, to enrich the proof, to bring further arguments, etc.

Truth then *jubilates.*

Spermatozoids flow into the feminine slit, willing and

Telle est l'unité par générosité (par génie) et non l'unité par manque (par austérité ou simplisme).

*

1. On nous dit que « Malherbe fonde une doctrine de la difficulté ». Non. C'est plutôt à mon avis, chez lui, ce que j'ai appelé « la difficulté *à plaisir* ». Sans doute serait-il plus exact de dire qu'il a *le goût* de la difficulté et qu'il le déclare, car à fonder la difficulté en doctrine? Non, il ne le fait pas. Mais un goût tel, oui, il le proclame. Ainsi : « Un bien sans mal ne me *plaît* pas ». « Où le danger est grand, c'est là que je m'efforce », etc...

2. On nous dit que « ses exigences techniques sont des impératifs catégoriques ». Peut-être est-ce exact. Mais voici comment je nuancerai cette affirmation (peut-être, ce faisant, la renverserai-je).

Je le vois bien, en effet, se refuser *jusqu'au dernier moment* toute infraction aux règles posées d'abord : règles qu'il a pu formuler verbalement, c'est possible, ou à l'occasion de sa lecture critique de Desportes, car il faut bien rappeler encore qu'il n'a jamais publié aucun traité. Pourtant, l'on n'a pas manqué de constater qu'il n'était aucune règle qu'il n'ait lui-même transgressée en quelque occasion. Qu'est-ce à dire? Qu'en conclure plus justement?

Il me semble que les règles (exigences techniques) sont posées d'abord comme impératives, pour que la difficulté qu'elles soulèvent, l'obstacle qu'elles dressent, oblige à piétiner, à marquer le pas, à faire comme on dit du « sur place », voire à s'enfoncer, à s'enterrer sur place, comme un assiégeant devant un mur. Cela, à la vérité, dans quelle intention (secrète)? Eh bien, je crois que c'est pour obliger à *attendre*, je crois que *c'est le moyen* d'attendre; mais d'attendre *quoi*?

welcoming in a state of rut, in a state of emptiness (a condition that Nature abhors and where everything rushes in to fill it). Phonetic relationship between *viduage* and *evidence*.

That is so apparent in Shakespeare, for ex.

Such is unity by generosity (by genius) and not by absence (austerity or ignorance).

*

1. We are told that "Malherbe made difficulty into a doctrine." False. It is rather, in his case, as I see it, what I have called *"an abundance* of difficulty." It would certainly be more appropriate to say that he had a *taste* for the difficult and that he admitted it. As for making difficulty into a doctrine? No, he doesn't do it. But a taste for it, yes. He proclaims it. For example: "Pleasure without pain does not *please* me." "Where the danger is the greatest, there I do my best," etc.

2. We are told that "his technical demands are categorical imperatives." That may be. But I would modify that affirmation in the following way (perhaps in so doing, overturn it).

I see him, quite clearly, refusing *up to the last moment*, to break any of the established rules: rules that he may have formulated verbally, that's possible, or during his critical reading of Desportes, because one must always remember that he never published any treatises. Still, it has been noted that there were no rules that he himself did not fail to break at some time or other. What does that mean? And, what conclusions can be drawn from this?

It seems to me that rules (technical requirements) are

D'attendre, je crois, que se vérifie qu'il n'existe pas de meilleure formulation (que celle qu'on a trouvée d'abord); d'attendre au besoin d'autres tours; de laisser à d'autres expressions ou formulations le temps matériel d'arriver, le temps de sortir de l'oubli et de se présenter, d'apparaître sur le champ de bataille ou sur l'établi où l'on travaille. Pour créer une *accumulation* de forces.

Il faut bien se rappeler en effet (et cela, seul un « créateur » sans doute peut un jour se le rappeler, parce qu'il l'a éprouvé lui-même) comment *cela se passe* dans le travail de l'expression verbale (je n'ose pas dire poétique).

Bien qu'il me semble qu'il sera toujours plus juste de comparer à Malherbe, plutôt que Flaubert par exemple, Cézanne, prenons pourtant Flaubert, puisqu'il s'agit d'expression verbale (et par ailleurs d'un normand). Le comportement de Flaubert est sans conteste celui d'un *artiste*, c'est-à-dire quelqu'un dont les intuitions dominent l'intellect, quelqu'un pour qui tout commence par une sensation, par une émotion. Qu'on songe par exemple à ce qu'il a dit que, dans Mme Bovary, il voulait tout simplement exprimer un certain ton jaune. Eh bien, Flaubert, certes, plus que personne, connaît les affres de la phrase, les supplices de l'assonance, les tortures du rythme recherché, les tortures de la période, mais il n'a formulé à ma connaissance, non plus, aucune règle. Tout n'est jamais chez lui, chaque fois, qu'un cas d'espèce. Bien noter cependant que dans Flaubert il s'agit d'une sorte de réalisme, d'antériorité du monde extérieur et de la sensation ou de l'émotion qu'il en a reçue, tandis que dans Malherbe, il s'agit d'un nominalisme, il ne s'agit que d'une certaine perfection absolue de la Parole. Mais les tortures sont les mêmes, elles viennent d'un idéal fermement aperçu d'abord, quoiqu'informulé et auquel l'artiste ne peut que rester farouchement fidèle, avec lequel il ne peut en aucun cas transiger. Il attend,

initially layed down as imperatives so that the difficulty they raise, the obstacles they erect, force us to mark time, to wait, and, as the saying goes to "step in place," even more than that, to dig in, to entrench oneself like a besieging army in front of a wall. And all that for what (secret) purpose? Well, I believe it is meant to make us *wait*, I believe it is the *way* that allows us to wait; but to wait for *what*? To wait, I believe, for proof that no better solutions exist (than the one initially found); to wait, if needs be, for other opportunities; to allow other expressions or solutions the material time to arrive, the time to be recalled from memory, and present themselves on the field of battle or on our workbench. In order to create an *accumulation* of forces.

One should in fact remember (and only a "creator" one day may remember it, because he himself experienced it) how *this occurs* in working out a verbal expression (I dare not say poetic).

Although I will always find it more accurate to compare, for example, Malherbe to Cézanne, rather than to Flaubert, nevertheless, let us take Flaubert, since we are discussing verbal expression (and besides, by a Norman). Flaubert's behavior is indisputably that of an *artist*, that is to say, someone whose intuition dominates his intellect, someone for whom everything begins with a sensation, with an emotion. Consider, for example, as Flaubert said himself, that all he wanted to express in *Madame Bovary* was a particular shade of yellow. Undoubtedly, Flaubert, more than anyone else, knew the anguishes of the sentences, the torments of assonances, the tortures of perfect rhythm, the tortures of the rhetorical period, but, as far as I know, he also did not formulate any rules. Everything is always, for him, in each instance, a specific case. Note well, however, that Flaubert was involved in a type of realism, a precedence of the exterior

il essaye, il ne se satisfait jamais à bon marché, à bon compte. Il ne s'agit jamais que de cela. Primo, de ne pas désespérer de pouvoir réaliser un jour l'expression selon *son goût*. Secundo, de rester inexorablement fidèle à son exigence première, de laisser (tant que c'est nécessaire) permaner cette exigence ; je dis bien la première : celle antérieure à toute formulation, celle qui se manifesta au moment du choc, de la rencontre, de la nette vision du projet. Ainsi Van Gogh décrivant, en termes de couleurs (couleurs de marchand de couleurs) les paysages qui l'émurent.

Dès lors, comment faire ?

Peut-on dire que cette formulation idéale, que l'on sait possible, dont on sait qu'elle existe et qu'il ne s'agit que de l'attendre, peut-on dire qu'on la *cherche* ?

Certes oui, on cherche ; on cherche par exemple dans le trésor de Littré ; on peut chercher dans les dictionnaires de rimes, dans ceux de synonymes ; fréquenter les dictionnaires, s'entourer d'expressions, tenir son vocabulaire en éveil.

Mais non ! Il s'agit surtout d'*attendre*, d'être à l'affût, afin de capter au passage. Souvent l'on ne se rendra compte que beaucoup plus tard de certaines des raisons de l'élection.

Pourquoi ?

Parce que le *nombre* des tours et des formulations, bien qu'il soit *fini* — je veux dire bien qu'il ne soit pas *infini* — toutefois est très grand ; si grand qu'il ne peut être à notre disposition dans sa totalité à chaque instant. Ainsi faut-il attendre, et se borner *à refuser* tout ce qui n'est pas ce que nous attendons, et que nous reconnaîtrons à n'en pas douter, quand il se présentera.

Ainsi faut-il ressasser incessamment son exigence ; étant donné son « sujet » (qui *comporte* le lecteur, la situation tactique, enfin une sorte de point d'équilibre vital), ressasser incessamment la forme vide de son rythme initial, sa couleur,

world and of the sensation or the emotion that he received from it, whereas Malherbe was interested in a form of nominalism, only interested in a certain absolute perfection of the Word. But the tortures are the same, they come from an ideal perfectly understood initially, though nonformulated, to which the artist remains unalterably and fiercely faithful, and to which he will always be true. He waits, he tries, he is never satisfied by a cheap or an easy answer. Nothing else matters. *Primo*, never despair of being able to find, one day, a way of writing in conformity with *one's taste. Secundo*, remain inexorably faithful to one's initial exigencies, to maintain this exigency (as long as it is necessary), I repeat, the initial one: the one that preceded all solutions, the one that manifested itself at the moment of shock, of the encounter, when the idea of the project was first envisioned. This is the way Van Gogh described, in terms of colors (colors of the color salesman), the landscapes that moved him.

What is to be done after that moment?

Can it be said about this ideal solution, that one knows to be possible, that one knows exists, and that will come in time, can it be said about it that one really *searches* for it?

Of course, one searches: one searches, for example, in Littré's treasure; one can search in dictionaries devoted to rhymes and synonyms; one can befriend dictionaries, surround oneself with expressions, keep one's vocabulary awake.

Of course not! It is essentially a matter of *waiting*, lying in wait, in order to catch it on the go. It is often much later that one will have understood certain reasons for the choice.

Why?

Because the *number* of expressions and solutions, although *finite*—I stress that they are not *infinite*—still are very considerable; so considerable that we cannot dispose of

dans une certaine mesure sa forme (plastique), et ressasser tout cela avec une telle aspiration, une telle force d'appel, que dans cette exigence *vide*, dans cette forme, on appelle incessamment la matière verbale, exactement comme on amorce une pompe. Cette aspiration se fait par les moyens, les conduits, les tuyaux les plus étroits, les plus autoritaires, les plus impérieux : il faut aspirer très fort, créer une tension maxima et en même temps être assez adroit, savoir capter, appeler, retenir, enfin je ne peux mieux dire, c'est le travail d'amorçage d'une pompe.

Ainsi, si Malherbe édicte (ce n'est pas le terme exact) certaines règles si précises, si difficiles, si comminatoires, concernant la rime par exemple, c'est *justement* parce que *là n'est pas l'essentiel*; non, du tout, on ne peut dire que ce soit cela qu'il cherche; ce n'est que le moyen, qu'un des moyens qu'il connaît pour induire le courant, pour amorcer la pompe. De ces moyens peut-être en est-il bien d'autres? Ce genre d'exigences ne fait que dresser l'obstacle qui fera jouer les muscles du cheval, qui obligera la bête (le Verbe) à faire jouer visiblement tous ses muscles, à en faire bellement et utilement montre. Rimes « stériles », pourquoi? Parce que cela appelle des idées éloignées? Sans doute : c'est ce que l'on appelle créer une tension; — et qu'il faudra bien, dès lors, puisqu'on *ne peut* être que clair, limpide et simple (on n'est pas poète, on est positif), il faudra bien, dès lors, passer par toutes sortes d'harmoniques, de nuances, d'erreurs relatives, de valeurs proches, de degrés qui densifieront, et rendront indestructible l'ensemble, — et feront finalement de votre intuition, proverbe; de votre bon plaisir le plus arbitraire, loi-générale, obligation toute-simple pour tous.

La rime, visiblement, ne suffit pas comme obstacle : c'est le minimum. Les rimes ne sont que les deux touches initiales qui créent la tension. (C'est ce que dit Bonnard de

them in their totality at every moment. Thus, we have to
wait, to limit ourselves to a *refusal* of everything we didn't
expect, and that we will recognize, without a doubt, when it
does appear.

Consequently, and at all times, one must review again
and again one's demands; given one's "subject" (which
includes the reader, the tactical situation; and, in the end, a
sort of vital point of equilibrium), at all times, review again
and again the form, empty of its initial rhythm, its color, to a
certain degree, its (plastic) form, and review again and again
all that with such aspiration, such power of recall, that in this
empty exigency, in this form, at all times, one calls forth the
verbal matter, in a manner similar to the way one primes a
pump. This aspiration is determined by means, conduits,
pipes that are the narrowest, the most authoritarian, the
most imperious ones: one must inhale very strongly, create a
maximal tension and, at the same time, remain sufficiently
clever, knowing how to capture, bring forth, retain, so that,
in the final analysis, I can only compare it to the way one
primes a pump.

Thus if Malherbe decrees (that's not the exact word) certain rules concerning rhymes, for example, that are so specific, so difficult, so comminatory, it is *exactly* because the
essential is not there; no, not at all, one cannot say he is
searching for that; it was only a way, one of the ways he
knew how to induce a current, prime a pump. Are there
many others? This type of exigency only raises obstacles that
will exercise the horse's muscles, that will force the beast (the
Verb) to flex all of its muscles publicly, making a beautiful
and useful display out of it. Why "sterile" rhymes? Because
this evokes remote ideas? Most likely: this is what is called
creating a tension: and it will then have to be, since one *must
be* clear, limpid, and simple (one is not a poet, one is posi-

Cézanne : « Il suffit qu'il pose deux tons... ») Mais une richesse inouïe de consonances, d'assonances et d'allitérations, dosées d'ailleurs de telle façon que la signification l'emporte (très légèrement mais enfin l'emporte) sur le concert de vocables, sur la musique : voilà le fin du fin.

*

MECANISME ou MACHINERIE

Les impératifs techniques (rimes rares et stériles, césures, pas de hiatus, strophes à sens complets, sonnets réguliers, etc.) ne servent au fond que de clefs de tension.

On finit par les transgresser s'il le faut.

Ils sont là pour délimiter *le champ* de l'objet textuel, et peut-être pour le créer. Pour créer la tension, le champ de forces.

Mais, comme il est parfaitement impossible d'obéir toutes les règles à chaque instant, on finit, dis-je, par les transgresser (l'une ou l'autre, et finalement, au bout du compte, on les a transgressées *toutes*, une fois ou l'autre).

NOS règles véritables, celles qui ne peuvent être formulées, car ce n'en sont pas, ce ne sont que des censures instinctives; *nos règles*, dis-je, sont bien plus graves, bien plus impérieuses, bien plus arbitraires. Ce sont comme des obsessions impératives, des manies, des rites, des inhibitions, des phobies personnelles.

Peut-être, justement, est-ce dans la mesure où nous voulons les garder secrètes, dans la mesure où nous les concevons comme si arbitraires, et en quelque façon si maniaques, si honteuses (mais pour rien au monde nous ne nous en priverions), oui, peut-être est-ce dans cette mesure même que

tive), and it will then be necessary to consider all sorts of harmonics, nuances, relative errors, approximate values, of degrees that will become denser, that will make the whole indestructible—and will, finally, make a proverb out of your intuition; make out of your most arbitrary pleasure, a general law, a very simple obligation for everyone.

Rhyme obviously is not a sufficient obstacle: it is a minimum. Rhymes are only the first two keys that create a tension. (Bonnard said about Cézanne that "he only needed to put down two tones. . . .") But a staggering wealth of consonances, of assonances, and alliterations, distributed in such a way that the meaning is more important (very slightly, but more important, nevertheless) than the concert of vocables, than the music: that is the utmost in refinement.

*

MECHANISM or MACHINERY

Technical requirements (rare and sterile rhymes, caesuras, no hiatus, complete stanzas, regular sonnets, etc.) only serve, basically, to key up the tension.

They're all disregarded, in the end, if necessary.

They are present to delimit the *field* of the textual object, and perhaps to create it. To create tension, the field of forces.

But since it is impossible to obey all the rules all the time, in the end, as I have said, one disregards them (one or the other, and finally, in the last analysis, *all* have been disregarded, at one time or another).

OUR true rules, those that cannot be formulated, because they are not rules (they are only instinctive censures); *our rules*, I say, are much more consequential, much more

nous aimons donner l'illusion (et nous la donner à nous-mêmes, pour nous rassurer), nous donner l'apparence de nous être soumis à d'autres règles, celles qui se peuvent édicter, celles que tout le monde connaît et s'épuise, épuise ses ressources de vigueur, et de génie, à observer.

Ainsi faisons-nous notre opération secrète à l'intérieur (à l'abri, sous le couvert) de la cérémonie traditionnelle, de la messe rituelle.

(Comme d'ailleurs, de toute façon, nous employons un langage qui sert à de tous autres usages, et à de tous autres auteurs).

Nous répondons en réalité à de bien autres impératifs, mais nous n'avons à l'avouer à personne.

« ... Ange ou sirène, qu'importe!
Qu'importe si tu rends, fée aux yeux de velours,
Rythme, parfum, lueur, ô mon unique reine,
L'univers moins hideux et les instants moins lourds. »

Bien sûr, c'est dans la mesure où nous nous serons satisfaits de ce point de vue (du point de vue de nos manies les plus particulières) que nous trouverons, que nous conquerrons nos meilleurs lecteurs (dans l'avenir), ceux qui nous assureront notre survie, notre situation au Parnasse puis au Panthéon intemporels.

*

Ainsi me paraît-il évident que le fondateur d'un (tel) classicisme est par définition le plus riche et le plus vigoureux des esprits. Celui aussi qui montre un dédain aristocratique de la liberté. La liberté? Liberté vis-à-vis de qui et de quoi? La liberté? Pourquoi faire?

imperious, much more arbitrary. They are like imperative
obsessions, manias, rites, inhibitions, personal phobias.

Perhaps it is to the extent that we want to keep them
secret, to the extent that we conceive of them as being arbitrary, and, in a manner of speaking, so maniacal, so shameful (but we wouldn't part with them for anything in the
world), yes, perhaps it is to that very extent that we like to
pretend (even to ourselves, to reassure ourselves), to appear
to have submitted ourselves to other rules, those that can be
decreed, those that are known by everybody and that everybody wears himself out in observing, wears out his energy,
and his genius.

In this manner, we perform our secret operation within
the context of (sheltered, under cover) traditional ceremony,
the ritual mass.

(And, in any case, we use a language that is used for
other things, and by other authors.)

We are concerned, in reality, with a wholly different set
of imperatives, but we don't have to reveal it to anyone.

. . .Angel or siren, I care not!
Fairy with velvet eyes, who cares, if you make
Rhythm, perfume, light, o my one and only queen
The universe less hideous and moments less toilsome.

Assuredly, it is to the extent that we will have been satisfied by this point of view (the point of view of our most personal manias) that we will find, that we will win our best
readers (in the future), those who will assure us of our sur-
vival, our place on Parnassus, and then, in the timeless Pantheon.

*

Mais ici, il faut soigneusement distinguer encore.

Ainsi, prenons Valéry.

« L'homme vraiment fort, dit-il, tremble quand il n'y a pas d'obstacles ; il en crée. »

Et ailleurs :

« Pour réussir l'opération, pour sortir de ce que Valéry, dit Fromilhague, a osé appeler le barbotage de la conscience (c'est ce que j'ai appelé, moi F. P., « le magma analogique pur, qui ne m'intéresse pas comme tel »), pour faire, continue Fromilhague, surgir de ce limon un palais de marbre (*sic*), l'esprit a besoin de s'appuyer sur quelque chose, de se créer des résistances. Il les trouve dans le langage (...) dans les conventions de toutes sortes. Les règles de la prosodie traditionnelle, par exemple, sont comme des *brisants* ; l'idée vague, l'intention, l'impulsion y déferlent, et de ce choc résultent des figures imprévues (Paul Valéry, Cours de Poétique au Collège de France, cours du 10 décembre 1937, p. 142, coll. Ygdrasill, 1937-1938).

Eh bien, il faut absolument « fonctionner » *contre* cette conception. Rien de mieux à faire que de constater à quoi elle aboutit. Voici, en effet, comment continue et conclut Valéry :

« Est poète celui auquel la difficulté inhérente à son art donne des idées — et ne l'est pas celui auquel elle les retire. » « Donne des idées ! » Quelle pitié !

Hélas ! Valéry prouve ici qu'il n'est pas poète. Cela me semble évident. Trop évident.

Quant à moi, je dirai en effet qu'est poète celui qui a tellement fort quelque chose à dire, quelque émotion à communiquer, qu'il peut s'opposer toutes les règles, tous les obstacles, toutes les difficultés possibles, il n'oubliera jamais *ce* qu'il voulait dire et il finira toujours par le dire, par le faire passer comme une évidence.

Thus, it seems to me evident that the founder of (such) a classicism is, by definition, the richest and the most energetic of minds. The one also who displays an aristocratic disdain for freedom. Freedom? Freedom from whom? From what? Freedom? What for?

But here again, we must define very carefully.

Let us take Valéry.

"The truly powerful, he says, trembles when there are no obstacles; he creates them."

Elsewhere:

"In order to carry off the project, to get out of what Valéry," says Fromilhague, "dared to call the muddlings of consciousness (that is what I called, me, F. P. 'the pure analogous magma, that does not interest me *per se'*), in order," as Fromilhague continues, "to build a marble palace out of this clay (*sic*), the mind needs to lean on something, to create resistances for itself. It finds them in language . . . , in all sorts of conventions. Rules of traditional prosody, for example, are like *high explosives;* vague ideas, intentions, impulsions, break out of them, and from these shocks, unexpected figures result" (Paul Valéry, "Cours de Poétique au Collège de France" [December 10, 1937], p. 142, Ygdrasill, 1937-1938).

Well, one must absolutely "work" *against* this concept. Nothing is more convincing than to see where it leads. As a matter of fact, this is the way Valéry continues and concludes:

"A poet is one whose ideals arise from the inherent difficulties of his art—and he is not a poet when those difficulties are removed from it." "Ideas that arise!" how pitiful!

Alas, in this instance, Valéry proves he is not a poet. That seems evident to me. Too evident.

As for me, I would say that a true poet is someone with

Peut-on dire seulement que, *sans* ces difficultés qu'il s'oppose, il ne parviendrait jamais à le faire assez intensément et assez clairement pour le faire passer intégralement comme une évidence? Non, on ne peut même pas dire cela.

« Eh bien, si ce n'est un sonnet, c'est une sonnette! » répondit un jour Malherbe à Racan.

*

CONTRE LA SOI-DISANT MODESTIE ET LA SAGESSE « CLASSIQUES »

« Il me semble que les qualités que nous nous plaisons à appeler classiques sont surtout des qualités morales... dont la première est la modestie. » (Gide).

Non, ce sont des qualités d'intelligence : la première est le goût de l'efficacité.

« ... le premier des renoncements à obtenir de soi, c'est celui d'étonner ses contemporains. » (Gide).

Non, puisqu'il faut plaire, sans cela pourquoi écrire et que la surprise et l'étonnement jouent leur rôle dans les plaisirs esthétiques.

Oui, oui ! je vois bien ce que Gide veut dire. Je vois bien comme de tels préceptes pouvaient être utiles au temps de Paul Adam ou de Péladan, de Rostand ou de d'Annunzio.

Pourtant je vois aussi que plusieurs ne réussirent guère à *ne point étonner* leurs contemporains, et durent défendre sans modestie excessive, contre l'opinion des cercles influencés par Gide aussi bien que contre celle de leurs autres contemporains, la nécessité, la nouveauté et la prétention de leur oeuvre. Songeons à Proust, à Claudel. Songeons à Picasso, Braque, Paul Klee, songeons à Apollinaire ou Breton.

an overwhelming urge to say something, to communicate some emotion, that, though he recognizes all the rules, all the obstacles, all the possible difficulties, he will never forget *what* he wanted to say, and he will eventually end up by saying it, by having it accepted as evidence.

Can one assume that *without* those difficulties that he sets up, he would never succeed in doing it sufficiently intensely and sufficiently clearly to have it accepted as evidence? No, one can't even say that.

"Well," as Malherbe once said to Racan, "If it isn't a sonnet, it must be a sonatina!"[5]

*

AGAINST SO-CALLED MODESTY AND CLASSICAL WISDOM

"It seems to me those qualities that we like to call classical are really moral qualities . . . and the first one is modesty" (Gide).

No. They are intellectual qualities. And the first one is a taste for efficiency.

" . . . Let the first self-denial be the pleasure of amazing one's contemporaries" (Gide).

No, since we must please; otherwise, why write? Furthermore, surprise and amazement play their part in aesthetic pleasure.

Yes, yes, of course I know what Gide had in mind. I realize how such precepts might well have been useful at the time of Paul Adam, or Péladan, or Rostand, or d'Annunzio.

And yet, I also know that many never succeeded in *not*

5. Untranslatable pun based on the double meaning of *sonnette:* little sonnet and bell (S. G.).

*

« L'amour propre » et « la prétention » sont les princi-
pales vertus, ai-je pu écrire, contradictoirement, quant à moi.

Il me semble que la nécessité (le désir, le besoin) d'écrire
— de s'exprimer — est plus important que la modestie. Donc
le *quelque chose à dire* (départ dans l'émotion, la sensibilité).

Ce qui rend classique, ce n'est nullement la modestie,
c'est le désir de convaincre et l'expérience du ridicule et de
l'inefficacité du déchaînement, c'est le sentiment de la force
de persuasion de *l'unique*, du *simple*, du *rigoureux* (voire du
gracieux). C'est un *surcroît* d'orgueil qui rend simple, et un
redoublement de ténacité et de ressources qui permet de faire
d'obscurité, clarté.

amazing their contemporaries, and had to defend without excessive modesty, against the opinion of circles influenced by Gide, as well as against the opinions of other contemporaries, the necessity, the novelty, and the virtue of their works. Let's remember Proust and Claudel. Let's remember Picasso, Braque, Paul Klee. Let's remember Apollinaire or Breton.

*

As I have said, and it may have appeared contradictory, for me "vanity" and "pretension" are the principal virtues.

I believe that the necessity to write (the desire, the need), to express oneself, is more important than modesty. Consequently, *what has to be said* (based on emotions, sensitivity).

Modesty has nothing to do with what makes a classic. It is a desire to convince, and the knowledge that an outburst is ridiculous and ineffective. It is the feeling of the power of persuasion in the *unique*, the *simple*, the *rigorous* (the gracious, too). It is an *excess* of pride that leads to simplicity, and a doubling of tenacity and resources that transform obscurity into clarity.

Francis Ponge.

Bibliography

WORKS BY FRANCIS PONGE

1961. *Le Grand Recueil*. Paris: Gallimard. Vol. I: *Lyres;* Vol. II: *Méthodes;* Vol. III: *Pièces.*
1965. *Tome premier*. Paris: Gallimard.
   Douze petits écrits (1926)
   Le Parti pris des choses (1942)
   Proêmes (1948)
   La Rage de l'expression (1941-1947)
   Le Peintre à l'Etude (1950)
   La Seine (1950)
1965. *Pour un Malherbe*. Paris: Gallimard.
1967. *Le Savon*. Paris: Gallimard.
1967. *Nouveau Recueil*. Paris: Gallimard.
1970. *Entretiens de Francis Ponge avec Philippe Sollers*. Paris: Gallimard/Seuil.
1971. *La Fabrique du Pré*. Geneva: Skira.
1977. *L'Ecrit Beaubourg*. Paris: Centre Georges Pompidou.
1977. *L'Atelier contemporain*. Paris: Flammarion.
1977. *Comment une figue de paroles et pourquoi*. Paris: coll. Digraphe, Flammarion.

Some texts not yet incorporated into a volume:

1967. "Nioque de l'avant-printemps," *L'Ephémère*, 2.
1968. "L'avant-printemps," *Tel Quel*, 33.
1968. "L'Opinion changée quant aux fleurs," *L'Ephémère*, 5.
1968. "Deux manifestes indirects," *Manteia*, 5.
1971. "Ecrits récents," TXT, 3/4.

Bibliography

1976. "La serviette-éponge," *Digraphe*, 8.
1976. "Entretien avec Francis Ponge et textes écrits," *Cahiers critiques de la littérature*, 2.
1978. "Nous, mots français," *Nouvelle Revue Française* (March 1).

WORKS ABOUT FRANCIS PONGE

Besnehard, Pierre. "Francis Ponge: l'homme, le monde, et la parole." Ph.D. dissertation. Université de Provence, 1975.
Blanchot, Maurice. *La Part du feu.* Paris: Gallimard, 1949.
————.*Le Livre à venir.* Paris: Gallimard, 1959.
Camus, Albert. "Lettre au sujet du Partis-Pris," *Nouvelle Revue Française* (September 1956).
Douthat, Margaret Blossom. "Le Parti-pris des choses." *Yale French Studies.* New Haven, 1958.
Gavronsky, Serge. *Poems and Texts.* New York: October House, 1969.
————. "Interview with Francis Ponge, extracts," *Books Abroad* (Autumn 1974). (This commemorative issue also includes texts by Riffaterre, Morot-Sir, Robert W. Greene, and others.)
————. "Nietzsche ou l'arrière texte pongien," in *Francis Ponge, Colloque Cerisy.* Paris: 10/18, 1977. (This publication also includes texts by Riffaterre, Derrida, Maldiney, Thibaudeau and others.)
————. *Francis Ponge: The Sun Placed in the Abyss and Other Texts with an Essay, Interview and Translations.* New York: SUN, 1977.
Gavronsky, Serge, with Terry, Patricia. *Modern French Poetry.* New York: Columbia University Press, 1975.
Guglielmi, Jo. "De la résistance (à la) critique," *Critique*, 254 (1968).
Houdebine, Jean-Louis, "Lire Ponge," *Action Poétique*, 28/29, 31 (1956-1966).
Plank, David G. "Le Grand Recueil: Francis Ponge's Optimistic Materialism," *Modern Language Quarterly* (June 1965).
Prigent, Christian, et al. "Ponge Aujourd'hui," TXT, 3/4 (1971). Articles also include those by Sollers, Guglielmi, Clemens, Duatt, Steinmetz, and Denis Roche.

———. "La 'Besogne' des mots chez Francis Ponge," *Littérature* (February 1978).

Richard, Jean-Pierre. "Les Partis pris de Ponge," *Nouvelle Revue Française* (April 1964).

———. "Francis Ponge," in *Onze études sur la poésie moderne.* Paris: Seuil, 1964.

Sartre, Jean-Paul. "L'homme et les choses," in *Situations I.* Paris: Gallimard, 1947.

Scarpetta, Guy. "Ponge dans la serviette-éponge," *Promesse,* 22 (1968).

Sollers, Philippe. *Francis Ponge.* Coll. Poètes d'aujourd'hui. Paris: Seghers, 1963.

———. "La poésie oui ou non," *Logiques.* Paris: Seuil, 1968.

———. *Entretiens de Francis Ponge avec Philippe Sollers.* Paris: Gallimard/Seuil, 1970.

Spada, Marcel. *Francis Ponge.* Coll. Poètes d'aujourd'hui. Paris: Seghers, 1974 (contains the latest bibliography for the period 1965-1973).

Temmer, Mark. "Francis Ponge: A Dissenting View of His Poetry," *Modern Language Quarterly* 29 (1968).

Thibaudeau, Jean. *Francis Ponge.* Coll. Bibliothèque idéale. Paris: Gallimard, 1967 (contains the best bibliography for the period up to 1965).

———. "Les poésies de Ponge," *Critique* (August/September 1965).

Walther, Elizabeth. "Francis Ponge, analytiche Monographie." Stuttgart, 1961.

———. "Caractéristiques sémantiques dans l'oeuvre de F. Ponge," *Tel Quel,* 31 (1967).

TRANSLATIONS IN BOOK FORM

Archer, Beth. *The Voices of Things.* New York: McGraw-Hill, 1972.

Corman, Cid. *Things.* New York: Grossman, 1971.

Dunlop, Lane. *Soap.* New York: Grossman, 1969.